LIFE IN PROGRESS

LIFE IN PROGRESS:

WINNING WHERE IT MATTERS

Kyei Amoako

PUBLISHING

Columbus, Ohio

Copyright © 2018 by Kyei Amoako

All rights reserved. No part of this publication may be reproduced, distributed or transmitted in any form or by any means, including photocopying, recording, or other electronic or mechanical methods, without the prior written permission of the publisher, except in the case of brief quotations embodied in critical reviews and certain other noncommercial uses permitted by copyright law. For permission requests, contact the publisher at www.KyeiAmoako.com.

Cover and Interior Design by Ryan Magada
Cover Photo by Rick Buchanan

Life In Progress/ Kyei Amoako. -- 3rd ed.
ISBN 978-0-9998312-0-5 (Hardback)
ISBN 978-0-9998312-1-2 (Paperback)

DEDICATION:

To my mother, Rose Afriyiye, for her love and sacrifices.

SPECIAL THANKS:

To all the people who helped to bring this book to life.

VERY SPECIAL THANKS:

To Obeng Amoako, for the inspiration;
to William Ampadu, for the friendship;
to Mrs. Charlotte Akyeampong, for the nurturing;
to Kwabena Bediako, for leading the way;
to Eric Amankwah, for believing in me;
and to Elsie Osei-Tutu, for always being there.

CONTENTS

Introduction 1

PART I: STARTING OUT

1. Myself 7
2. Happy Are We 25
3. Hello, World! 45
4. Preparing for Take Off 57

PART II: FINDING MY PLACE

5. Welcome to America 71
6. The Pursuit of Happiness 91
7. Clarity of Purpose 103
8. Work and Happiness 115
9. Felt The Fear But Did It Anyway 129
10. Self-Awareness and Personal Power 141
11. What Matters Most 149
12. This I Believe 161
13. Making Sense of God 173
14. My Obituary 189
15. My Playlist 201

CONTENTS

PART III: TIES THAT BIND

16. What's Love Got to Do With it? 231
17. Love and Marriage 243
18. My Brother's Keeper 255
19. My Daughter In Whom I'm Well Pleased 273
20. Culture. Ghana. Me. 283

PART IV: I BELIEVE THAT WE WILL WIN

21. All I Do Is Win.. 297
22. My Appreciation 313

Index 323

AUTHOR'S NOTE

The stories referenced in this book take place predominantly in Ghana and in the US. Keeping in mind that some of my readers in the US and around the world may not be very familiar with the culture and geography of Ghana (and vice versa), I've done my best to provide enough context to bring everyone along throughout the book. Please bear with me when I do not provide enough (or provide too many) descriptions as I tell these stories.

INTRODUCTION

On the eve of my 40th birthday, I stayed up into the early morning hours and recorded a selfie video which I would eventually title "Note to Self." My birthdays had almost always come and gone with a humble acknowledgment and without any fanfare. I preferred it that way. This was the first time in a long while that I had thought of celebrating my birthday in a notable manner. I recognized that 40 was a milestone birthday, but I did not want a party. The thought of organizing a party or burdening others to coordinate one on my behalf felt overwhelming.

Active on Facebook, I knew I could expect the usual birthday wishes that would come my way later that day. I was passively combing through other people's Facebook pages and checking out their latest posts, when I had the idea to record and post a selfie video.

Recording and posting selfie videos was a new trend, and I had earlier dismissed it as a self-promotion tool for attention seekers. However, the idea of sharing my thoughts on life, as a more experienced and wiser version of myself, seemed interesting to me. I was hesitant because recording and sharing a selfie video would mean stepping outside my comfort zone.

Introduction

But then it dawned on me that if I were to die the following day, there would be a limited record of my existence in this life. As morbid and silly as that may sound, the thought of literally and figuratively disappearing in death was enough motivation to "do something before I die," as a popular Ghanaian saying goes. So, I went ahead.

My "Note to Self" selfie video project became a 100-second clip featuring me bopping my head to a mash-up of "Forever Young" (by Mr. Hudson and Jay Z) and "Lose Yourself" (by Eminem). It included these quotes: "Live today like it was your last" and "You Only Live Once...but if you do it right, once is enough." I closed with motivational speaker Les Brown belting out a thunderous rallying call, "When you step into your fears and continue to push yourself to go on, something happens for you!"

The video was very cool, and I watched it again and again, fine-tuning the cuts and making sure it was as good as it could be. After all, it was my big moment, and it had to be excellent. It received a modest response of fewer than 100 views and likes. But it didn't bother me that only a small fraction of my friends and acquaintances had seen or reacted to the video. What mattered to me was that I had accomplished what I set out to do – step outside my comfort zone and put a video of me on social media.

The day after my birthday was a feel-good one. I was 40 years old, and I didn't feel like what I thought, in my 20s, turning 40 would feel like. Physically, it didn't feel any different from when I turned 30. On the inside, I felt really good and happy. I was satisfied with my accomplishments and experiences, even though I was haunted by the dreams I had not pursued. Having embraced the selfie video idea and done something that scared me, I felt ready to embrace the years ahead and to focus on doing some of the things I had put off.

By making that video, I gave myself permission to fail at something that I, quite frankly, thought was a stupid idea until I leaned into it. A selfie video didn't seem like a grown-up thing to do, but it turned out to be a worthwhile endeavor. I had permitted myself to step into my fear.

I watched the video again, and again, and again, and reflected on my successes and failures, the lessons learned and lessons missed, my fears and my hopes, as well as my ambitions and bottled-up dreams.

The video was intended to convey my thoughts to others, but it turned into a pep talk to myself. Months later, that pep talk inspired me to get over my fear of sharing my life's lessons, my opinions, and my ideas with the world, and to write this book. I had in the past written essays on some of the topics discussed here and quietly tucked them away on a semi-private blog. But writing a book was a whole different beast – one that scared me.

There were three specific fears I had to confront: the fear that what I have to say may have already been said; the fear that my thoughts may not be profound enough to merit anyone's time and attention; and the fear that submitting my private thoughts for public examination would be the biggest mistake of my life.

I felt the fears but did it anyway.

The process of thinking through what I'm writing helped me examine, and in some cases, reexamine ideas, experiences, and beliefs that inform my decisions. I had no idea that writing about my experiences and sharing my point of view would be as psychologically rewarding to me as it has been.

Introduction

I hope reading it does for you what it's done for me – revive in you an appreciation for life, and inspire a desire to live like this life is the main event (and not a dress rehearsal for something in the future).

Even though I am not the world's leading expert on any of the subjects I discuss, I am the most qualified person to share my point of view and the ideas running around in my head.

This book is a conversation with friends – those I know and those I'm yet to meet. Sometimes, the conversation will be fun and lighthearted. Other times, it will be intense and passionate. But at all times, it will be good-spirited and sincere.

In the coming years, we may run into each other and share more stories. We may even meet at somebody's birthday party. It may be mine when I turn 50 – who knows!? Hopefully, we'll get to trade stories and celebrate the fact that each of us is living life fully and winning where it matters.

Until then, this is my "Life in Progress."

PART I: STARTING OUT

• ONE •

MYSELF

"I am fundamentally an optimist.
Whether that comes from nature or nurture, I can't say."
– **Nelson Mandela, South African president**

Somebody once asked me, "If your life is made into a movie, would you pay money to go see it?" My answer was a resounding "Yes!" not only because the movie would be about me, but also because my story to date has many of the necessary ingredients of a good movie.

There's the part about where I came from and where I'm headed; the part about why I believe the things I believe; and then the part about navigating relationships. All these pieces, I believe, could fit together to tell an exciting story about a bright-eyed teenager who leaves home to launch into adulthood in a new country. From one adventure to another, he realized that his contentment with the way things are often neutralized most of his best efforts. Now an adult, this optimistic nice guy learns to trust his instincts, face his fears, and live life on his terms.

Myself

Yeah, sometimes I speak about myself in the third person.

I had forgotten, or just didn't take the time to recall many of the stories of my childhood and my younger years, until my daughter Afriyie started asking about what life was like growing up in Ghana. Telling the stories almost always brought smiles to my face, and I would sometimes go on and on until someone or something interrupted me.

My first attempt at telling stories about myself was as a six-year-old elementary school student in Ghana. As was typical for most students at that age, the "Myself" essay was a writing exercise in which I was expected to share things like my name, when and where I was born, who my parents are, the things I liked the most, and who my best friend was. Back then, life was simple and a one-pager sufficed.

A lot has happened since then.

My story started out in Alajo, a small town in Ghana's capital of Accra. Alajo is often the butt of jokes because it used to flood regularly during the rainy season. The neighborhood I grew up in was a modest one where most people within a two-mile radius knew each other. It was a very diverse town of rich, poor, and people in the middle. My family belonged in the middle – neither rich nor poor. There were compound houses – single, walled households with multiple family units who were often unrelated. A compound house may have seven-to-ten different families with each usually occupying a living room and one or two bedrooms, and all the residents usually sharing an outhouse bathroom. There were also single-family houses, like ours, which were usually walled and gated for privacy. Most people communicated in the Twi and Ga languages. Most people spoke English only in formal settings like schools and work, and sometimes at church. There were Christians, Muslims, and people who practiced other religions. You were as likely to be awakened at dawn by the early morning prayer of the Pentecostals as you were to be awakened by the call to prayer by the Chief Imam.

My memories of my childhood are happy ones. They include many, many recreational activities such as playing soccer with other kids in the neighborhood; playing in "counters ball" tournaments with my brothers; playing "police and thief" the Ghanaian version of "cops and robbers;" eagerly looking forward to the 6pm start of the weekday television broadcasts; singing along to highlife music on the radio; and playing in a make-believe band with my brothers.

I have many siblings, but for a majority of the time, I grew up in the same household with three brothers, my oldest sister, and my twin sisters. My brothers and I listened to a lot of highlife music, learned the lyrics, and often challenged one another to singing and dancing competitions. Since there were four of us boys, it was very instinctive to split up into teams of two and turn most things into competitions. Such was the case with our counters ball games.

Bottle caps are often referred to as "counters" in Ghana because kids used them to learn how to count and do basic arithmetic. Counters ball is a simulation of a soccer game where we used bottle caps as the teams' players. Using another bottle cap as a control device, the players (counters) are moved around the floor to advance the ball into the opponent's goal post. This game was our version of the Xbox or PlayStation, and we took our counters ball tournaments very seriously. We had jerseys for our players, kept league tables, and even had trophies for the winning teams.

Myself

Music, specifically highlife, was a big part of my childhood, and I was drawn to the underlying storytelling devices many of the songs used. Highlife is a popular West African genre of music, which during the 1990s, went through an evolution by infusing pop and funk musical styles from Europe and America into indigenous Ghanaian guitar-band music. When we played in our make-believe band, we often played highlife music.

The make-believe band my brothers and I played in was something we invented to simulate the happenings at a beach party. Beach parties, often referred to as Meet-Me-There, were very popular on holidays such as Ghana's Independence Day. Some kids' families took them to places like Labadi Pleasure Beach where they would enjoy live band music and run around in the ocean. My mother, on the other hand, feared that events with large and sometimes-out-of-control crowds were unsafe, so we never went to any of these beach parties.

Through the power of our active imaginations, we brought the Labadi Pleasure Beach experience to our home. Our band's instruments were all homemade: the drums were made from old pots and pans, the keyboard and guitars were cobbled together with scraps of wood, and the microphones were made out of empty milk cans attached to the end of sticks. We jammed, sometimes quite accurately, to many of the highlife hits on the radio at that time. Kids in the neighborhood would often stick their heads over the walls to take a peak. Most of these experiences make me smile and sometimes laugh out loud as I recall them.

There were also moments that I did not enjoy as much. Like my father waking us up at dawn to listen to the news on BBC Radio. I liked the news part, but I did not like the early wake-up part. News was usually boring to me but I liked the current affairs facts I picked up from listening to news from around the world. On other mornings, my mother would wake us up at dawn to listen to advice from our father. That was another constant feature of my childhood – my father giving us advice about life, morals, and values, and telling stories from his life. Again, I liked the conversations but only wished I didn't have to wake up that early to participate.

Not long after I could cobble words together into sentences, my parents taught me various songs and nursery rhymes. I also started learning the English alphabet at a very young age. My father's approach involved the phonetic method, which emphasized the sounds of the letters as opposed to their names. That approach, which was different from what teachers typically used in Ghanaian schools, made for a smooth transition into combining letter sounds into two-letter words and eventually into multi-syllable words. That was how I learned to read early.

I attended pre-kindergarten for one year and left when I turned five. My mother, who taught Class 1 at an Alajo public primary school, enrolled me in her class. I had to be six years old to be in Class 1, but she brought me along with her anyway. Most good kindergartens were private and expensive but this was a cost-free alternative. Besides, I was ready for Class 1 at the time. I always loved getting ready for school. At my mother's school, I liked not having to go far from home to get to school. I also liked being by my mother's side throughout the day.

After a successful Class 1 in my mother's classroom, I was now almost six and eligible to start Class 1 as a regular student in what my parents deemed a more challenging and ideal school. I would be attending this new school with my older brothers

Oliver and Arthur. Oliver was three years older than I was, and Arthur was one year older than I was. The thought of walking to school in the company of these older siblings was exciting. When the time came on one early September morning, I headed off giddily to my first day of school, away from my neighborhood and far from the comfort of my mother's classroom.

Accra New Town 1 Experimental School (A.N.T. 1) was located about seven miles from my Alajo home. The school was considered an "experimental" school because it was designed to mimic the instructional format and quality of private preparatory schools in Accra at the time. Even though it was a public school, we did things slightly differently from other public schools. Most of A.N.T. 1's students, like private preparatory school students, sat for the Common Entrance Examination in Class 6 unlike other public schools where students usually sat for that exam after a year or two upon completing Class 6.

My brothers and I, and a few other kids from the neighborhood, would usually walk in groups to and from school. That seven-mile walk would take about an hour if we were not distracted. Many times, especially when returning home from school, we would take alternate routes and explore other neighborhoods, and sometimes stop at friends' houses to play or get a drink of water. There were many adventures involved in those daily commutes. Some were hilarious and others were embarrassing.

Being the child of a teacher came with being known. Most of my teachers knew my mother quite well and knew my name even before I was their student. My seat was often a desk or two away from my teacher, and I was usually appointed the cupboard boy. A cupboard boy is a teacher's assistant responsible for the class cupboard, the closet where textbooks and classroom supplies were kept. I would often pass out the textbooks at the beginning of class and ensure that they were returned at the end of the day.

While other kids clamored to become the class prefect, I had no interest in that. A class prefect was the teacher-appointed leader of the class (or sometimes elected by his or her peers) whose primary job was to keep his or her peers in line. A class prefect would usually write down the names of talkative students – those individuals who would talk or misbehave whenever the teacher stepped out of the classroom – and submit the list of names to the teacher. Usually, the teacher would punish the talkative students by cane-whipping them on the butt or in the palm, or assign them tasks like picking up litter from the school compound. Being a class prefect was often a contentious role and I was happy to leave that to the students who really wanted it. I loved my gig as a cupboard boy, and I was one for about four out of my six years in elementary school, often because my previous teacher recommended me.

The last day before the end of each term for elementary school children in Ghana is called "Our Day." That's when kids were allowed to wear clothes other than their school uniforms and bring to school special home-cooked meals, special beverages, and snacks. It was a party commemorating the end of the school term. The climax of the "Our Day" celebration was an assembly where the top three students in each class were announced. With the assembly held outside, the food vendors and kids from nearby schools would converge on our compound to get a peek at the top-ranked students in the school.

Coming in first place on final exams was a big deal to us elementary school kids. In Class 1, I ranked eighth and then fourth in my class. From Class 2 onwards, I was on top of the class at the end of most grading periods. That made me quite popular among my peers both at school and at home.

That popularity was enhanced when my younger brother Obeng enrolled in the same school, and emerged at the top of his class year after year. While I enjoyed being celebrated as a smart kid, I was slightly embarrassed by the attention. Having Obeng to share the spotlight with made me comfortable about embracing the idea that it was OK to be smart. Even with that newfound comfort, I would often deflect the attention directed at me by saying, "If you think I'm smart, you should meet my brother – he's double smart."

In secondary school, however, my raw academic abilities were not enough to get me through exams as successfully. In elementary school, I had relied on my ability to easily recall what the teacher said in class and from the homework I completed. I had not learned the skill of taking notes during class and how to prepare for tests. I struggled mightily during my first two years in secondary school and got by with average grades. Thankfully, I got myself together and bounced back in time to have a successful secondary school career.

When I started Form 1 at West Africa Secondary School (WASS), I was 12 years old. WASS was an all-boys secondary school in Accra and very well known at the time for its rowdy students. At the time, the school was attempting to turn a new leaf and trying to shed it's long-standing "bad boys" reputation. With a new administration, relocation to the new premises in the then-sprouting Accra suburb of Adenta, and the introduction of new school uniforms, it promised to be a much more normal experience than the rowdy ones I had heard about.

My older brother Oliver had attended WASS for the two prior years and told me stories about bullying and the students' unruliness. Part of me was excited about starting secondary school, and another part of me was scared by the thought of the hazing and unprovoked bullying that were the destiny of most first-year students. With the changes at the school and the fact that I would be attending with my two older siblings (Arthur was also enrolling that year), I knew that there would be some people looking out for me. With that in mind, the next chapter of my young adult life kicked off.

At WASS, I was extremely playful and more interested in clowning around than paying attention to what was taught in class. The demands of the secondary curriculum were such that my little-effort approach from elementary school was not going to cut it. I didn't realize that right away.

I was winging it, for the most part, as far as academic work was concerned. I told my parents that I was doing fine and they believed me. It would take the kindness of Yakubu Kassim to get through most examinations with semi-decent grades. Yakubu was my classmate and neighbor. He always had notes for each class and was diligent with completing his homework.

Many times, I would check with him, while we waited for the school bus, about which assignments were due. He would rebuke me for my lack of seriousness and then tell me what I needed to know. During the week leading up to end-of-term exams, I would spend most nights at Yakubu's house making a copy of his notes and asking for explanations to things I didn't understand. Of course, cramming at the last minute only got me so far. My grades were just average in those first two years. As a matter of fact, most of my first two years of secondary school was a blur.

Myself

My wake-up moment came in Form 3 when I was confronted with the fact that if I wanted to be selected for the science program, I would need very high math grades throughout the year. The secondary school curriculum was such that after Form 3, the students focused on one of three areas: arts, business or science. The science focus was highly coveted, and that's what most of the brightest kids chose or were expected to choose.

I wanted to become a pilot, and a science focus was the only way to get there. I needed to amend my ways and make it into the science program, lest I disappoint my parents and me.

Before deciding to become a pilot, I wanted to be a journalist. If I were going to become a journalist, I probably wouldn't have bothered with fixing my learning habits and getting serious because the arts program, which comprised the path to becoming a journalist, was relatively noncompetitive.

I wanted to become a journalist reporting the news like Sam Yeboah or Nana Ohene Ntow on Ghana's GBC TV. My grandfather had been a journalist and worked as a reporter for Ghana Broadcasting Corporation (GBC) and the Ghana News Agency (GNA) in the 1960s. Seeing pictures of my grandfather reporting from the field also fueled my interest in the career. When I was selected in 1985 as one of six elementary school students from the Greater Accra Region to read the news on the nationally-televised children's program, Children's Own, I was convinced that was a sign from the heavens that I was meant to be a journalist. For a 10-year-old touring the studios of GBC, meeting and greeting on-air personalities, and appearing on TV, there couldn't have been a more fantastic experience than that to reinforce my career interest in journalism. My father, however, talked me out of becoming a journalist, citing the persecution of journalists by the military government at the time who did not respect press freedom.

So, now that I wanted to become something other than a journalist, I needed to make the cut for the limited number of seats in the science program.

I had been the class clown for my first couple of years at WASS. Many of the stories about my clowning around involved my teasing the older classmates, their running after me, and other students cheering me on. When a teacher failed to show up as scheduled, I would stand in front of the class and imitate the teacher with funny impressions of him or her. Most of my peers loved it and urged me on. I enjoyed goofing around and entertaining my classmates – until my wake-up moment.

Along with my resolve to get serious, Form 3 was the first time Mr. Boye was not going to be my math teacher. I'm not the only one among my peers who thought Mr. Boye was not an effective math teacher. He didn't seem to care about what he was doing. And with my playful attitude, introduction to algebra was worse for me than it was for many of my classmates. But with a new math teacher in Form 3, who seemed to care more, along with my renewed focus, math became less intimidating. I looked forward to going to class. I even joined math study groups.

By the way, the short form for mathematics in Ghana is "maths" whereas it is "math" in the US. I write it as "math" because that's how I've said and written it for the past 20 years. You can read it either way. You can also read it as "mass" since that is what the Ghanaian pronunciation of "maths" sounds like.

Months later, all the hard work and new discipline in Form 3 paid off. I earned a spot in the science program. For the next two years, my core subjects were physics, biology, chemistry, math, additional math and English language. My two elective courses were economics and geography, rounding up my course load to eight subjects.

After two years of titrations, dissections, logarithms, essays, scientific calculations, and hundreds of hours of instruction and independent study, the General Certificate of Education (G.C.E.) Ordinary Level (O-Level) Exams was near. Given my earlier struggles with math, my mother wanted to eliminate any surprises. She sought a math tutor for me, as well as for my brother Arthur. Arthur found a high-end math teacher at the Achimota School and convinced my mother that this was the best math teacher in the country and that he wanted to go there. The teacher, Mr. Awuah, charged a lot for his services. I thought the services were overpriced, so I was not enthusiastic about the class. But my mother insisted that I attend anyway. She enrolled my brother and me, and paid the fee in installments. I spent most of my Saturdays traveling about an hour by public transportation to get to the tutoring sessions. The session lasted about two hours, but I thought they were a waste of money my mother didn't have. She was single-handedly taking care of most of the financial obligations in the household as she had been doing for a while. By that point, my father had decided to be only a passive member of the family and couldn't be bothered with paying for private tutoring sessions.

Out of consideration for my mother, I quit going to the tutoring sessions and told my mother someone else was helping me. Nobody was helping me. I was confident enough in my group of study partners that I felt I could rely on them to explain concepts I didn't understand. I knew if I did what I had to do, I would be fine.

With about six months until the exam, I went to live on the campus of Presbyterian Boys' Secondary School (PRESEC) in the home of a teacher, Mr. I.O. Yeboah. This was a referral by Sissi Bediako. Sissi Bediako is the mother of my friend and mentor Kwabena Bediako, and she knew Mr. Yeboah from the days when Kwabena attended PRESEC. Mr. Yeboah and his family graciously took me in. This new living arrangement also minimized my daily commute to and from WASS since PRESEC was only a 30-minute bus ride away. The commute from my home at Alajo would have been about two hours each way.

My younger brother Obeng had been at PRESEC for three years before I moved into Mr. Yeboah's home. My neighbor Kwame Sampong (a.k.a. Batista) was also a student at PRESEC, lived in the campus dormitories, and was also getting ready to take the O-Level exams. With guidance from my brother and Batista in navigating the school's culture and community, I settled in nicely, made some new friends, and maintained my dedicated focus on preparing for the exam.

Being in an environment where my routine involved mainly going to class during the day, napping for a couple of hours and then studying late into the night, I was as prepared for the exam as I could have possibly been. I would eventually pass the exam with honors and enroll at PRESEC for the final two years of my secondary schooling. The last two years of the Ghanaian secondary school system then was called Sixth Form – Lower Six and Upper Six for the first and second years respectively. More on that later.

My years at WASS laid a solid foundation for the next steps of my academic journey. I had learned to rid myself of the foolishness that distracted me from being successful. My experiences at WASS also gave me a first-hand appreciation for social and economic diversity.

In addition to the long-standing reputation for being a rowdy bunch, students from WASS often came from the rough and tough neighborhoods of Accra. My classmates and I enrolled at a time when the school was relocating from Accra New Town, a congested inner-city neighborhood, to Adenta, a remote suburb on the edge of the Greater Accra Region. This move was part of the grand plan by the then-headmaster Mr. Owusu Ansah to change the culture and reputation of the school.

That plan worked. When the school was at Accra New Town, some non-students would wear WASS school uniforms and misbehave around town or at interschools events, and WASS would get the "credit" for those misbehaviors. After the relocation to Adenta, with its distance away from the hustle and bustle of the inner-city, and the more inspired teaching staff, WASS became a different school.

WASS had become more attractive to some middle-class and affluent families. More families across the city gave WASS a second look and enrolled their children there. The population evolved to include students from different parts of the city, and from across a broader social and economic spectrum.

Per the linguistic code of the day, a student from an affluent home was called a "dadaba," which loosely translates as "the child of an affluent man." The plural version of the word is "dadabas" or "dadamma." Most teenagers of my day measured a school's sophistication by the supposed percentage of "dadabas" or "dadamma" the school had. Coincidentally, the percentage of children from affluent homes a school had seemed to correlate with a school's overall academic performance.

Celebrated schools like PRESEC, Achimota School, Adisadel College, and Wesley Girls' High School were, and are still, perceived to be on one end of the affluence and academic excellence spectrum whereas a school like WASS was generally perceived as being on the other end. Some of these perceptions, however, are slowly changing as more and more schools, including WASS, have become academically competitive.

The perception of a correlation between affluence and academic performance was a fascination of my teenage mind. Students' test scores and educational outcomes lent some truth to the stereotype. I observed that students from affluent homes were usually more exposed to sophisticated experiences, had more confidence when it came to social interactions, and usually performed better academically. WASS had a modest number of "dadamma" and I took consolation in that fact.

Like my Alajo community, WASS was very economically diverse. I had close friends from the affluent neighborhoods and close friends from the other parts of the town. I had the benefit of experiencing the very different worlds of my rich friends and that of my not-so-rich friends. I saw first-hand how economic disparities impacted student outcomes. And even though my family's financial situation did not seem to have had any impact on my academic results, I sometimes wondered if kids from affluent homes were more intelligent, considering the overall higher test scores from the predominantly "affluent" schools. I concluded that the affluent kids had access to resources that gave them an advantage, and that what my not-so-rich friends and I didn't have in financial resources, we had in intellectual ability.

While PRESEC's high-performing reputation and sophistication made it one of the "affluent" schools in Ghana, it was the one "affluent" school I had always been comfortable associating with. Most of their students were what I considered then as regular "dadamma" – not as aloof as most "dadamma" tended to be at the time. I harbored a sincere admiration for the school.

I had always wanted to attend PRESEC because that is where most young people aimed to go for secondary school if they wanted to attend the best science school in the country. Furthermore, several of my neighbors whom I admired very much went there. So while at WASS, I would sometimes remind myself that I was destined to be at WASS to learn street smarts and then continue at PRESEC to add to my academic training and eventually become a professional who is both accomplished and resilient.

My reason for wanting to attend PRESEC evolved from being heavily influenced by the academics to being heavily influenced by extra-curricular activities. I had heard so many good things about the PRESEC Drama Club and wanted to be a part of it. It may sound frivolous to the academically inclined but to me it was a good enough reason for choosing a school. I had always been interested in acting in well-planned stage plays, so I figured PRESEC would be an excellent two-for-one deal – I get an excellent education as well as be part of a highly regarded drama club.

When I gained admission to PRESEC for my Advanced Level (A-Level) secondary education, I was supposed to be a science student studying biology, physics, and chemistry. I opted out of that program and signed up for math, geography, and economics as my core subjects. That way, I figured, I would stay on track to becoming a pilot and at the same time carry a slightly lighter academic workload, and fit the Drama Club into my schedule.

The PRESEC Drama Club is one of the best things to have happened to me during my secondary school years. My involvement paid dividends during and after my years in the school, helping me develop a deeper interest in public speaking and in the creative arts. The drama club was the group I would eventually, in September 1994, travel with to the US for a two-week student exchange program hosted by the University of Toledo's Excel program.

Mrs. Charlotte Akyeampong, the beloved English teacher who managed the drama club, was a big reason the drama club attracted some of the brightest students to become actors, regardless of what courses of study they were pursuing. The nurturing environment Mrs. Akyeampong provided to all her students and the emphasis she placed on academic excellence set the stage for many students' success.

I tell the story of myself and where I'm coming from – and there's more – because I think it is an important backdrop to my present and my future. From Alajo to A.N.T. 1, to WASS, and then to PRESEC, the foundation for the adult I would become was laid. That foundation set the stage for subsequent events that would mold me from a boy into a man.

These life experiences and lessons shaped my worldview, and have certainly contributed to the nurturing that has made me into an eternal optimist.

· TWO ·

HAPPY ARE WE

"The future always starts out in the imagination."

- Mensa Otabil, pastor and entrepreneur

Presbyterian Boys' Secondary School (PRESEC) is one of the highly regarded secondary schools in Ghana. The school has produced many of the country's prominent leaders and luminaries in business, healthcare, government, academia, entertainment, and in other areas of the society. It has also produced some lesser-known individuals who are doing amazing things in Ghana and around the world. This boarding school is located in Legon just a few miles from University of Ghana's main campus on the outskirts of Accra.

When I enrolled at PRESEC in 1992, I joined some of the brightest young people from around the country. There were students from as far north as Bolgatanga in the Upper Region, from major cities in the middle belt, across the southern coast of the country, and also from rural towns I had never heard of. Five of us from West Africa Secondary School (WASS) – me and four other students in my graduating class – were admitted to PRESEC that year. PRESEC promised to be an experience that would springboard me to a successful career and a future I had dreamed of. As it turned out, it was all that and more.

I had been accepted into the science program, and my primary subjects were supposed to be physics, chemistry, and biology. These subjects were going to require a lot of my time in order to keep my grades where they needed to be. I intended to be an active part of the school's drama club but didn't want my grades to suffer as a result of stretching myself too thin, or worse, be forced out of the drama club because my grades had slipped. Since I was under the impression that the academic demands of being in the science program would be too rigorous to leave any room for me to pursue any extracurricular activities, I petitioned the admissions office to change my subjects to geography, economics, and math. The reason I gave for that change request was that those were the subjects necessary to prepare me for a career as a pilot.

I was confident in my abilities in geography and economics. I knew I was pushing the envelope with math, but I was going to have to make it work. My request was granted, and life in Sixth Form was in full effect.

Let me digress and share a quick overview of Ghana's educational system then and now, and how that relates to what I'm talking about. You might find it useful.

Preschool, sometimes called nursery school or day nursery, comprises all early childhood education up until kindergarten. After a year in kindergarten, most children enroll in Class 1 or Primary 1 (P1) in a primary or elementary school, and would be six years old by then. Primary school, whether privately-run or government-run, lasts six years.

Before 1986, students in Class 6 (which is the US equivalent of Sixth Grade) sat for the Common Entrance Examination to go to a secondary school. Students who did not qualify to sit for the Common Entrance Examination continued to middle school where they would have an opportunity each of the next four years to sit for the exam, and then enroll in a secondary school if they passed.

In secondary school, students attended for five years (from Form 1 to Form 5), and then sat for the General Certificate of Education (G.C.E.) Ordinary Level (O-Level) exams. In Forms 1, 2 and 3, which is the equivalent of most US middle schools or junior highs, the curriculum comprised subjects such as math, English, English literature, general science, agricultural science, art, geography, history, bible knowledge, Ghanaian languages, French, music, and physical education. In Form 4, a student focuses on arts, business, or science subjects. Based on whether a student focuses on arts, business, or science, he or she takes on eight subjects including general requirements, core subjects, and electives.

Chronologically, the next two years after Form 5 should be Form 6 and Form 7. However, both years are referred to as Sixth Form, with the first year called Lower 6 and the second called Upper 6 (or just as Lower and Upper respectively).

After two years in the Sixth Form, students sit for the General Certificate of Education (G.C.E.) Advanced Level (A-Level) exams. Based on a student's results, the student may continue to a university or other tertiary institution after working for a year as part of what is called national service.

Beginning in 1986, the phasing out of the Common Entrance Examination and the G.C.E. system from Ghana's mainstream educational system started. That is when the Junior Secondary School (J.S.S.) system was introduced, and the two educational systems existed concurrently until about 1994.

In the new educational system, Class 6 students continued automatically to a J.S.S. After three years, the students sit for the Basic Education Certificate Examination (B.E.C.E.) and then continue to a Senior Secondary School (S.S.S). After three years in an S.S.S. (also known as Senior High School or S.H.S.), the students sit for the Senior Secondary School Certificate of Education (S.S.S.C.E.) and then, based on the student's results, continue to a university or other tertiary institution.

The transition from the old system to the new one was not as chaotic as most people feared it would be. The two systems coexisted fairly well throughout my time in secondary school.

Now, back to the story.

So, here I was in Sixth Form at PRESEC excited and looking forward to the beginning of classes. After the couple of days it took to settle into our respective dormitories and get ready for classes, we were on with the academics. It started off slowly and ramped up very quickly with the introduction of new concepts and various assignments.

Around the same time, new friendships and cliques were forming. Some of my peers had begun actively lobbying for student leadership positions. Various extracurricular clubs were also recruiting members.

I had always wanted to act in a play but never found the right circumstance. This was going to be the first time I unleashed a skill I knew all along that I had but hadn't been enthusiastic enough about putting into practice. I wanted a part in that year's school play and having a line or two would have sufficed. I didn't care what part. I was eager to get on stage as quickly as possible, and I looked forward to my first drama club meeting like a child looks forward to Christmas.

My first time meeting Mrs. Charlotte Akyeampong, the English teacher who ran the drama club, occurred when I stood in front of the old PRESEC administration building waiting for the club members to gather. I arrived in the company of my friend Ben Tawiah (a.k.a. Impa), greeted Mrs. Akyeampong, and waited around awkwardly while other students dominated the conversation.

Moments later, Mrs. Akyeampong turned towards me, and in a very welcoming voice, smiled and asked, "How are you?"

I responded with, "I'm fine, thank you," and then Ben jumped in, as he did on many occasions, and introduced me.

"Madam, he's my friend," he began exuberantly. "He's been asking about the drama club since he got here."

I don't remember the rest of what Ben said that afternoon, but he went on with a few more sentences until Mrs. Akyeampong pointed us to the large bench under the big tree in the middle of the compound. There were about 20 of us with some of the students eager to claim a big part in the play; they signalled that by voluntarily reminding everybody present of the previous school play roles they had, and how experienced they were as actors.

Mrs. Akyeampong handed out the scripts for a cold reading. I flipped through the list of characters and checked out some of the dialog. I was ready to go. She randomly assigned characters, each student reading at least one role, and then we called it a day.

Of my classmates who joined the drama club that year, I was the only one who hadn't been in the group before. I was indeed a rookie because I had never acted in a stage play. I had recited poems on stage, and delivered Scripture readings in church but had no experience in acting. No one needed to know that. All I wanted was a role in this play, even if it were a small one.

When Mrs. Akyeampong announced roles a week later, I was pleasantly surprised that I had been selected for the lead role as Casper. That took some of my peers by surprise. I was surprised too that I would be picked over students who had been involved much longer than I had been. As honored as I was by the selection, I was anxious. I felt the weight of the production had been placed on my shoulders, and that the play would sink or swim, depending on how well I carried my role. I convinced myself that Mrs. Akyeampong had made the right choice and all I had to do was just relax, memorize my lines and just "bring it" like I did during the audition.

When I received my copy of the script, I flipped through the pages to see if my character had as many lines as I expected of the lead role. Yes, my character had many lines, and songs to sing. So, with my restrained excitement, I was ready to get on the stage and begin rehearsing.

Written by Mrs. Akyeampong, the play was titled "The Search" and it was an adaptation of Chaucer's *The Pardoner's Tale*. It was the story of three good-for-nothing fellows who went on a delusional quest to avenge the death of their friend Bolton. They believed Bolton would have helped them find jobs, had he not been taken away by cruel Death. They set out in search of Death – and to kill him.

Crazy, right? You bet.

But the character I played, Casper, was very effective in convincing his two compatriots to come along for this unimaginable mission.

The three lead characters had girlfriends in the play. That filled me with a healthy mix of excitement and nervousness. To my teenage mind, the many rehearsals and performance hours I will be spending with my female counterparts held possibilities for closer friendships. At the same time, I was just beginning to get used to the idea of having female classmates, as this was my first time since elementary school.

PRESEC was an all-boys school except for the Sixth Form, so there was a disproportionately large number of boys compared to girls. Out of the 150 or so students in my Sixth Form class, less than ten percent were girls. Three of these girls were going to be in the play with me, and I was likely going to befriend them. What teenage boy wouldn't get excited – and nervous – about this prospect?

Female friends were a big deal because, well, we were hormonally driven teenage boys. But more than that, having female friends at that age was a big deal given how big a boost it was to any guy's "street cred" or reputation. Fortunately for me, I was going to be in a play with three of them.

But just like some of my colleagues had jockeyed aggressively for lead roles in the play, I knew there would be serious attempts by others at getting the attention of our three female drama club colleagues. There was one person who was rumored to have joined the drama club with the hope of winning the affection of one of the girls. That didn't end very well. Even though I wished for some attention from my female colleagues, I didn't care as much if I were the subject of anyone's romantic affection.

My budding acting career was the most important thing to me at the time. And besides, the competition for girls' attention was pretty keen. Some students were wooing girls with gifts I couldn't afford, so I hoped for the best and carried on with being the best stage actor I could be.

My biggest concern with clamoring for a girl's attention had to do with the embarrassment that usually followed when word started to spread about a boy having been rejected or bounced by a girl he expressed interest in. Many boys had tried unsuccessfully to win the affection of some of our female classmates, generating fodder for the rumor mill and creating awkward social situations for the individuals involved. The last thing I wanted was to be the subject of one of those rumors.

Moreover, I was a naïve seventeen-year-old and had no business being attracted to these sophisticated girls. At least, that is what I told myself. Suffice it to say that I developed healthy friendships with all the girls in the drama club and worked well with them. Even some of their non-drama club friends became my friends, too.

Rehearsals went on, the play started taking shape, and we were off to a great start. The director of the play, Ababio Gyebi, and the choreographer, Terry Bright Ofosu, were at the time students at the University of Ghana's School of Performing Arts. Ababio Gyebi was a seasoned TV and stage actor who was famous for his role as Kwashi Papa in an episode of the then-popular television show called TV Theater. Terry Bright Ofosu was the 1989 National Dance Champion and was studying at the university. Through Mrs. Akyeampong's relationships with the university faculty, she got these gentlemen to work with us. And when Ababio or Terry could not attend our rehearsals, Eric

Ansah Brew or Kwaku Duah Berchie, also students at the university, came instead.

I learned various acting techniques, learned some dance moves for the choreographed parts of the play, and got more comfortable with delivering my lines on stage.

Our first full-blown production was at the PRESEC assembly hall before an audience of students and staff. The students' expectations were high. Previous years' productions had been stellar; our play was going to have to keep up.

We delivered. We may have received a standing ovation; I don't remember. I was relishing the fact that I did not forget or fumble many of my lines. Not bad for a first time. "This acting thing is really happening," I thought to myself.

Word started to spread among the student population about the play and the actors. We received lots of positive feedback. We worked out the kinks in the production and headed out to share our play with the general public.

We booked two evening performances at the School of Performing Arts' Drama Studio and performed to a full house on both occasions. We also performed at the Ghana Institute of Management and Professional Studies (GIMPA), the Armed Forces Officers' Training School, and were scheduled to take the show on the road to several schools around the country. But those plans fell through. Even though I was disappointed that the nationwide tour was not going to happen, I was floating on "Cloud 9" as a result of my successful debut.

I had not told my parents about my acting or about being in the drama club. I was in a boarding school, therefore my parents did not know what I did on a day-to-day basis unless I told them. I did not tell them because I feared they might think it wasn't the best use of my time. I finally told them after the performance we staged for the entire school. Even if they disapproved of my acting, it would be too late to pull me out of the cast. I also told them because I had to invite them to come see the play.

My mother and my brother Arthur were at the first public performance at the Drama Studio. After the show, they both commended my performance, and my mother added that I could continue acting as long as I maintained good grades.

In the Arts section of the *Weekly Spectator*, a national newspaper, the reviewer gave high praise to the cast and referred to me as an acting prodigy. I had to look up the word "prodigy" in a dictionary for its meaning, and I smiled at the praise but resisted the temptation to let it swell up my already-big head. I was, however, very excited to have been mentioned in the newspaper article. I kept a copy of that article but lost it eventually.

Participating in the drama club helped me integrate smoothly into the PRESEC community. Students who enrolled at PRESEC at the Sixth Form usually integrated cautiously. That's because as a new student, you were plugging into existing relationships, and it was only wise to proceed with caution. For me, having my younger brother in the school and the fact that I had lived on the campus a year before gave me a head start. Even some of my colleagues assumed that I had been a student there prior to the Sixth Form because it was pretty easy to tell a new student from an old student. I suppose I blurred that line because I arrived in Sixth Form familiar with many of the key aspects of life in the school, and took a more active route to becoming a part of the community.

And yes, headlining the school play was a massive boost to my popularity, and gave me many opportunities to make new friends. With the new female friends I made following the debut of the school play, some of those held the potential to have evolved into something more. But, again, I was too intimidated by the possibility of embarrassing myself if I got turned down. I was content with being just friends with these colleagues, so those friendships remained that way.

Around the same time as my drama club popularity was taking off, I was casually lobbying for a role in the student leadership body. Prefects, as the student leaders were referred to, were either voted on by the general student body or appointed by the school's faculty. These were highly coveted positions for which students lobbied, and some even campaigned heavily. One of the ways by which students lobbied for these posts were by showering their predecessors with gifts in exchange for their support and/or official recommendation. And following the recommendations, nominations, and vetting, the candidates for the various positions had to campaign for votes from the general student population.

Being a prefect was a big deal partly because of the perks, including special privileges that came with eating at the special prefects' table in the dining hall, the respect of your peers, and the authority to discipline younger students who disobeyed school rules.

Most new students didn't submit themselves for consideration as prefects, due mainly to a tendency of the school's administrators and the voting students to prefer students who had been at PRESEC for their O-Levels. Also, many new students viewed themselves as outsiders and were hesitant to seek such positions of authority. To me, the perks of being a prefect were enough motivation to submit my name for consideration.

The agriculture (agric) prefect was in charge of farm tools and the school farm, and most students didn't care much for that position. I saw it as an opportunity to enjoy the same perks as any other prefect and possibly change the misconception many students had about that post. That position was by appointment, so I would not have to stand for elections.

As part of the vetting process, a panel of teachers interviewed me, and I made my case for why I would be an effective agric prefect. I talked about how I was going to help transform the school farm into a major source of vegetables for feeding the student population and, in effect, save the school money. One of the teachers on the panel asked how I was going to make the students comply with my leadership of the school farm since I didn't seem like the intimidating type. I wasn't expecting follow-up questions to my prepared remarks, so I had to think quickly. I started by trying to convince the teacher that I had an intimidating side, which I could use to get students to comply when necessary, and that I prefer to use my people skills in convincing the students to do what they know they are supposed to do.

I fumbled through that answer but left the interview feeling good about my prospects as the future agric prefect. The other students went through the vetting process, and the students who were contesting for the elected positions busily campaigned and made all kinds of promises to the student population.

The election day came and the students made their choices. Fred Kwawuvi (a.k.a. Yelloo) was selected as the head prefect. Nana Addo-Dankwah and Joseph Caiquo were elected as his deputies. Kwaku Daaku, Joseph Anim-Addo, and Alhaji Sanhoon were elected as grounds prefects. Eugene Osae, Kwame Sampong Bediako (a.k.a. Batista) and William Ampadu (a.k.a.

Odo Yewu) were elected as dining hall prefects. The appointed positions were announced, and I was not the next agric prefect. Rather, I had been appointed as a prep prefect, along with Nii Otu Okunor and Lawrence Owusu Sekyere. That was a pleasant surprise. Prep prefects were responsible for making sure that all students attended evening independent study sessions known as "prep" (short for preparations), making sure they stayed awake and quiet during the two-hour sessions. I made friends and enemies in the discharge of my duties. I would sometimes have to discipline unruly students by assigning extra tasks – nobody liked me for that. I would occasionally turn a blind eye to minor infractions – everybody loved that.

The experience of being a peer leader in secondary school is an excellent training for real-world leadership. I didn't know at the time how much this leadership role was preparing me for life after secondary school, but it surely was.

I balanced my active involvement in the drama club and my role as a student leader with the rigorous academic demands and maintained decent grades, keeping my parents and Mrs. Akyeampong very pleased. Mrs. Akyeampong was as interested in her students' remembering their lines as she was in their maintaining good grades. She demonstrated that to me with her frequent inquiries about how my classes were going. With the drama club and Mrs. Akyeampong, I had a family away from home. My time with the drama club had been notable because of how that experience set the tone for the path my life took at the school and even beyond.

When we brought down the curtains on "The Search" to prepare to sit for the G.C.E. A-Level exams, most of us in the drama club shared the sentiment that it was going to be the last time we performed as a group. Little did we know that the best was yet to come.

Toledo is a city in northeast Ohio. Until around July 1994, I had never heard of it and barely knew about Ohio. I had no idea then that the state of Ohio was going to become a huge part of my adult life, beginning with a visit to Toledo.

Dr. Helen Cooks, the director of the Toledo Excel program, while on a visit to Ghana, heard about a play by a group of high school students from PRESEC. That piqued her interest because Toledo Excel was a scholarship incentive program at the University of Toledo that prepared African-American high school students for success in college. She had been thinking of creating a cultural exchange program for her students, so she connected with Mrs. Akyeampong after the play.

Following a series of conversations, and with the help of Dr. Titus Glover Quartey, Dr. Quarcoopome, and others, the Toledo Excel students were going to be our guests that summer.

During this time, somebody in the drama club started a rumor that since the Toledo students' trip was supposed to be a part of an exchange program, we would visit Toledo later in the year. That assertion made sense, but I refused to believe it.

About a year earlier, I thought we would be going on a nationwide performance tour, but was disappointed when that fell through. It seemed reasonable to expect to visit Toledo if this was truly an exchange program, but I wasn't buying into it – yet.

The Toledo students spent two fun, activity-filled weeks in Ghana. Numbering about fifty, along with their adult chaperons, our respective families hosted them in our homes. As part of the well-planned itinerary, we all participated in lectures on Ghanaian culture at the University of Ghana, visited various tourist destinations around Accra, and staged "The Search." We performed a second play, "Ananse and the Gumman," which featured the classic Ghanaian folk villain Kwaku Ananse in a scheme to selfishly have the fruits of his family's farm labor all to himself.

During the second week, we all traveled to Kumasi and to several tourist destinations outside Accra, and returned after four days to hold a private beach party at the Labadi Pleasure Beach. We then bid our guests goodbye and began our wait for word on whether the second leg of the exchange – our visit to Toledo – was going to happen. The grown-ups only said that they were trying to secure funding, both locally and internationally, for a possible trip to Toledo.

I had lowered my expectations about the possibility of a trip to Toledo. I refused to believe we were going, even after I submitted my passport and the required payment towards the cost of the travel. Ababio Gyebi, who was very involved in the trip coordination, offered mild hints with his vague answers to my specific questions about the travel plans. For example, I asked him why we were being asked to submit passports for visas if the trip had not been confirmed. He responded that I was free to hold on to my passport if I so wished, and then smiled wryly.

Within a week or so from the submission, each of us received our passports back with US visitor visas stamped in them. I was finally convinced we were Toledo-bound.

All I wanted was a part of a school play and to live out my long-held acting dream. I got the lead role, had a blast on stage, and didn't think it could get any better. But it was about to. We were taking the show on the road to the United States of America!

I knew enough about America for my imagination to start running wild with what I was going to see and experience when I arrived in America. I knew about Bill Clinton, Jesse Jackson, and a little bit about the civil rights movement. I knew about entertainers like Arnold Schwarzenegger, Rambo, and Eddie Murphy from their movies. I also knew about LL Cool J, Kriss Kross, and several musical acts of the time. I hoped I would run into someone famous. I had also seen TV shows like "Sanford & Son," and "Apartment 227" so I had an upbeat expectation of living with host families. Additionally, I wanted to experience winter and see snow, even though I was not thrilled about winter's cold. However, traveling in September meant we were a couple of months removed from winter and snow.

We left Accra on the inaugural Ghana Airways direct flight from Accra to New York, and arrived at the J.F.K. International Airport. It was a late fall afternoon. We huddled inside a comfortable charter bus and journeyed for about 13 hours to Toledo. The flight from Accra to New York took 10 hours, and that felt long. Our young and restless bunch of teenagers having to endure a longer bus ride to our final destination was the most grueling "are we there yet" scenario you could imagine. I was tired and restless. The excitement of seeing the New York City skyline through our windows eventually gave way to the boredom of staring at cars and trucks drive by on the freeway.

In Toledo, I lived with the Hearn family who was very kind to me. John P. Kee's "Colorblind" album was playing on their car radio when they picked me up. I heard bits and pieces of the album's songs at low volume during drop-offs and pick-ups, and I was intrigued. One morning, I asked Mrs. Hearn if she could turn the volume up a little bit more. She smiled and raised the volume. It was an excellent gospel album based on how many of the songs talked honestly about many real-life issues. It also had an eclectic, contemporary sound that I loved very much. As a parting gift, Mrs. Hearn gave me a copy of that album, which I enjoyed for many months after leaving Toledo.

Members of my group stayed with other Toledo African-American families. We attended various community events including several at Braden United Methodist Church. We performed our two plays, participated in a choral concert, visited places of interest including the zoo and the museum of art, and even took a day trip to a tire factory in Michigan. We also participated in lectures organized by the University of Toledo, and visited their mayor's office where he issued a proclamation naming the day of our visit Ghana Day in Toledo.

My short stay in Toledo was as much fun as I had anticipated, but I couldn't wait to return to Ghana to share my experiences with my family and friends. Although it was for only two weeks, the trip felt much longer. After the first week, I, like most of my peers, was homesick and longed for some regular Ghanaian food. The cheeseburgers and pizza and other American foods were great for the first several days but not for the latter parts of our stay. Lunchtimes during the second week were not as exciting as they first were, and the looks on the faces of my peers seemed to beg the question, "This same food again?"

On our way to New York for our flight back to Ghana, we stopped over in Washington D.C. My longtime neighbor from Ghana, Mr. Amoah, at the time lived with his family in the Washington D.C. area. He and his wife brought my group fufu and light soup at our hotel, which made most of us extremely happy. I didn't even know then that fufu, a staple food made out of boiled and pounded cassava and served with a spicy African soup, existed in America. So you can imagine my pleasure when they showed up with several big bowls of fufu. Those bowls of fufu and light soup arrived like manna from heaven arrived to the Israelites in the wilderness. That moment was undoubtedly one of the highlights of our US trip, and we talked about it for many days and months.

We returned to Accra in early October of that year, went about living our lives and, of course, sharing the stories of our American adventures with our families and friends. There was no social media or smartphones back then, so we could not share pictures online or tweet about our experiences. Through old-fashioned word of mouth, however, word quickly spread around town about the Toledo trip. I gladly shared my stories, including the story about the fufu.

I often got asked if I was going back to live in Toledo. I didn't know. I was interested in and had inquired about attending college there, but I was not going to jinx any opportunity by talking openly about it. So I would often answer the question by explaining that I was nowhere near certainty with my plans for the future, and that I would thoughtfully weigh the Toledo option when the time came.

The results for the G.C.E. A-Level exams were in, and my options for university were the University of Ghana in Accra, the Kwame Nkrumah University of Science and Technology in Kumasi, and the University of Toledo. Each of these options had its unique set of circumstances that appealed to me. I was still interested in becoming a pilot, so I researched flying schools as well. The Ghana Institute of Journalism was also an option I considered since Ghana's political landscape was changing for the better, and journalism no longer seemed like a dangerous profession. I was going to explore them all and then weigh my options later.

The months following my graduation from PRESEC were some of the best times of my life. I was very involved in activities at church and around town. I enjoyed my post-Sixth Form freedom, which included visiting friends in their homes, making new friends, and seriously entertaining the idea of choosing a girlfriend. At this point, I had become pretty adept at making friends with female peers, but it would be several months later before I would find the confidence to express interest in a girl.

PRESEC gave me an opportunity to grow and expand my worldview. I had taken advantage of the academic and extracurricular opportunities, and had made the most of them. My life so far had been happy, and I felt a strong sense of belonging to my communities, especially my PRESEC community.

PRESEC's school anthem opens with the lines, "Happy are we, studious are we; students of Presbyterian Secondary School. Onward we march, we trudge along to happy victory…" During my years there, I sang this song many times as part of student assemblies or during important school events. After graduation, I have on occasion joined former PRESEC students to sing the anthem and pay homage to the school we credit for a significant portion of our upbringing.

As a student, the words of the song affirmed for me a bright future that I had imagined, and was happily working my way towards. As a former student and now an adult, the words remind me that the opportunities that the school afforded me were meant to prepare me to become a positive contributor in my community.

Through the holistic education received and the relationships formed, I built a "sure, solid foundation to take my place in the future of my country and church," as the closing lines of the anthem states.

Today, I am happy indeed about the path my life took. And because I have been given much, I know that much is expected of me.

· THREE ·

HELLO, WORLD!

"Go forth and do great things!"
- **Anonymous**

I have been fortunate that most of my teachers, both formal and informal, taught me how to make a living as well as how to live life. After all, teachers, they say, ought to teach students how to do both. With my elementary and secondary school education, I had been given a firm foundation upon which I was going to build my adult life. Following my graduation from PRESEC, I felt I had acquired the skills I needed to figure out what I wanted to do for work and to go pursue that. I was optimistic about the future but suspected that the real world was more complicated than the life I had known up until that point.

My first real job was as a teacher at a local junior secondary school. This was my national service, the one-year employment within the Ghana Civil Service expected of all Sixth Form graduates. It was the first time I was expected to spend most of my days working for an employer, and I was going to be paid a salary. Previous jobs I had involved helping my mother with one of her many petty trading enterprises or running errands for neighbors. National service was a real job, and I was excited.

I was assigned to Kotobabi 1 Junior Secondary School, which was about ten miles from my home at Alajo. I was going to teach mainly math and English language, and maybe general science. I had been looking forward to national service and teaching, but the prospect of spending my days with a group of kids who may not take me seriously because of our closeness in age, dampened my excitement a little bit. As a 19-year-old, the responsibility of managing a classroom of 12- to 14-year-olds was a tad bit intimidating.

My preference was a junior secondary school at Alajo. That was my home turf, and my mother taught in a nearby primary school. Most students I would have taught at an Alajo school would have at one point or another been my mother's students, so they were likely to know me or my mother. I felt such students were more likely to accept me as their teacher merely because they knew me or whose son I am.

Tough luck! I was going to have to teach somewhere else and figure out the new relationships on my own. There would be no hiding in my mother's shadow.

While I was lamenting how tough my teaching assignment was going to be, I admonished myself to quit whining and get on with it. I was one of the "lucky" few who didn't have to spend their national service year in a remote village with limited infrastructure. Many of my peers had been posted to far off rural areas, some of which had no electricity or running water. My best friend Elsie Osei-Tutu (nee Acquah), for example, had been posted to Ajumako Bisease, a village in the Central Region, but she was not complaining.

Elsie lived in my neighborhood and her house was about three miles away from mine. Because she attended a boarding school for most of her secondary school, I rarely ran into her. We later became acquainted with each other through mutual friends, and our friendship took off not long after that. This was during the long vacation break before Sixth Form, and I still felt awkward about interacting with female peers. But Elsie was easy to talk to, and she turned out to be even more down to earth than I thought.

We traded stories about life in our respective secondary schools and talked about what each of us was looking forward to in Sixth Form and beyond. I went to her house frequently. Our conversations went on for hours on most days, and we always found something new to talk about. For a brief moment, I entertained the thought that Elsie could become my girlfriend. But then I found out that Elsie was a year older than I was, and that immediately disqualified her from becoming my girlfriend.

A neighbor had previously told me that it was the worst idea for a boy to date a girl who is older than he since girls tend to mature faster than boys. I took this neighbor's words very seriously, especially when he added that any boy who dates a girl older than he is would become the butt of jokes. So, that fleeting thought of Elsie's someday becoming my girlfriend evaporated as quickly as it entered my head. Our friendship, however, grew.

With our birthdays just days apart in September, we often joked about being twins born a year apart. Elsie became my confidant on matters relating to my interest in girls, and like a sister to a brother, she often patiently listened to my detailed assessment of girls I was interested in. In return, she provided thoughtful feedback that helped me put things into perspective.

When she learned that her national service would not be in Accra, Elsie never complained. She was looking forward to making a difference in the lives of her students in Ajumako Bisease and was not troubled by the lack of social amenities. I was staying near home in Accra, so I had no reason to complain.

National service was my first real experience with the working world, and I was expected to show up to work on time each day, report to a supervisor, be accountable for completing daily responsibilities, and not leave until the close of the school day. My job was to help shape the young minds entrusted into my care. To my idealistic self, this was an opportunity to inspire young people, share my academic expertise, and contribute to Ghana's social and economic development. With that in mind, I set out to impact my students as much as possible.

During my early secondary school years, other national service personnel who taught in the same school as my mother were extremely helpful in expanding my worldview. Anthony Darby was the first national service person my mother hired to tutor my brothers and me. Frederick Opare-Ansah (a.k.a. Watuse) tutored us the second year. These young men helped my brothers and me with math, and would often spend time chatting with us about books they had read or something cool that was happening in another part of the world. Many of these mind-opening conversations I had with Tony and Watuse stayed with me through the years. Being the avid readers that they both were, they told us stories about how computers and other emerging technologies were changing the world, and also about Jason Bourne's adventures in *The Bourne Identity*. They made a strong impression on me, helped to shape my young mind, and stirred up my imagination about the future.

With my role as a national service person, I was determined to extend a similar learning experience to the young people I would be working with. I would teach them math and science; additionally, we would talk about current affairs, have quiz competitions, learn songs and hold debates on various topics.

I braced myself for the first day of my professional teaching career, filled with many bright ideas of how I was going to engage my students. Susan Prah, my national service colleague who had been on the job a couple of days before me, seemed less nervous than I was. She graciously shared her experience and offered some classroom management tips.

I don't remember what I taught on my first day, but I remember that the students in this J.S.S. 1 classroom were much better behaved than I had anticipated. Even the known troublemakers sat in their seats and paid close attention as I told them about myself. I supposed the fact that I graduated from WASS, and then from PRESEC highly impressed these students. This was because most of them knew of WASS' tough reputation, so they may have concluded that I was not to be messed with. Similarly, most of the students knew of the academic prowess of students from PRESEC, so they may have thought that I was very smart, and that they might learn something from me if they listened. Those alleged conclusions were fine with me. I continued giving an overview of the topics we would be covering during the year.

One student raised his hand and asked if it was true that I had recently visited America. I didn't know how they found out about my trip to Toledo, but I was happy to talk about that if that was what they wanted to talk about during our first session together. After all, I was getting to know them, and they were getting to know me.

As I spoke about my experiences, they listened with so much focused attention that it dawned on me that they may have been more impressed with my travel to America than they were with what schools I attended. Many hands shot up when I offered to answer their questions.

They were keenly interested in what I did when I was in America and which famous people I met. They were somewhat disappointed that I did not run into Bill Clinton or Michael Jackson or Arnold Schwarzenegger or any of the famous Americans who were often shown on Ghanaian television. Some of them were disappointed that I hadn't stayed long enough to experience winter to tell them what snow felt like. Some of them wanted me to show pictures from the trip, which I eventually did. Most of them were impressed with the fact that I had visited a country most of them imagined visiting someday.

It appeared the students had decided I was a cool enough guy from whom they could learn a thing or two, and have fun doing so. Therefore, over the course of the year, they remained respectful and did not give me as tough a time as I feared they would.

Teaching came naturally to me, and that did not surprise me. I had observed both of my parents teaching my siblings and me at home. On several occasions, I assisted my mother in teaching her elementary school students. I had also helped my younger sisters with their homework and other assignments. I knew the basics of teaching a class, and I learned more about classroom management as I went along.

The only thing about teaching professionally that didn't seem interesting to me was the part about preparing lesson notes. My mother spent most of her Sunday evenings preparing lesson notes, and that seemed very tedious to me. I was hoping the head teacher at my school would not ask for my lesson notes. He never did.

The real teachers, those on staff who had attended teacher-training colleges, served as the lead teachers, and they prepared the lesson notes. I taught math to their students and filled in wherever they needed help. It was an ideal arrangement. And just like I had pictured it, my teaching was a mix of academic instruction, random quizzes, and the sharing of songs and poems. About half of my students loved almost everything I did. For the other half, the honeymoon period lasted only a couple of weeks after which they weren't as interested in what I had to say.

With all things considered, national service had been the perfect transition into adulthood. It came with just the right amount of responsibility to expose me to the working world. It had been a fun experience, but I was happy when the school year drew to a close. I was a busy young adult and had other things on my to-do list.

Being in Accra for my national service allowed me to also continue with my introduction to the world of business. I had been helping my friend Kwabena Bediako with his pharmaceutical supply business by running errands for him.

Kwabena and his brother Amakye, just like most of the Bediako siblings at the time, supplied pharmaceutical products to independent pharmacies around Accra. The nature of the business was such that these pharmacy shops paid for the products in installments, and the payments had to be picked up weekly or a couple of times each week. I ran these pick-up errands, brought the money to Kwabena or deposited the funds into their bank account, and updated the accounting records. I began running these errands during my time in Sixth Form and continued through my national service year.

Around the time of my national service, both Kwabena and Amakye lived in Kumasi, about five hours north of Accra. They were both students at the Kwame Nkrumah University of Science and Technology and could not travel to Accra as often. Thus, I was now entrusted with more responsibilities – collecting more substantial payments, making more deposits, tracking product inventory, and paying for products. The perks of that gig were pretty good, and included a generous stipend and the opportunity to often meet and interact with some prominent business owners around the city. I felt like I was doing a very important work, so I was very dedicated.

In addition to teaching and running errands for Kwabena and Amakye, I was very active in my church. I was the drama director of my church's youth group, The People of Tomorrow. I was a member of the youth choir, a member of the main church choir, and a member of the main drama ministry. With membership in all these groups, I was at the church three or four evenings each week either for a rehearsal or a mid-week service. This was in addition to the Sunday morning services and the weekend outreach events for the choir or the drama group.

As busy a young adult as I was, I loved having every hour of my day occupied by something productive. All those activities during my national service year and the year that followed exposed me to many people and situations that contributed to my growth and development. And I enjoyed being busy doing various things.

Life at home, however, wasn't as good. I was about 19 at this time, and my parents' marriage had continued to decline into turmoil. My mother ended up leaving the marriage and moved a few miles down the road from my father's house at Alajo. She had built a modest house on a piece of land she had co-inherited from her father. While I wished my mother didn't have to leave, I knew enough about what had been going on to believe she was doing what was best for her under the circumstances.

My parents had five children together, and my father had other children. Of the children my parents had together, Arthur is the oldest, a year older than me. I am three years older than Obeng, who is two years older than our twin sisters, Panin and Kakra. We grew up in the same household as our half siblings, Barbara, Agyapongmaa, Joe and Oliver, who are all older than Arthur. Until I was 12 years old, Arthur and I did not know that Oliver was our half brother. It took a talkative tailor, Anokye, to casually spill that fact. Nonetheless, my half siblings I grew up with in the same household viewed and related to my mother as their mother for the most part.

When my mother moved out, Arthur and I continued to live with my father in his Alajo home. Panin and Kakra went with my mother, and Obeng lived away from home in his PRESEC boarding house.

The crumbling unit had finally disintegrated.

For me, errands for Kwabena Bediako and activities at church were a welcome distraction. I didn't have to spend most of my time absorbed in the dysfunction that was going on at home. Before my mother finally left, I found myself a couple of times in the awkward position of rebuking my father for not doing the right thing. It wasn't a pleasant experience having to express my displeasure to my father - I risked being branded as a disrespectful young man - but I felt it was necessary to speak out.

From the way I saw it, my father had gotten away with many unacceptable actions for far too long, and somebody had to say something to him. Unfortunately, he had taken to drinking often and heavily, and would often hurl insults at my mother and all of us at the least opportunity. Verbal abuse and altercations became so commonplace in our home that there was a welcomed psychological relief every time my father stayed away from home.

Many of the adults around the house whispered among themselves that my father's actions were willfully cruel, but none of them would say anything to his face. They were afraid to offend my father. Earlier, I was also worried about offending my father by protesting his actions. But when physical violence towards my mother became imminent, I didn't need any more reasons to speak up.

I adored my father who was a self-made businessman. His charm and wit made him my hero. I wanted to give him the benefit of the doubt, but I had witnessed several of his indefensible actions that I couldn't give him that benefit. At this point, my father had become both the hero and the villain in the true-life story that was unfolding before me.

Some of my earliest experiences with my father were about learning to read and write. My father would write the letters of the alphabet across the floor or on a wall to teach us how to read. When we walked somewhere, my father had us reading almost everything in sight. From billboards to book covers to newspaper headlines, my father never missed an opportunity to have us practice reading. I loved reading billboards and gladly walked to many places with my father, and looked forward to reading out loud anything he handed me or pointed to. Occasionally, my father would encourage me to write letters to pen pals abroad.

Life In Progress: Winning Where It Matters

When my father wanted to disperse the crowd of kids playing in the compound of our home, he would usually show up with a book in hand. Fearing that he would call on them to read, these kids from the neighborhood will begin disappearing at the sight of my father with a book in hand. After the other kids left, my brothers and I would usually have to read. I didn't have a problem with the reading; it's his timing that often upset me. On days we didn't have school, we would plan to play all day. My father had a way of spoiling that fun, with reading.

Many other moments with my father were also opportunities to learn random but interesting facts. My ears would perk up every time he started off with, "So, did you know...?"

My father also gave us our haircuts. He was the best barber we knew until barbershops and real barbers began springing up in our neighborhood. The only haircut style my father could offer involved evenly trimming the hair to a close fade. He used a pair of scissors and a comb, so it was not often as smooth as it could have been. The occasional scissor cuts on the ears were painful, so we longed for an alternative haircut provider. The real barbers used electric shavers and provided some of the trendy haircuts that were popular with famous athletes and entertainers. When my brothers and I stressed that we needed more fashionable haircuts, my father would often respond calmly with an explanation about how most of the so-called trendy haircuts were worn by people who were not gentlemen.

When it came to yard work, my father was not afraid to get his hands dirty. We spent many Saturdays and Sundays outside together. Sometimes we would make flower beds by tilling the soil that lined the driveway inside our house, and then plant flowers in them. Other times, we'd dig a trench in the backyard to make a well for watering the flowers. When the trash that had been dumped for months behind the wall at the back of our house piled up, we would use shovels and rakes to push back the heap. There were also times when we would break boulders into smaller pieces of rock to fill the potholes in the street in front of our house.

These memorable experiences and the positive, refreshing side of my father is what I had known for most of my life. Thus, when the discord between him and my mother ramped up, it was extremely difficult to stomach. The beautiful childhood experiences had been replaced with unpleasant ones, and my father was slowly slipping out of my lineup of heroes.

But I was older now, and the reality of life was staring me in the face. To a large extent, my father had checked out of our lives even before he and my mother parted ways, and there was no going back to the way things used to be. My parents were not going to be together anymore, and that's a reality I needed to accept and move on.

Navigating relationships with two feuding parents and at the same time forging ahead with building my own life was a lot of work. It was also an awakening to the fact that the real world was not always filled with rainbows and butterflies.

My enthusiasm for life, however, did not wane. I was convinced of the bright future ahead of me, so I went about living my life and wearing a bright, cheerful smile most of the time.

• FOUR •

PREPARING FOR TAKE OFF

"One important key to success is self-confidence.
An important key to self-confidence is preparation."
- Arthur Ashe, athlete and philanthropist

Before I wanted to become a pilot, I wanted to be a journalist. I would watch the news and imagine myself reporting from an event's location. I pretended to be a journalist by interviewing my siblings who would pretend to be famous people. I listened to journalists on the radio and TV interviewing important people and memorized some of their questions for use in my make-believe world as a journalist.

My father didn't think journalism was a safe career choice. Journalists, especially those who the government of the day didn't think were helping their cause, were usually targets for persecution. It was common knowledge that some journalists suffered violent attacks; others' families were threatened with violence. Fearing that the authoritarian rule of that era would not be changing anytime in the near future, my father suggested that I study to become a pharmacist instead.

His recommendation of pharmacy was informed by the fact that one of his brothers, who owned a pharmacy retail store, had a well-paid pharmacist on staff. My father believed the pharmacist got paid well for not doing much. He added that, according to his brother, pharmacists would continue to be in high demand because of increasing government regulation limiting the kinds of medications that retail stores could sell without having a pharmacist on staff.

Coincidentally, my mentor Kwabena Bediako and his family operated a pharmaceutical distribution network, and he was studying to become a pharmacist. I had spent a great deal of time around Kwabena and his family, and was aware of how lucrative the pharmacy business could be. Kwabena had encouraged me to consider pharmacy as a career, and I did, at the O-Level stage of my secondary school career. However, studying to become a pharmacist was no longer an option for me after I switched courses in the Sixth Form.

So, here I was after national service and weighing all my options: a university in Ghana or America, journalism school, or flying school. Flying school was the least likely of the options since the cost was astronomical. But airplanes fascinated me so I continued to nurse the idea of someday becoming a pilot.

I would watch planes fly across the sky and wonder what it would feel like to be floating up there. I longed to see what the cockpit of an airplane looked like. I liked the sharp uniforms airline pilots wore. I also liked the idea of visiting destinations around the world as part of my job as an airline pilot. It didn't matter to me that there were limited job opportunities in Ghana for pilots. I knew it was a long shot, but I was a teenager then so it was all right to have big dreams.

I developed a sharper focus on my future career as a pilot and researched flying schools around the world. The cost of attending such a school, coupled with my limited family resources, plus the lack of scholarships, put a mild chill on my flying ambition.

I was eligible for admission to both the University of Ghana and Kwame Nkrumah University of Science and Technology. I purchased application forms but never submitted them to either university. Ghana Airways, then the premier national airline, was recruiting flight attendants, so I thought that would be my way of getting my foot in the door of the airline industry and eventually becoming a pilot. Therefore, I applied for a job there. I also considered joining the Ghana Air Force and had a couple of serious conversations about that with my uncle who was a retired military officer.

I decided to hold off with the Air Force and see how the flight attendant interviews would turn out. After several rounds of Ghana Airways interviews and tests over a two-month period, I was not selected. I was disappointed but because I believed I still had options, I was unshaken.

The government of the day was loosening its firm grip on the news media and private radio stations. Private stations like Joy FM and Radio Gold had appeared on the scene and were thriving. My friend Cyril Heyman had been hired as a sales and marketing representative at Joy FM after his national service. I saw that as the perfect opportunity to tag along and network my way into a gig as an on-air radio personality. The path seemed clear but getting on air turned out to be harder and more competitive than I thought.

Preparing for Take Off

In between running errands for Kwabena Bediako, I ran errands with Cyril as he called on business owners to encourage them to advertise on Joy FM. Cyril was good at what he did. He was born to sell, and he would often redirect my interest from being on the air towards the business side of the radio industry.

As much as I longed to be on the air, and believed I would be good at it, I only hoped to pursue it as a serious hobby. So, for the time being, I was okay with running errands with Cyril and learning from him. There was the possibility that I would have the opportunity to do voiceovers for commercials, if I stuck with Cyril. So, I hung on.

Joy FM was a big deal around 1995. It was a very sophisticated radio station that had the attention of most people – young and old – around Ghana's capital of Accra. When Cyril secured a client, he would hire a writer to produce a script for a commercial, hire a voiceover professional, and then book a studio to record the commercial.

After following him around on several of these productions, I was ready to try my hand at writing scripts for the radio commercials. However, I could not convince Cyril that I could match the quality of the professionals. I even offered to work for free just to prove myself, but he kept reminding me of his clients' high expectations, which he thought were too high for me to meet. I protested his lack of confidence in me but nothing changed.

One day, he had a problem. He needed someone to translate a script from English to Twi, but the professional he usually called on was not available. With no other option, he turned it over to me to give it a shot. It was done within about an hour. He vetted it with his peers at the radio station. And even though he did not tell me this, I knew he was impressed.

He gave me money to pay for studio time, and to record the commercial. Cyril did not bother to come to the studio to supervise the production like he usually did. I was on my own as the producer, and I was not about to fail. I had a feeling he was expecting a mediocre product by which he could finally prove to me that I was not ready for the big stage. But this was my one big shot, and I wasn't going to miss it.

Together with my friend Elizabeth Armstrong-Mensah, who also had no experience with voiceover work, we created what I thought was a respectable production. Cyril listened to the tape of the commercial and seemed mildly impressed. I guess he thought to himself that it didn't suck. He played it for his client, and, according to him, they loved it. So, it was on! The "Living Bitters" commercial was set to air. My voice was going to be on the radio!

And it was indeed! The unanimously positive reception various people gave to the commercial gave me the feeling that this was only the beginning. In the months that followed, I produced several radio commercials for Cyril. Even though we both knew he was paying me much less than what he would have paid the professionals, it seemed like a fair arrangement and I did not complain. He was giving me a shot and I was more than grateful.

Even though it was nice that my voice made it onto the radio many times (in the form of voiceovers), I wanted to do more than that. However, I was not as hungry as I needed to be in my pursuit of a full-time radio gig. I liked the idea of being on radio but didn't think it would suffice as a viable long-term profession for me, so I considered my other options.

I had never considered acting as a career option. As much as I loved to perform and believed I would be good at it profession-

Preparing for Take Off

ally, the economic prospects of becoming a professional actor in Ghana at that time deterred me. Most actors were very popular but seemed to be struggling financially. Thus, when my brother Arthur suggested that I consider studying acting at the University of Ghana's School of Performing Arts, I acknowledged the suggestion as a compliment but didn't seriously consider the option. I had a lot of respect for some of the prominent professional actors of the time but becoming an actor was not on my list of viable options.

I abandoned the idea of joining the Air Force. Given the overly politicized nature of Ghana's military at the time, I wasn't as enthusiastic about joining as I had been a few years earlier. My political views were firming up, and I disagreed with some of the strong-armed tactics of the country's leaders who were also in charge of the Air Force. I was concerned that my progressive views on national and political issues would place me on the wrong side of the partisan divide and adversely affect my career in the armed forces.

At this point, I had narrowed down my options to one; I was headed to the US to explore my options for colleges. I figured that if I could visit a few schools in person, I had a higher likelihood of convincing an admissions officer to award me a full-ride scholarship to allow me to attend at no cost.

I loved the comfort of home and enjoyed being around the people I was most familiar with. I wanted to experience university life in Ghana, especially the Hall Week celebrations and the variety of fun activities the students participated in. I was also fascinated by the long-term opportunities that could come with launching out into the brave new world of the US. I renewed my US visa from my Toledo trip and made plans to head out.

It is worth noting that while renewing my visa was an over-the-counter activity, that was an anomaly. A young Ghanaian who wanted to travel to the US for school or for a visit had a less-than-likely chance of obtaining a visa. This was especially the case when he or she didn't have a college admission with a scholarship in hand, or his or her parents didn't have a huge bank account to back that visa application. A very popular song at the time by Reggie Rockstone was about the pain of being denied a visa. That song was a major hit mainly because many young people could relate to the sentiments conveyed in the song.

I dropped off my passport and visa application in the morning and then picked it up at the end of the day, with my US visa renewed. No interview and no hassle. That was certainly not the case for most people.

But before leaving for the US, I had an idea to pursue a business venture that involved producing t-shirts for high school graduating classes. I was familiar with the ink-on-paper kind of printing because my father operated a printing press for many years. I was not familiar with the type of printing that placed inscriptions on t-shirts, but I was curious. T-Shirts Tomorrow, a screen-printing shop, had opened a production facility next door to Kwabena Bediako's house. The owner of the business was very gracious to me when I stopped by to check out what they did and how they did it. He explained the process and showed me around. They were producing t-shirts for a high school's graduating class. The t-shirts had the school's name across the front. On the back, it had the inscription "Class of 1995." That sparked an idea. Instead of writing a generic class year on the back, I wondered about customizing the shirts by adding a list of the names of the people in the graduating class on the t-shirts.

Preparing for Take Off

I could start with my graduating class from PRESEC because I could quickly get the official list of that graduating class. But it had been more than a year since graduation; so finding most of my former classmates to sell to them was going to be difficult. So, producing about 25 t-shirts as a test of the concept, and then producing more shirts later seemed like the perfect next step. I pitched the idea to the folks at T-Shirts Tomorrow. They wanted my business, but they required a minimum order of 200 shirts. I knew I had a cool idea, but I wasn't ready to risk ordering that many shirts. I couldn't sell to enough people to break even.

Oliver Asante, a local artist, agreed to do 24 shirts as long as I paid for the artwork and materials up front. That sounded good to me, so he had my approval to proceed.

The artwork he created comprised a torch, which is the central part of the PRESEC school emblem, and eight words. He represented each letter in the acronym PRESECAN with a matching word. A student from PRESEC is known as a Presecan, so I picked out adjectives that I believed most of my peers would identify with. As best as I can recall, there was "P" for "Positive," "R" for "Responsible," "E" for "Enlightened," "S" for "Studious," "E" for "Energetic," "C" for "Confident," "A" for "Academic" and "N" for "Noble." In the artwork, I wanted the words to radiate from the flame of the torch. Mr. Oliver convinced me that those words would be easier for people to read if they are neatly listed across the chest to the right of the torch. So that's what he did.

Within a week from when the shirts were produced, I sold the first 24 and ordered another 24. Mr. Oliver artfully decided to double his unit price unless I ordered a minimum of 100. I couldn't convince him to change his mind, and I was not going to be able to sell 100 shirts. So, I decided to move on to creating similar shirts for other student groups who would be graduating soon.

I recruited my friend Godfred Osei-Boakye (a.k.a. Gobbay), and he enlisted a friend of his who had contacts in schools in the Eastern Region. We pitched the idea to influential students on various secondary school campuses. They bought into the idea and became the points of contact at their respective schools, and took in hundreds of orders. Each of these middlemen was going to get a cut of each sale.

I struck a deal with two middlemen in a school in Accra. It seemed like a fair arrangement, and it looked like it was going to be a big payday. But as it is with most ventures involving middlemen, things don't always go as planned. Some human beings are just dishonest, and I had to learn that lesson the hard way.

These two young men, who were also my neighbors from Alajo, had taken in one of the largest orders as of that time. I produced the t-shirts per their instructions and delivered as agreed. When they claimed they hadn't received all the money for the shirts, I should have held on to the shirts until I had all my money in hand.

But I didn't. I turned over the t-shirts to them trusting that they would keep their word. I was wrong. I would visit the school a few times, and these guys didn't have my money ready. They did not return the t-shirts when I asked for them. They claimed they had given the shirts out to people who promised to pay, and they were still trying to collect the money.

That was a lie, and it became clear to me that I had been scammed. People I thought I knew quite well had scammed me. I was very sure they didn't need the money that badly; they were just greedy and dishonest.

Up until this point in my young life, I had been fortunate to deal mostly with people who kept their word in financial transactions. This episode, even though it did not completely erase my faith in handshake deals, was one of my early lessons about the fact that dishonest people do exist, and sometimes they come wearing a bright smile.

I was disappointed that I couldn't pass my working capital on to my brother Obeng who was going to take over from me since my departure from the country was imminent. That bad experience was not significant enough for me to lose sleep over, so I let it roll off my back. I didn't have as much money to pass on to my brother, but I was passing on an idea he could use to make more money than I could have given him. As it turned out, after I left for the US, the t-shirts business became profitable for my brother and some of our friends who later came on board.

When I was starting out with the t-shirts business, I did not know exactly where that venture was going to go, and almost did not pursue it because I had one foot out the door. But I was glad I created something that transcended me. Pursuing that business idea added to the foundation I would be building my life upon.

In the two years following Sixth Form, I had made several life-defining decisions, maneuvered complicated relationships, and embraced life as an adult. I had grown up. I had lost some of my inexperience about life and human beings, and was ready to step out on my own.

I did not fully know what the future had in store for me, as I got ready to head out of Ghana. The path I had chosen would involve my leaving the comfort of home and moving away from my familiar support system. I was giving up the comfort and safety of home but I dreamed of a future full of possibilities.

Life In Progress: Winning Where It Matters

Traveling to a destination more than 6,000 miles across the Atlantic Ocean meant literally leaving home. I was excited about the future and the many opportunities I would be tapping into.

The future was here, and I was ready to find my place in it.

PART II: FINDING MY PLACE

· FIVE ·

WELCOME TO AMERICA

> "What makes someone American isn't just blood and birth but allegiance to our founding principles and faith in the idea that anyone – from anywhere – can write the next chapter of our history."
> - **Barack Obama, 44th president of the United States of America**

Eddie Murphy's "Coming to America" is a hilarious movie. It is a story about the prince of a fictional African nation who on his 21st birthday decided that he was fed up with the pampered lifestyle he had known all his life, and that he was venturing out into the land of opportunity – America. He wanted to do more for himself, including choosing his bride. So, he arrived in Queens, New York, in search of a woman who would "arouse his intellect as well as his loins."

This movie is funny in part due to the manner in which many instances of the immigrant experience were exaggerated and humorously portrayed. I have watched this movie many times, and

Welcome to America

I enjoyed it every time. I know that it is not intended to be an accurate reflection of the reality of the millions of immigrants from around the world who have come to America, usually for more serious reasons.

It is a fact that most immigrants, especially those of us from Africa, share many experiences with Eddie Murphy's Prince of Zamunda. Examples of experiences that are common to the prince and real-life immigrants include the process of assimilating into the mainstream American culture, reconciling one's expectations of life in America with the reality of life in America, managing the expectations of family members back home, and weeding through solicited and unsolicited advice. At the top of the list of immigrants' shared experiences is the belief in the idea that there is enough room in America for everyone's dreams.

Like the Prince of Zamunda, I had come in pursuit of the idea that everything is possible in America. I had come to tap into the promise of America. But unlike the Prince of Zamunda, I lived in the real world where a happy ending was not guaranteed.

On that September morning in 1996 when I arrived in New York, I had an idea of what life and living in America would be like. Looking back on that day more than twenty years ago, I humbly concede that my ideas then about America were soaked in youthful optimism and naivetés. I was, however, in the right place at the right time, so I was going to have to live and learn.

My cousin Peter Ntiamoah was my host for my first two weeks. Peter is my father's nephew and he was my classmate in Sixth Form at PRESEC. He arrived in New York a year earlier and lived with his older brother, Benjamin Boateng. They graciously welcomed me into their Bronx apartment and treated me well. Peter showed me around the Bronx and New York City, "interpreted" to me what the Subway conductor was announcing over train's PA system, and oriented me to life in America.

Newark, New Jersey, which is about an hour by train from the Bronx, was my final destination. After two weeks in New York, I hopped on the New York City subway, switched to the PATH train in downtown Manhattan, and eventually arrived at Newark's Penn Station. Then on Bus 39, I arrived at my stop at the intersection of Lyons and Chancellor Avenue, and hauled my single suitcase to my new home, which was a brief walking distance away.

My host, Albert Edusei, welcomed me and introduced me to a couple of his neighbors. I was eager to get out there and get my piece of the American Dream. I was open to starting out with odd jobs or any opportunities that would come my way. Even though my host did not immediately expect me to contribute to the rent and the other household expenses, I knew it was only a matter of time that I would have to carry my own weight.

I waited around a couple of days for Albert to help me find a job, and got restless sitting at home flipping through TV channels. I decided to head downtown to see what was out there and possibly come across a job opportunity.

The money I had left on me was just enough for a one-way bus ride to or from downtown. I could either ride the bus downtown and walk home, or walk downtown and ride the bus home. I chose the latter. I was going to use my walk as a sightseeing stroll and to check out the neighborhoods.

I headed down on Chancellor Avenue towards Weequahic Park, and then turned onto Elizabeth Avenue towards downtown Newark. That was a 45-minute bus ride, and I leisurely walked it in about two hours. I was warmly bundled in layers of clothes so I enjoyed the cool crispness of that fall morning weather. There were, however, not many interesting sights along the way, but I was picking up on the vibe of the city.

Newark felt like a heavily scaled down version of New York City, and that was just fine with me. It was not crowded with people and skyscrapers, and people didn't seem to be rushing around as they did in New York City. I was unimpressed with how littered the streets were. I used to bemoan people littering the streets of Accra and assumed sophisticated Americans would not litter their streets as much. That was not entirely true. There are unsophisticated people in Accra and in Newark, and they didn't care about where they dropped their trash. For a brief moment, I wondered how the people who were paid to sweep the streets felt about littering.

Downtown was vibrant with cars, buses, shoppers, and pedestrians filling the streets and sidewalks. I entered one store, looked around, and then move on to the next. In one of those stores, McCrory's, I stumbled into Eric Amankwah.

Eric was four years my senior at WASS. He was in Sixth Form when I was in Form 3, so the two of us had limited interactions while we were both in the same school. Several years after WASS, Eric lived in a house near my father's office at Accra New Town, where I saw him more often. It had been about six years since I had last seen him.

Walking around downtown Newark, I was hoping to run into an African or a Ghanaian, thinking that it would be easier to have that person point me towards a store that was hiring. That is the main reason meeting Eric in the McCrory's store made me so delighted. I had not seen him for a few years, but he quickly recognized me and walked towards me when he saw me come through the door. I couldn't remember his name, but I remembered his very distinct face. I don't think he remembered my name either.

"What are you doing here?" he said with a broad smile.

"What are you doing here?" I replied, and we both burst into laughter.

I told him that I was strolling around in hopes of finding work, and that I would appreciate any help or referrals. He worked in that store and had been doing so for about a year.

He checked with the store's assistant manager and then informed me of an assignment that was available. He gently cautioned me that the assignment was not a very glamorous one. I was excited just to have a paying gig and to make an honest living, so I agreed to take it on.

The store's fourth floor, an open space meant for storing inventory, had been filled up with heaps of trash. They had been dumping up there for months bags of trash from the store, and the city's building inspector had issued them a citation. They had to get rid of the trash within 30 days or face further sanctions.

I scoped out the floor and figured out my game plan. This was not tougher than the chores I had done in Alajo clearing trash in the backyard. I donned my work gloves and got to work hauling bags of trash down the freight elevator and out to the dumpster on the side of the building. Some of the bags were broken, so I had to temporarily hold my breath, repack the trash into new bags, and then haul them away.

Earlier during my walk downtown, I had wondered how the people who were paid to sweep the streets felt about littering. Here I was, a few hours later, sweeping up trash that someone at the store had kept. I did not realize then the coincidence, and it wouldn't have made any difference to me even if I did. I also did not ask why they kept the trash instead of just throwing it away. Years later, Eric told me that he thinks it may have started with one person, instead of taking only cardboard boxes upstairs, took the bags of trash upstairs as well and left both there. The City of Newark required that empty cardboard boxes, which were to be recycled, be broken down and tied together into a bundle before being placed on the sidewalk for pickup. The compactor, which the store used to crush the empty boxes and then tie them up into a bundle, was located on the fourth floor. It is very likely that this person taking the empty boxes upstairs found it convenient to just leave the bags of trash with the cardboard on the fourth floor. Or maybe this person left the trash there accidentally, and then other people followed suit. And after months of this going on without anyone addressing it, they now had a problem. And I was now assigned to provide a solution.

One trip after another, I chipped away at the mountain of trash. A few hours later, Eric came upstairs to check on me. The wide-eyed look on his face gave away his amazement at how much of the trash I had cleared within that short period. That is when he told me that each of the last five people who had been hired for that assignment lasted less than 30 minutes before each of them quit. I shrugged and thanked him for recommending me. I stuck with it for three more days until the fourth floor was as clean as a whistle.

McCrory's was a departmental store that sold all kinds of items: canned goods, snacks, detergent, housewares, cosmetics, school supplies, clothing, and a whole lot more. It was a bustling store. According to the store's general manager, they didn't have any openings, but he was too impressed with my work on the fourth floor to let me go. He hired me to help out on the sales floor and to help clean up at the close of the day. I made myself useful, helping out wherever I was needed. Stocking shelves, keeping an eye on shoplifters, sweeping and mopping floors; I did it all.

There's a scene in "Coming to America" where Prince Akeem was handed a mop and a bucket with a wringer and asked to get to work cleaning. He did not know how to work the mop and the wringer, so he wheeled the bucket around until Mr. McDowell showed him what to do with the mop. I laugh out loud at that scene every time because I can relate to that. That was me trying to mop the aisles at a McCrory's store for the first time. For several months, I earned my keep at McCrory's, sweeping, mopping, and doing much more.

The store closed in the spring of 1997 shortly after it filed for bankruptcy. Before the store's doors were shut for the last time, almost all the staff was laid off. The few of us who were left had significantly reduced work hours. I spent the extra time I now had at the Newark Public Library.

The library was a 10-minute walk from McCrory's, and I loved the time I spent there. Personal computers and the internet were not as easily accessible then as they are now, but the library had them available for free to the general public. All I needed was a website address, and I was exposed to a treasure trove of information. I researched US colleges and scholarships.

Getting into college that year was a top priority. It was never lost on me that many of my peers in Ghana were in college at the time and I needed to keep up. It was also evident to me, from my interactions with other Ghanaians living in the US at that time that a college education was going to open more doors for me. I was singularly focused on trying to gain admission into a college. From my job at McCrory's and subsequent jobs as a gas station attendant, package handler at a UPS sorting facility, and housekeeping staff at a hotel, among others, I was able to save up some money to get started with school. My quest to find a full scholarship to attend college on a full ride had not yielded the desired outcome.

My pastor at the Franklin-St. John United Methodist Church in Newark, Rev. Lloyd Preston Terrell, had taken a keen interest in helping me get a scholarship to his alma mater, Payne College in Augusta, Georgia. He was able to get me a scholarship that covered tuition but not room and board. In spite of his best efforts, things didn't work out financially for me to attend Payne College.

Kean University was another option. It was a half-hour by bus from my home in Newark, and the cost of tuition was reasonable. I found out that I could pay for my tuition in bimonthly installments. This way, I could pay what I could and get started, and then pay the rest over time. I spent some time visiting the campus and hanging out with my friend Abena Nyanteng, who I knew from Ghana and who had been at Kean for a year. I applied, gained admission and started in September 1997.

Kean had a diverse population including students from African, Asian, European and South American countries. The students seemed to mix in quite well and that was very refreshing to me. In addition to Abena Nyanteng, there were about twenty other Ghanaian and African students I got to know. Most of us were a part of the African Students Association, a group that sought to help its members assimilate into the Kean community. That association served its purpose well by helping me and most of my peers form a network of friendships that proved helpful for thriving on campus. Additionally, the two Ghanaian professors there, Dr. Yamoah and Dr. Boateng, had an open-door policy and often welcomed us into their offices whenever we had questions about academics or questions about life on campus.

My routine, during most of my time at Kean, involved attending classes, working on campus as a tutor at the Learning Lab, and hustling away at an off-campus job. Even though I wished I had more time to engage in social activities on campus, I made the most of the little social time I had by hanging out with my friends as often as possible. There were no crazy parties, just casual outings to bowling alleys or hanging out at the apartment I shared with my friends Francis, Egbert, and Legge. At other times, we camped out in Abena's dorm room past visiting hours until an R.A. (Resident Assistant) asked us to leave.

My self-funded educational endeavor relied on the benevolence of others. One of the main reasons I appreciated Eric Amankwah as much as I do is the financial and moral support he provided towards my college education. Together with his uncle George Afful, they looked out for me in major and minor ways.

Another person who sacrificed to help me through my early years of college was my "Uncle" Ed Mettle. We met at Franklin-St. John United Methodist Church and developed a father-son relationship that would provide me with critical guidance and support in the years that followed. I felt a kinship with him after learning that he had migrated from Ghana many years earlier to attend college in New Jersey. He was very encouraging when it came to my academic goals and even lent me money at times to help with my tuition.

My Uncle Yorke Afriyie, my mother's brother whom we affectionately called Wofa Moto, chipped in significantly from time to time. During one of my telephone conversations with him, he closed with asking for my bank account information. When he subsequently wired a couple of thousands of dollars into my account, it felt to me like what winning the lottery must feel like. He did that twice, and he did that without my asking.

It was the benevolence of people like Wofa Moto, Uncle Ed, Eric and all the people who chipped in to help me fund my education that reinforced my belief in the idea of paying it forward. Since I couldn't fully pay back every contribution others made towards my education, I do the best that I can to pay it forward and help others pursue their dreams, be it with education or otherwise.

I settled on accounting as my major because the people I had conferred with told me that my job prospects upon graduation were much brighter with a business or computer science degree. A conversation with Dr. David Yamoah, who was then a professor of finance and the assistant dean at the university's College of Business, helped affirm my decision to go with accounting. My childhood interest in journalism popped up again, and I considered communications as a major. However, I did not know much about the career options in communications and most of the people I spoke with didn't either. Furthermore, I was a black immigrant with an accent and feared that opportunities to work in the radio or television industry would be hard to come by. I could become an unemployed graduate if I did not make a careful, realistic career choice. So I went with a safer bet: accounting.

I was able to get my A-Level coursework in math, economics, and geography from Ghana evaluated by the World Education Service, and credited to me at Kean. That took care of eight credits hours of required coursework, almost a semester's worth of work. During my first semester at Kean, I took on 13 credit hours of coursework. Halfway through the semester, I realized that the cost of tuition was the same whether I took on 12 credit hours or up to 21 credit hours. Being that I was paying out of pocket, I wanted to get the best value for my money. So, for the next semester, I signed up for 15 credit hours, upped it to 18 credit hours the following semester, and at one time 21 credit hours. I carried this much workload while working a full-time or two part-time jobs. It was a grind but I powered through. I took as many courses per semester as possible, some summer courses, and graduated in three years.

In the summers of my junior and senior years, I had internships with the accounting firm, Coopers and Lybrand, which eventually became PricewaterhouseCoopers through a merger. I secured this internship through Inroads, an organization that recruited and placed talented minority youth in business and industry. Inroads is a phenomenal organization that prepared many young people for corporate and community leadership, and they helped me and some of my friends start out our careers on firm foundations.

Before my internships, my idea of an accounting career was limited to the mundane numbers-crunching kind that I wasn't enthusiastic about. As an intern in a global public accounting firm, I was exposed to various aspects of accounting and life in corporate America that my opinion about the accounting profession evolved. Going to work daily dressed in a suit, I loved being an audit intern and could see myself working as an auditor in the oncoming future. Upon graduation in December 2000,

I accepted an offer from PricewaterhouseCoopers and started working there the following January.

Life was good and I was "the man." I enjoyed my work as an auditor and felt very fortunate to have the opportunity to do what I considered very important work. I was working for one of the "Big 5" accounting firms auditing financial records of major corporations. As the basis for big decisions, many investors and shareholders relied on the numbers that I verified for inclusion in audited financial statements. So while accounting wasn't my first love when entering college, I had found something meaningful about the profession and was going to dig my heels in. I was going to sit for the CPA exam and grow my career in public accounting.

Nine months in, the terrorist attacks of September 11, 2001 happened, and everything changed. The US economy took a hit, and PricewaterhouseCoopers laid off many people, including me. Surprisingly, I wasn't upset about losing my job. The writing had been on the wall for a couple of weeks as audit teams became smaller and work assignments were required to be completed in fewer days. I understood the company had to do what it had to do.

However, I became frustrated when finding another job proved to be more difficult than I had imagined. I had figured my "Big 5" accounting experience would make me a very attractive candidate for other accounting jobs. The reality then was that with the abundance of qualified candidates in the market, supply exceeded demand and jobs became hard to find. About three long months later, I was hired into a staff accountant role at Weichert Realtors, a real estate brokerage firm near Morristown, NJ.

There was nothing particularly exciting about this position. There was a very predictable routine of booking journal entries, processing accounts payable and closing the books at the end of the month, and repeating that cycle month after month. I was bored out of my mind on most days at work and I wanted to do more. I missed working at PricewaterhouseCoopers.

At that point, I had also grown tired of living in New Jersey, with its high cost of living and congested roads. I was ready to experience life in other parts of the country. I was also considering starting a family and wanted to live where I thought was more conducive to a young family on a budget. The time felt right to move on to greener pastures.

I had visited Columbus, Ohio, a few times before I decided to move here. My friend Kwame Agyakwa lived in Columbus then and spoke very highly of the city. I was sold on the city when I drove through a very clean and uncongested downtown and arrived at the Bureau of Motor Vehicles (BMV) to the politeness of the people behind the service windows. The people behind the service windows were extremely polite, unlike what I was used to in New Jersey. I remember telling myself that if the people at the BMV were this nice, I am sure this would be a city of very nice people and that I could see myself developing roots here for the foreseeable future. I've been living in Columbus since 2001, and I've never regretted the move.

From a naive young adult who arrived in a brave new world in pursuit of his dreams, I had grown into a sometimes-naive-but-wiser man. I have come very far from where I started out. Everything has not worked out exactly as I imagined, but I've had a pretty good run. I have dreams I'm still working on, and I believe the best is yet to come. I am mindful to pause, when life gets overwhelming, to appreciate all aspects of my journey so far.

There were times during my early years in the US when I got homesick. I belonged to a community that embraced me well, but I missed my family and friends and the familiar routines that I had left behind in Ghana. By my third or fourth year, I had assimilated reasonably well into life in America and had become very comfortable with the idea of making my home here beyond the foreseeable future. Before then, I had a 10-year plan that culminated with me returning to Ghana in nine years.

I would eventually switch from the I-am-getting-ready-to-go-back-home mindset, which was understandable given my love for Ghana and my desire to apply my skills and ideas there, to the this-is-my-home-and-I-belong-here mindset. That struggle of where to consider "home" was real for me, as it had been for many immigrants I know. When it came to fully embracing America as home, the nagging thought that I was abandoning the country of my birth worried me. I had a silent pact with Ghana that we were meant to be together for life.

America had been good to me. I had felt nothing but a warm welcome from America, my gracious host. But calling any country other than the country of my birth as my home was easier on my mind than it was on my heart.

The decision to call America home was initially an economic one. I had to work, live and build a future. The prospects of doing that successfully in America were much higher than it was anywhere else, including in Ghana. That was the part that had to do with my mind.

I was anxious about the part that had to do with my heart: my emotional connection to my birth country and the people with whom I shared certain innate values and cultural practices. There was awkwardness about switching identities (as frequently as a hip-hop artist changes hats) in order to simultaneously stay connected with my Ghanaian and my American identities. In predominantly American circles, I had to be as American as possible to blend in and not feel like an outsider. In predominantly Ghanaian circles, I had to be as authentically Ghanaian as possible lest I be branded pretentious or a sell-out. Chief among the things I did as part of the switching identities was the manner in which I pronounced words like "quarter" or "water" – whether with a silent "t" or not. I also had to be mindful of whom I spoke to in only Twi or only in English, or in a mix of both languages. The struggle was real, and this was a feeling that was commonly expressed by many of my peers with backgrounds similar to mine. I knew I needed to resolve this awkwardness, but it was not happening quickly enough.

In the early 2000s, a population growth spurt of Ghanaians in Columbus made the city begin to feel more like home. Before that, running into a Ghanaian around town was for me a noteworthy event. The word about Columbus as a destination city for immigrants spread quickly. Many Ghanaians from mainly New York and New Jersey relocated to Columbus, and the size of the Ghanaian community grew rapidly from less than one thousand into several thousands. Ghanaian businesses, churches and civic associations sprung up all over the place with many of the people, just like me, figuring out the cultural assimilation process. Together, we were building a hybrid community by merging elements of Ghanaian culture and values with those of mainstream America. I was fully immersed in the affairs of the growing community helping organize community-wide picnics, mobilizing friends to tutor children who needed help in school, and documenting private and public events as a video producer.

Certain things take time. An immigrant getting to a place of peace about his or her identity as an American, and fully embracing the ideas that make America the nation that it is takes time.

Musician and international activist Bono describes America as an idea. He says his native Ireland is a great country but not an idea. Great Britain, he says, is a great country, but not an idea. He added that the rest of the world sees America as one of the greatest ideas in human history. The idea that ALL men and women – no matter where they were born – are created equal; the idea that life is not meant to be endured but enjoyed; the idea that if we have liberty and justice, we'll figure out the rest. These are the ideas that, when put together, make America one of the greatest ideas in human history, according to Bono.

America, indeed, represents the idea of like-minded individuals banding together "in order to form a more perfect Union, establish justice, insure domestic tranquility, provide for the common defense, promote the general welfare, and secure the blessings of liberty to ourselves and our posterity."

The quoted portion above is from the preamble to the US constitution, the document upon which migrants from Europe founded the nation now known as America.

America, admittedly, has some ugly sides to it. From a history of racism that has not been adequately addressed, to the present existence of discrimination in its various forms, America and each of us who subscribe to the idea of America have our work cut out for us. The longing to go back to the way things were, on which Donald Trump rode to victory as the 45th president of the United States of America, is inconsistent with the ideas that this country was founded on. Some of those sentiments, which often came across as anti-immigrant and racist, are some of the ugly sides of America. It is in that same bucket of ugliness that I place the disturbing reality of gun violence that takes thousands of young and old lives year after year. As I wrestled with embracing the idea of America, I wrestled with becoming accountable for these ugly sides.

"This is America, and this is all of us," I would often whisper to myself when the inconvenient truths about the country stared me in the face. As an American, I would be embracing the good, the bad and the ugly of America.

When then-senator Barack Obama addressed the controversial comments his former pastor Jeremiah Wright made about injustices in America, he said he could no more disown him (Rev. Wright) than he could disown the black community who shared a similar view or his own white grandmother who once confessed her fear of black men and who on more than one occasion uttered racial or ethnic stereotypes that made him cringe. These people are a part of him, he added, and they are a part of America, this country that he loves.

I wasn't the only one wrestling with America's imperfections. Barack Obama had to give the "A More Perfect Union" speech to remind American voters that America is still a work in progress and that each of us has a role to embrace the ideas that make us stronger together, and work to bring us closer to a more perfect union.

It is no secret that I am a huge fan of President Obama and love him for his exemplary leadership. More than his many professional accomplishments, it is the sincere manner in which he navigated the many facets of his identity that I admire most. As the son of a black father from the African country of Kenya and a white mother from Wichita, Kansas, who spent part of his childhood living in Indonesia, earned a law degree from an Ivy League school and worked as a community organizer in inner-city Chicago, I drew inspiration from Obama's embrace of all the pieces that formed the man that he had become. President Obama, the person, and not just his election as the 44th president of the United States was one of the major catalysts for my full embrace of the idea of America.

Being an American, or for that matter a national of Ireland or Great Britain or Ghana or any other country, I think is more than merely carrying a passport of that country or claiming a birthright. It took the time that it took, but I came to realize that nationality means more than confining oneself to the geopolitical classifications that separate us one from another. The idea of who we are as Americans and citizens of the world is bigger than any one passport or national flag can contain.

And on a personal note, the birth of my daughter in 2004 was another notable catalyst that inspired my full embrace of the idea of America. I would be raising her as a black child in an imperfect America. As imperfect as this country is, it became clear to me that I had a responsibility to contribute fully towards creating a more perfect country for me, for my daughter and for the people I care about.

A few years ago, I produced a documentary for a friend who leads a Columbus church of more than 1,500 members, mostly Ghanaian and other African immigrants. We discussed what our respective experiences had been with fully embracing America as home. He acknowledged that many African immigrants live with an internal conflict regarding whether to see America as "home" or continue to think of their birth country as "home." Apostle Bismark Akomeah added the following in the documentary:

"A lot of our people have this mindset that they want to go back home and live their lives there. But I know that God brought us here for a reason and a purpose; that we have come to stay. Our children may one day go back to visit the continent of Africa and the individual countries that we come from. But we all know for sure that this is the place they call home."

He continued, "We cannot resist the need to invest financially, emotionally, spiritually and in the civil affairs of the city and country we currently live in. We have an obligation to build this community because this is home, too."

In keeping with the mindset of making Columbus home, Apostle Akomeah and his congregation in 2016 broke ground on a 14-acre piece of land adjoining their multi-million-dollar church property to build an elementary school to serve the Columbus community.

It goes without saying that such an investment in the community and the various contributions of natives and immigrants are how we are together writing the next chapters of Columbus' and America's history.

I am an African. My connection to the African continent is a cherished, inerasable part of who I am. That comes with a set of natural gifts, expectations, and idiosyncracies. Also, I am an American. I fully embrace the ideas that make the country great, and I work collaboratively with others to improve those things that need improvement. I am an African-American, both in the sense of being an African who is also an American, and also in the sense of being a black man in America.

I recognize that an immigrant is often a complex blend of several significant cultures and experiences, and that the immigrant experience is unique for everyone, even though huge similarities exist. Settling on where to call "home" has been an intellectual, economic, emotional and cultural process. On most days, "home" means more than a single physical location.

America's founding fathers, according to conservative commentator and political historian Matthew Spalding, expected that immigrants would add to the moral capital of the growing country, bringing with them the attributes necessary for the workings of free government, and promised advantages to those "who are determined to be sober, industrious and virtuous members of society."

I feel like the founding fathers were expecting me when they said those words.

Too bad they were gone when I got here.

· SIX ·

THE PURSUIT OF HAPPINESS

"I don't want to get to the end of my life and find that I've lived only the length of it; I want to have lived the width of it as well."

- Diane Ackerman, author and naturalist

The pursuit of happiness is one of the "unalienable rights" that America's Declaration of Independence says has been given to all human beings by their creator. Life and liberty are two others. It did not mention the right to happiness but instead, the right to pursue happiness. Big difference. At first glance, the right to pursue happiness may seem to mean the same thing as the right to pursue the material things that make us happy. As it turns out, there is more to this pursuit than accumulating stuff.

As a well-intentioned young man growing up in a country founded on the principle that each person has seemingly abundant opportunities to go after this cherished idea called happiness, I had my life planned out to pursue the things that would

The Pursuit of Happiness

bring me happiness. I planned to have a good job, a beautiful house, a lovely wife, healthy kids, great friends, occasional vacations, see Kirk Franklin or Michael Bolton live in concert, give to others in need, return to Ghana within ten years to establish a television and film production company, travel the world to see people, places and things, and live happily ever after. That is what I imagined would be happiness for me.

Happiness means different things to different people but almost everyone pursues some form of happiness. Pursuing the things that make us happy or that bring us joy or fulfillment is something most people around the world do to one degree or another. Even the monk who stays away from worldly pleasures to concentrate on spiritual matters pursues some form of happiness. So does the shopaholic who buys everything under the sun with money he or she doesn't have. So is the African migrant making a deadly voyage to cross over into Europe for better economic prospects. So is the teenager monitoring Instagram to see how many "likes" her latest glamor post has accumulated.

The more I have learned from others and from my own experience, the more apparent it has become to me that happiness is not something that I need to pursue actively. Happiness is the outcome of decisions and choices I make. My happiness is my emotional feelings ranging from satisfaction to intense pleasure that result from decisions and choices I make from moment to moment.

Some people have argued that the idea of pursuing happiness has made many people into nervous wrecks and victims of scams. There is some truth to that argument. The prominent Jewish psychiatrist Victor Frankl says, "It is the very pursuit of happiness that thwarts happiness."

Life In Progress: Winning Where It Matters

Opinions about happiness abound. Psychologist, priests, prophets, psychics, social scientists, entertainers, politicians, marketers, motivational speakers, and all the experts, including your friends and my friends, have opinions on what happiness is. There are hundreds of studies that describe what happiness is, measure why people are happy (or not), and how people find happiness. Some of these studies distill their findings into catchy bumper sticker slogans like "happiness is a choice" or "happiness is a scam." Others take a more nuanced approach, providing helpful ideas about how to perceive and pursue happiness, and taking into account the variations of what happiness means from culture to culture and from person to person.

While all these views and ideas about happiness have some truth to them, my pursuit of happiness started off with developing the skills necessary for making a living and then evolved into taking on responsibilities of adulthood. Along the way, I have learned that happiness is not a destination, but moments or periods that put a smile on my face or make me laugh out loud. Mingled with the happy periods have been periods of unhappiness, as well as periods of neither happiness nor unhappiness.

A 2013 article in the *Atlantic Magazine* declared, "There's more to life than being happy." The article, which emphasized the pursuit of meaning over the pursuit of happiness, cites Viktor Frankl's optimistic view of mankind as laid out in his celebrated book, *Man's Search for Meaning*. Curious, I looked up Victor Frankl to find out who he is, what he had to say, and how his work related to the article's bold assertion.

Frankl was an Austrian neurologist, psychiatrist, and a Holocaust survivor. His experiences as a prisoner in a Nazi concentration camp, where his wife and most of his family died, led him to discover the importance of finding meaning in all forms of existence. As the story goes, he helped others in the concentration camp discover meaning in life as well as helped them appreciate the "why" for their existence. In effect, he helped them towards decisions that enabled them to endure the painful life that they were subjected to by the Nazis.

Frankl strikes me as a naturally optimistic, glass-half-full kind of guy who didn't focus on his circumstance but on what he could make out of his circumstance. I don't think he went into the concentration camp with a gloomy view of life and then, after he'd been stripped of every practical way of pursuing happiness, he suddenly discovered that there is more to life than having material things. It is possible that may have been the case, but I doubt it.

He tells a story of two people in the concentration camp who were suicidal because they said they had nothing to expect from their lives. Frankl says he responded almost instinctively with, "Isn't it considerable that instead, life expects something from you?"

The idea that life might be expecting something from us, instead of our expecting something from life, is a note that should probably be printed on each person's birth certificate. It could shake off the entitlement mindset out of any perceptive person.

Before you conclude that Frankl was just a guy high on his own ideas, consider the examples of the Lou Gehrig and Dr. Martin Luther King Jr. who are two people with good reasons to be upset or bitter because life and circumstances seemed to have been unfair to them. These men conducted themselves in such ways that strongly suggest there may be more to life than just being happy.

Gehrig, the talented, seven-time Major League Baseball (MLB) All-Star player who spent 16 seasons with the New York Yankees and racked up numerous accolades for his talent and championship pedigree, was diagnosed with a very rare form of the degenerative disease, ALS, which is now called Lou Gehrig's disease. There was no chance he would ever play baseball again, and he was going to die soon. He was only 35. In his retirement speech, he said:

"Fans, for the past two weeks, you've been reading about a bad break. Today, I consider myself the luckiest man on the face of the earth."

And he finished with:

"So I close in saying that I might have been given a bad break, but I've got an awful lot to live for."

Dr. King, a Baptist minister, championed the advancement of civil rights through nonviolent civil disobedience in an extremely antagonistic society that practiced lynching, enforced discriminatory laws and was in no way ready to accept black people like him as fellow citizens. In a speech delivered during the 1963 March on Washington for Jobs and Freedom, he veered from the prepared remarks and shared a vision of the country that was a complete opposite of his reality at the time. He said:

"I say to you today, my friends, so even though we face the difficulties of today and tomorrow, I still have a dream. It is a dream deeply rooted in the American dream. I have a dream that one day this nation will rise up and live out the true meaning of its creed: 'We hold these truths to be self-evident: that all men are created equal.'"

I am not in any way saying these men were happy with their life circumstances. I'm suggesting that the path of our pursuit of happiness is sometimes paved with unpleasant situations. However, seeing beyond those unpleasant situations could mean the difference between experiencing happiness or not.

I tend to see a half-filled glass as half-full, and that fuels my hopefulness about the future. Others have a right to see a half-filled glass as half-empty. My glass-half-full outlook has been a major contributing factor to my overall happiness. That is not to say another person's glass-half-empty perspective is leading him or her away from happiness. Maybe all that person wants is a half-filled glass, and there's nothing wrong with that if that's what he or she truly wants. I like my glass to be all-the-way full, therefore when it is half-filled, I celebrate the fact that it is half-full and look forward to what's to come.

I have found the attitude of gratitude to be a major contributing factor to my happiness, regardless of where I am in my life. As long as I have life and good health, I have something for which to be grateful. So in moments of celebration, in moments of disappointment, or in the moments in between, the opportunity to give, receive, succeed, fail, learn, teach, and participate in life's diverse activities fills me with gratitude, and that makes me happy.

Some people tend to exaggerate their misfortunes to attract attention and pity. Psychologist Wayne Dyer told the story of a gentleman he met at the gym who was complaining about having a severe cold. When he asked how long the man had been dealing with the cold, the gentleman answered, "In three weeks, it will be a month!"

The tendency to see, anticipate, and emphasize bad outcomes or conditions, I think is a sure way to be unhappy. Based on his answer, this guy in Wayne Dyer's story is either expecting to have the cold for a whole month or is simply a person wired to be unhappy. People who are wired to be unhappy may pursue happiness all-day long and may never be happy because they are prone to readily finding reasons for which not to be happy.

Some experts say happiness is partly due to genetics, partly circumstances and partly our response to our circumstances. Frankl acknowledges that theory, but heavily emphasizes the part that has to do with our responses to our circumstances.

There are conflicting views on what the percentages are for each of these three categories that are believed to contribute to a person's happiness. Arthur Brooks of the American Enterprise Institute says genetics is 48%, significant life events are 40% and the remaining 12% come from lifestyle decisions about work, faith, community and work. Sonja Lyubomirsky, author of *The How of Happiness*, says genetics represents 50%, circumstances represent 10%, and the remaining 40% goes to our voluntary actions and decisions.

Even though the exact percentages are debatable, I find them helpful as a starting point for affirming the idea that I am not totally helpless when it comes to my happiness. These percentages suggest that more than half of the factors that drive my happiness are outside of my control. However, it is undeniable that a decent portion of the factors that determine my happiness is within my control. As long as I have some control over my happiness, I'm good to go.

I will even venture to say that for each of us, these percentages are flexible and an adjustable dial of sorts. And depending on how we each moderate our responses to circumstances around us, each of us could dial down the impact of the circumstances or the impact of genetics.

The Pursuit of Happiness

In a random sampling of people in most metropolitan cities in the world, a majority of the people surveyed are likely to agree that they have a right to happiness. When ask the follow-up question of whether it is a right to happiness or a right to pursue happiness, some of the respondents are likely to say it is the same thing. Thanks to advertisers, who have conveniently repackaged the right to pursue happiness as the right to happiness, most of us have bought into the idea that we have a right to happiness and not just a right to pursue it.

One of advertising's primary goals is to stir up a desire for the things we do not have. That desire, when stirred up long enough, often leads to a discontentment with what we have. And when that desire persists long enough without being met, that discontent turns into unhappiness. So, we decide we have to buy the things being advertised in hopes of becoming happy.

I like nice things, and they make me happy. In acquiring nice things, I've learned to get these nice things because I need or really want them, and not merely because they are on sale at a discounted price. Discounted prices do not always mean value. In spending money to pursue happiness, I find my happiness in the value I receive in exchange for the money I spend. I hate it when I feel like I've been coerced by an advertisement into buying something I did not need or really want.

The pressure that comes from advertising's constant reminders that you have to have the latest and greatest of everything makes it difficult to ignore the implied connection between happiness and having things. However, the extent to which I can dial down the impact of advertising on my desire to have things I don't need or really want contributes to my happiness. So whether it is Arthur Brooks' 12% that comes from lifestyle decisions or Sonja Lyubomirsky's 40% that comes from our voluntary actions and decisions, my response to marketing and social cues about the connection between happiness and having things goes a long way towards my happiness.

Ghanaian musician Kofi Kinaata sings a song titled "*Susuka*," which translates into "take a measured approach to complaining about your misfortunes." The song echoes the idea that there is always someone somewhere who would trade places with you. He sings that, no matter how far your house is, another person's house is farther than yours, and that instead of crying about having no shoes, think of the man with no feet. Happiness, I have learned from this song, is about perspective and about the blessings or misfortunes we tend to focus on.

An African folktale tells the story of a man who decides to commit suicide because he was convinced life was not worth living. He didn't have much to expect from life, so he took off all of his clothes and walked into the forest to hang himself from a tree.

Another man came along, found the suicidal man's clothes and believed that to be the answer to his prayer for new clothes. He therefore thanked God and walked away with the clothes. The suicidal man, realizing that he forgot to carry a rope for the hanging, returned to get dressed in order to go get a rope. But his clothes were gone.

In the movie version of this folktale, the moment the suicidal man discovers that his clothes were gone will be the moment that God, played by Morgan Freeman, shows up dressed in a white suit. God will recite Victor Frankl's words to the suicidal man saying, "Isn't it considerable that instead, life expects something from you?"

The Pursuit of Happiness

There is no doubt that there is more to life than happiness. Happiness is an important part of life, and each of us wants to be happy. Each of us pursues some form of happiness.

Maybe the "pursuit" in the phrase "pursuit of happiness" was intended as a reminder that happiness requires effort. Perhaps it is a reminder that we are not entitled to anything but that which we have pursued or gone after. Maybe it was intended by the authors of America's Declaration of Independence as a reminder that happiness is an ongoing process that spans the entirety of our lives.

Even though the list of goals I had when I set out as a younger man in my pursuit of happiness have not all come to fruition the way I anticipated, I have learned many things that help me put the pursuit into perspective. I have learned that being happy and pursuing happiness are not the same thing. I have learned how valuable my attitude of gratitude contributes to my happiness. I have learned that my happiness is connected to the contributions I make towards the happiness of others. I have learned that even though there is no one way to happiness, there are actions that could almost guarantee one's happiness, just as there are actions that could almost guarantee one's unhappiness. And I use the word "guarantee" very guardedly because nothing in life is guaranteed. I have also learned that no matter how good things are, they could get better (or worse), and no matter how bad things get, they could get better (or worse).

With all these lessons I have learned, I tend to expect things to get better no matter how good or bad they are. Even when bad things happen to me, I look for the silver lining. That is not a technique to dismiss the reality of the misfortune but rather a technique to keep moving towards happiness.

As a well-intentioned younger man, I pursued many things apparently in pursuit of happiness. I have found some of the things I pursued, and I'm still pursuing some others. With the things I found, I realized that some did not bring me the happiness I had dreamed of. Some of the things I pursued disappeared even before I could find them.

As a more enlightened older man, I have several things I am pursuing, and I am trusting that those things will bring me some form of happiness. Whether the pursuit or the results bring me happiness or not, I am grateful for the inalienable right and the opportunity to pursue what I consider happiness.

• S E V E N •

CLARITY OF PURPOSE

"If you make a conscious effort to find out what it is that you're supposed to do [with your life], it can literally save your life."
- Les Brown, life coach and entrepreneur

The question of why each of us is here on Earth will have to be asked (and answered) individually, and probably several times throughout a person's life. Some people claim to have known from a very young age what their purpose (the reason they are on Earth) is, and have been working on it ever since. Most people, myself included, had an idea of what we were passionate about but not necessarily an answer to the philosophical question of why we are here on Earth.

As I recall, the question "What do you want to be when you grow up?" was my introduction to the idea of purpose. I don't remember thinking of it as a question about purpose, but I probably should have. Maybe I might have thought of the question of purpose much earlier if the question had been followed with "Why do you want to be what you want to be?" Even then, I doubt if it would have had the appropriate context to figure out what my purpose was.

Maybe a serious discussion about purpose is better suited for young adulthood and in adulthood when a person has had some life experience. By then, the person may also have a better idea of what he or she is good at, and how those abilities could serve the people around him or her. Certainly, it doesn't hurt to set the stage early and prompt a child or teenager to begin thinking about purpose.

In my early teen years, I thought of purpose and vocation (or profession) as the same thing. I continued to think that way for many years. It made sense to me that the reason I am here on Earth is to grow up and become successful at something that I do for work. I wanted to be a journalist. Why? The idea of reading the news on TV seemed like an important, fun job. And I wanted to do that. The question of how that was connected to why I am here on Earth never really came up. I was only a kid, and it was all right for me to want to do something simply because it seemed like fun.

As the years went on, however, the question of purpose – my purpose – often came up when I was trying to figure out how to make something meaningful out of my skills. As a teenager, my primary sources of information on important life matters were Christian authors and church leaders. Many of the books I read and the sermons I listened to on the subject often defined a person's purpose to be the service that God requires of him or her. From the way I understood it, my purpose was about what I did in service to God, specifically within the church and in expanding the influence of the church. Several adults I admired served actively within the church so that was the standard I embraced.

In my late teens and early 20s, I was actively involved in my church and was being mentored for leadership within the church. My interpretation of the message I received about purpose was that my professional career was just something I would be doing to earn a living, but my purpose was to be of service in the church. That never really sat well with me because as much as I enjoyed being a part of my church, I had never been too fond of active leadership within the church. Even though I welcomed opportunities to serve and to lead, I was always hesitant about confining my service and leadership to within the walls of the church.

The church-centered interpretation of purpose seemed limiting to me. There were things that I wanted to do that did not necessarily fit within the confines of the church, so I struggled with the burden that I may not be living purposefully by pursuing those non-church interests. For example, when I considered becoming an on-air presenter on a radio station in Accra in the 1990s, I was bothered by the silent protests from my Christian friends who viewed being a radio DJ who presented secular content as straying from the faith. Reluctantly, I chose to exclusively pursue opportunities with Christianity-based radio programs. A career as a pilot, which I was also considering at the time, was not going to be in service to the church, but I didn't think anybody cared whether it did or not.

I concluded that making lots of money and contributing some of that to the church would suffice as using my skills and talents in the service of God, albeit indirectly. Since I was still privately evaluating how my career choice would align with my understanding at the time of purpose, I rarely discussed the career options I was considering.

Clarity of Purpose

While I agreed with the idea that my purpose is God-ordained, in that my creator has endowed me with certain gifts and talents to be used in the service of others, I wrestled with the idea of where the appropriate place was for me to focus that service. It was important to me that whatever I chose to do professionally, whether as a journalist or as a pilot or as a presenter on a radio or TV station or as any other professional, was pleasing to God, and that I was operating within my purpose. Leading Christian voices such as Pastor Rick Warren who authored the bestselling *Purpose Driven Life*, as well as the leaders of my church, understandably, advocated for my purpose (and that of all Christians) to be directed towards the work of the church.

In my 30s, I contended with several existential questions without getting satisfactory answers. This was a period where I earnestly tried to reconcile the cultural and religious ideas I had embraced as a young adult with the ideas I had been exposed to as part of my expanding worldview. My purpose was one of these ideas that I sought clarity about.

It took me several years, and a lot of questions, conversations and observations to find that clarity. With time, I came to discover that my purpose on Earth is to share my gifts with others and to help make situations better than I found them. That is what I had been doing all along, but I hadn't wrapped my mind around it in such a way that affirmed the things I like to do as being in line with my purpose.

Boiling my purpose down into a single sentence made it easier to recall in answering the question of why I do the things I do. It also makes it less complicated to explain to others. Having a clear purpose in life reduces the likelihood of being distracted by things that do not matter nor contribute to success.

Life In Progress: Winning Where It Matters

Serving others is a noble activity that takes many forms. In the various roles I play as a parent, as a professional, as a volunteer, and in many other ways, the common theme is that of service to others. I feel a great deal of satisfaction from seeing others do well and from helping them overcome challenges. So, I find myself many times reaching out and lending a hand, or welcoming individuals who have a need that I can help meet. The more I share my skills and talents by contributing to the well-being of others, the more I feel like I'm doing what I was placed on Earth to do. Of course, I cannot help everyone who needs help but I do the best I can.

Mentoring or tutoring young people, for example, is one thing I had always done but didn't realize was aligned with my purpose. As the son of a teacher, I picked up an early interest in teaching others. Helping my sisters practice their ABCs was a part of my daily chores as a 10-year-old, and I was more than happy to do that. The many hours I spent hanging around in my mother's classrooms nurtured my interest in teaching. During my post-secondary school national service, I happily took on my role as a teacher. In college at Kean University, I worked for several years as an accounting and math tutor. Since moving to Columbus in 2001, I have from time to time tutored individuals or groups. I always thought I did that just because it was just something I liked to do.

More than just something I like to do, tutoring or teaching fits right within my purpose of sharing my gifts with others and helping make situations better than I found them. It took me some time to realize the connection that exists between helping others understand math concepts and my purpose in life. I realized that the question about purpose is not merely answered

Clarity of Purpose

with what I do, but instead with why I do what I do. Why I do most of the things I do is to help others do well.

A favorite example, which helped me realize that helping people to succeed is how I lead my purpose-driven life, is that of my tutoring relationship with a young man named Ezra.

I met Ezra and his family in 2001 when his father hired me to produce a video during a traditional Ghanaian ceremony to celebrate Ezra's birth. I lost touch with the family but occasionally ran into the father at community events.

Many years later, when Ezra entered eighth grade, his father hired me again - this time as a tutor. In our initial conversation, Ezra admitted to having fallen behind in school because his previous school did not demand much of him and he didn't challenge himself academically. I admired his honesty and agreed to work with him, not only on math concepts but also coaching him on helpful study habits.

I worked with him alone and in small groups, and observed him work independently. He gradually overcame his tendency to second-guess himself, developing competency in various areas of his study. He successfully completed middle school and passed the entrance exam for one of Columbus' prestigious Catholic high schools, St. Francis DeSales. I still maintained a mentoring relationship with Ezra, offering as much guidance as I can as he navigated the academic and social aspects of his young adult years.

Helping young people like Ezra navigate life feels like a worthwhile thing to do. It is so worthwhile that spending parts of my days helping him and other young people feel heard and empowered leaves me feeling like I am doing exactly what I was placed on Earth to do. Likewise, helping adults gain clarity about goals they're trying to accomplish or helping them take their game to the next level brings me a satisfaction that reinforces for me the idea that I am operating within my purpose.

It was relatively easier to see how my purpose is connected to service. What was not easy to embrace was how my purpose is connected to leadership. I often tripped myself up with the false idea that leadership was a role certain people are appointed to play. I eventually figured out that leadership is a mindset. Leadership is an accountability mindset. Leadership is the mindset that reminds me to be the best version of myself and help others do likewise. Leadership is the mindset that reminds me that I cannot do it all by myself, and that I need to empower others to contribute to the common good.

Until I came to this realization, I thought that leading people was one thing and serving people was something else. In reality, service and leadership always go hand-in-hand. I was comfortable with viewing myself as serving whereas I was in fact doing both most of the time. Whether it is with leading at home, in the community, at work, or among my friends, I had been hesitant to accept credit for the leadership I provide. It is a weird delineation, but in my mind, I separated the two for a long time.

Service and leadership are connected to purpose because I believe you cannot truly serve people without a sense of accountability. Neither can you truly lead people without serving them.

When I eventually made the connection between service and leadership, and how both formed the core of my purpose, I shed the mindset that erroneously reserved the "honor" of leadership to a chosen few who were in charge of things. I have fully embraced the idea that leadership and service are intertwined and both are vital aspects of my purpose-driven life. In serving people, I often provide information they need to make decisions. In leading people, I often offer motivation and feedback they need to pursue their goals or overcome hurdles. In most situations, this two-pronged approach has been my secret formula for helping others and making situations better than I found them.

The most effective leaders I have learned from are the ones who empower others through service and leadership. These are the leaders who identified opportunities for me or pointed me in the right direction, and then supported me with their guidance and feedback. From having been on the receiving end of that kind of service and leadership, I have endeavored to practice more of that as well.

Basketball superstar LeBron James is one of my favorite professional athletes. He is also a person who exemplifies the idea that service and leadership go hand-in-hand. I admire his exceptional abilities and the manner in which he carries himself on the big stage of global stardom. Above and beyond those fine attributes, how he empowers others to lead is what I admire the most about him. While it is probably easier for someone as rich and powerful as he is to exert the kind of influence he exerts, it is the manner in which he leverages this talent and influence to make other lives better that makes me a huge fan of his. That service-cum-leadership quality is something that many successful athletes and people with more money and influence have not demonstrated as well as he has.

Drafted into the National Basketball Association (NBA) in 2003 at 18 years old, LeBron has built a successful career highlighted by many accolades, including leading the Cleveland Cavaliers to their first-ever NBA Championship and ending a

52-year championship drought for the city. When he returned to the Cleveland Cavaliers after winning two championships with the Miami Heat, his reasons were thoughtfully conveyed in a manner that cemented my image of him as someone who had a vivid clarity about his purpose.

He announced his return to Cleveland in a July 2014 *Sports Illustrated* article. The article opened with the following words:

"Before anyone ever cared where I would play basketball, I was a kid from Northeast Ohio. It's where I walked. It's where I ran. It's where I cried. It's where I bled. It holds a special place in my heart. People there have seen me grow up. I sometimes feel like I'm their son. Their passion can be overwhelming. But it drives me. I want to give them hope when I can. I want to inspire them when I can. My relationship with Northeast Ohio is bigger than basketball. I didn't realize that four years ago. I do now."

He closed the article with the resolve of a self-aware leader who understands the difference between being important and being relevant:

"I feel my calling here goes above basketball. I have a responsibility to lead, in more ways than one, and I take that very seriously. My presence can make a difference in Miami, but I think it can mean more where I'm from. I want kids in Northeast Ohio, like the hundreds of Akron third-graders I sponsor through my foundation, to realize that there's no better place to grow up. Maybe some of them will come home after college and start a family or open a business. That would make me smile. Our community, which has struggled so much, needs all the talent it can get. In Northeast Ohio, nothing is given. Everything is earned. You work for what you have. I'm ready to accept the challenge. I'm coming home."

Clarity of Purpose

LeBron was important in Miami but he is relevant in Cleveland. Being important is good but being relevant is better. The results of his decision affirmed the wisdom of his decision. I am more than happy that Cleveland won a championship the year after his return. Even if they didn't win one, I would still regard his decision to return to Cleveland as one of the finest examples of operating with a clarity of purpose.

On and off the basketball court, LeBron has empowered his teammates, friends, and associates to become more than just people who depend on him. I remember reading some of the criticism he received when he appointed his friend and high school teammate Maverick Carter as his business manager. That was in 2006. Not knowing much about Carter's background then, I feared the critics might be right.

But after the string of lucrative business deals and operations he's put in place – including a successful Hollywood television and film production company, a wide-reaching scholarship program, and the billion-dollar lifetime deal with Nike – it is clear to me that Carter was and is the best man for that job.

LeBron's practice of empowering people around him is a leadership lesson that is not lost on me. More than his talent, the clarity he demonstrates concerning his purpose has made him one of the most influential people in sports and life around the world.

In my young adult years, the idea that God required my purpose to be in service in the church was a struggle because I felt my sphere of influence should reach beyond the walls of the church. I have always been happy to contribute to initiatives in the churches that I've been a member of but have rarely been interested in permanent leadership roles. This disinterest may have been due to my sometimes contrarian views on theology and Christian culture.

Being a pastor, elder or another leader in the church is noble, and I felt guilty for many years that I wasn't interested in any of those roles. And as a member of a Ghanaian (and predominantly Christian) community where a very high premium is placed on leadership in the church, it felt like swimming against a tide every time I sought to discover my purpose outside of the church. It took me a while to see clearly what exactly I was placed on Earth to do. But when that clarity came, it fueled my purpose.

My mother once told me that discovering your purpose is one thing, and having clarity about your purpose is another. She described the lack of clarity as the reason a person might fumble around incompetently and be unsuccessful even though they may be doing what they were placed on Earth to do. She added that clarity comes from seeking divine guidance and from the counsel of wise people.

My purpose is clearer today, so I am thankful for the divine guidance and to all the people who've guided me along my way. I have learned that work that is pleasing to God is work that serves people and makes conditions better for others.

For the rest of my life, I want to inspire people. I want to enable ideas. I want to connect people to opportunities and give them tools and resources to bring ideas to life. I want to learn and teach what I know. I want to share my talents with people, and leave conditions better for others.

That's my purpose. That's why I'm here.

· EIGHT ·

WORK AND HAPPINESS

"The only way to do great work is to love what you do."
- **Steve Jobs, inventor and businessman**

The conventional wisdom about career choice suggests that a person should follow his or her passion when choosing a career. That is not always a clear-cut option for everyone. Some passions easily translate into careers that are in demand. Some passions do not lead towards gainful employment and do not have a track record of economic viability. Deciding to pursue such a passion, especially when it involves financial obligations, sets the stage for some tense conversations with oneself and with loved ones.

Others' career choices have happened by default: he or she took on whatever was offered or available and continued on that path until that job was interrupted by circumstances or events. Others are still searching and may be wondering why there is no easier way to find work that brings them happiness.

Economic practicality drove my career choice during my early years in college. When I graduated and landed a good job as an auditor with a "Big 5" accounting firm, I was on the fast track to becoming a well-paid CPA in a few years. A few more years after that, I would have probably become the controller or an auditor in a well-respected organization in corporate America. I may have continued on that path because I had no compelling reason not to.

My company paid for my CPA exam preparation course and also made scheduling accommodations to allow all first-year associates to sit for the exam. I started the preparation and registered for the exam even though I didn't have a burning desire to become a CPA. My lukewarm interest in becoming a CPA further eroded when I was laid off and was not going to be reimbursed if I continued with the exam preparation course or the exam itself. As undesired as that lay-off event was, it may have been a blessing in disguise. At the time, I had an accounting degree, so I was going to figure out what I was going to do moving forward. I thought about doing something other than accounting but, again, economic practicality made me stick with it.

In order to find enjoyment and fulfillment in the work I do, I wanted to spend my time doing something I was passionate about. The idealistic part of my brain gave me that idea. The practical part of my brain reminded me of the economic and social realities that I needed to consider. It took the idealistic and practical parts of my brain working together to take me on the winding road that eventually set me on the path of pursuing a profession that matched my passion, and made economic sense.

Before enrolling in college, I couldn't simply search on Google or YouTube to find out what I needed to know to confidently choose to pursue a communications degree. In the pre-Google days of the late 1990s, I had to go to the library to find a book on the subject or find someone with experience in that career field to seek his or her opinion.

Going to the library to research careers felt like too much work, so I skipped that. I did not know anyone who had a communications degree or worked in communications. My limited idea at the time of what you did with a communications degree had to do with working in radio or on television.

Most of the people I knew and sought career advice from were successful MBAs and computer science professionals. They were candid about my job prospects with a communications degree, citing the fact that an immigrant with an accent like mine was not what recruiters looked for when they looked for communications professionals. There was some truth to that sentiment as I found out from my unscientific research of observing the lack of racial diversity in TV jobs. With degrees in computer science or business, I knew many people who were doing very well so I began leaning in that direction.

Dr. Yamoah, a trusted advisor and the associate dean of my university's College of Business at the time, told me his story of successfully changing careers from engineering to finance. He spoke approvingly of the various ways in which I would be able to apply my business education, even if I decided to do something else in the future. He advised that I should not focus on the degree but rather on the skills I would be developing. He pointed out that no matter where my career eventually took me, I would need business skills to think strategically and to solve business problems.

That made sense to me.

Work and Happiness

I majored in accounting and it turned out to be a good choice because I landed a good job just before graduation. I liked what I did for work as an audit associate: examining accounting records, testing internal controls for the issuance of audited financial statements, and performing due diligence testing for mergers and acquisitions. I was paid decently for my work. I could have continued this work for a few more years.

But when my company no longer needed my services because of the economic downturn at the time, I had to move on and find another way to make a living.

It would be two more months before I would earn another paycheck. That next full-time job was as a staff accountant at the real estate company, Weichert Realtors. This was a decent job with nice people, a respectable salary, and a 30-minute commute. But the predictable routine did not offer any excitement or a sense of fulfillment. I worked there for about six months before resigning and relocating to Columbus.

As committed as I was to finding an accounting-related job in Columbus, I was seriously entertaining the idea of going back to school for a communications or marketing degree, and making a career switch. Also on the table at the time was my interest in attending film school at Ohio University in Athens, about two hours southeast of Columbus.

Within a month of arriving in Columbus, a temp agency assigned me to a four-week clerical project at Nationwide Insurance. The four-week assignment turned into a two-month assignment. During the last week of the assignment, another temporary position opened up at the same company and I took it. This new assignment involved supporting brokers who invested the company's money in bonds and other securities. After coordinating trade settlements, reconciling accounts and analyzing portfolios for about six months, my temporary role was converted into a permanent one. I stayed in this position for a little more than four years before finally making a career shift to marketing and communications.

That career shift did not happen at the flip of a switch. It took a combination of several things: a careful assessment of my situation, a decision to face my fears by stepping outside of my comfort zone, and a confluence of events.

This was 2006 and it had been nearly six years since graduation, and I hadn't felt the happiness that I expected to come with a career. Among other reasons, I was convinced that I would enjoy my professional life more if I were engaging my natural abilities more. My natural abilities leaned more towards writing and other creative tasks, and not towards the repetitive, numbers-heavy tasks that my job as an investment analyst consisted of.

As a side hustle, I had started a business producing event videography. I viewed event videography as excellent preparation for my film production aspirations, and passionately spent a great deal of time figuring out how to use various equipment, software, and production techniques. I loved every minute of my life behind the camera and at the editing desk. I was consumed by my passion for video production and longed to do more of that kind of work. While in the office during the day, I often looked forward to returning home and continuing editing or beginning the next video project.

My attempts at transitioning into a communications or marketing role at Nationwide Insurance ran into walls time and time again. I had a decent portfolio of video projects, writing samples and some marketing materials, but I couldn't land any communications or marketing jobs. I was convinced that the HR people who looked at my resume didn't bother to look further once they saw that my degree was in accounting.

"I think I should go back to school for a communications or marketing degree," I told myself.

I was aware of the fact that obtaining a communications or marketing degree in itself would not guarantee me the kind of job that I wanted. But I was also aware that my chances of landing a communications job with an accounting degree were slim to none.

I had been taking part-time classes at Franklin University towards an MBA. I was pursuing an MBA because that was the only course of study for which Nationwide would reimburse me since the requirement for reimbursement included the education being directly related to my role at the time.

My dilemma: Do I stay at Nationwide and take one course per semester (since that's what tuition reimbursement covered) and graduate with a free MBA in about ten years, or take the leap and pay for a graduate degree in something I wanted to do? This way, I'd be done in 12 months and get to work doing something I loved.

I knew which decision made more sense, but I had a different idea: to pursue my passion for acting and filmmaking! I was determined to become a professional actor, as well as write and produce my own movies.

In my early college years, I tested the waters in acting. I attended weekend acting workshops in New York City and even took private lessons with a theater professor at Kean University. I auditioned for roles and got selected for a few small roles in some student films. Because of conflicts with my class and work schedules, my acting pursuit did not take off then.

So, in the middle of 2006, when I considered the acting and filmmaking idea, I was really serious. I was very confident with my camera operation and video editing abilities, and figured I would earn a living with that while I wait for acting opportunities that would pay a living wage. I thought of heading to New York City or Los Angeles, giving it my best shot and seeing what will happen next.

A year earlier, when I was still married and my daughter was less than a year old, my idea about going off to become an actor and filmmaker would have sounded crazy, even to me. However, my marriage had fallen apart at this point. I was starting over in my personal life so leaving town to start over in a new profession as an actor and filmmaker made sense to me.

Part of my hesitation with leaving my job at Nationwide had been the affordable health insurance coverage that I was going to lose. Voluntarily losing my job and the related health insurance coverage meant that I would have to buy expensive private insurance. But my infant daughter, who needed the coverage the most, was now living in Ghana with her maternal grandparents. She was not likely to return to the US for a few months to a year. Thus, it made sense to launch out at that time when I could risk not having health insurance coverage for myself (and for my daughter) for a few months while I tried to get my new career off the ground.

I quit my job at Nationwide that September. I was not going back to school for a degree in marketing and communications. I was headed to New York City to pursue my dreams in acting and filmmaking with what I felt was a rational plan.

I had my bags packed, my 401(k) retirement account cashed out, and counting down to the beginning of my new adventure. Before I could leave town, I had to shelve my plans until further notice. Afriyie's mother, who I had been feuding with over the manner in which she sent Afriyie off to live with her parents, became ill with an infection to her spinal chord. The paralyzing ailment required multiple surgeries, hospital and extended nursing home stays spanning more than seven months. This was a life-threatening condition for her. With the life of a person I cared about being on the line, my priorities shifted. I suspended the New York City plans and stayed in Columbus as her primary caregiver until she got better and literally back on her feet again. We eventually parted ways for good after her full recovery.

In figuring out what I was going to do next, since I was not going to New York City, I alerted several employment agencies that I was available to consider job opportunities, including accounting-related jobs. That December, I had a phone call from my contact at the temp agency. This was the same person who helped me find my Nationwide job, and she had a communications job interview lined up for me. She described the job as one that required a unique combination of writing and design skills, along with the ability to interview people and document processes.

That interview went well. I was offered the job shortly thereafter, and I started work as a communications coordinator at this lifestyle management company in January 2007. I didn't have a clear idea of what a lifestyle management company was at the time of interviewing for the job. I eventually found out that it involved helping a very high-profile family manage their property, schedules, social events and a whole lot more. I had a communications role on this team of six, and it was one of the best jobs I have ever had. I was finally doing communications-related work and was getting paid slightly more than I was paid in my last position at Nationwide. Work was fun, and there was something exciting to look forward to each day.

This communications coordinator job was supposed to be a one-year contract. However, it lasted three and a half years. That job ended because I worked myself out of a job by gladly training other colleagues to do the things I did. When it came to a time when there wasn't much for me to do, I was ready to move on. My employer and I agreed to a severance package, and I was off to the next thing.

I didn't know exactly what was next, but I was hopeful something interesting would come my way. I had earned a master's degree in marketing and communications from Franklin University by attending classes in the evenings over course of three years and half years. With my latest work experience and my master's degree in hand, I believed I would be marketable as a candidate for a communications or marketing job.

The offers didn't come rolling in as quickly as I had hoped. In that seven-month unemployment stretch, I spent most of my time launching an online radio station and learning about web analytics.

The online radio venture, Sahara Radio, was a fun experiment that evolved into a partnership with three other friends. It operated on a 24-hour programming schedule and offered African-centered music, talk and news to listeners. With a fair working knowledge of radio stations and my comfort with figuring out how things work, I cobbled together the required equipment and began operation in April 2011.

One mixed blessing of an online radio station, compared to a terrestrial radio station, was that geography did not restrain our broadcasts. Listeners tuned in from all around the world. On the other hand, listeners had to be very motivated to tune in since internet access via a computer or smartphone was required for listening. Keeping the opportunities and limitations in mind, I worked closely with a team of volunteers and other contributors to develop and present several engaging programs, and achieved modest success.

Sahara Radio became part of the fiber of the Columbus West African community. We developed several local talents into on-air presenters, served as a forum for discussions on topics of interest to the community, and provided a means for creating awareness about local events and services. For me, it was an excellent platform for putting my leadership abilities and creative ideas to use in a new setting. I enjoyed the experience as well as the fact that I had helped to create a valuable resource for the community. I probably would have continued running this radio station if it generated enough revenue to make it a viable business over the long-term.

Even in the midst of the frustration of unemployment and the radio station not bringing in significant revenue, I felt thankful that I had the time on my hands and the opportunity to pursue an idea that I have been passionate about.

I continued to apply for jobs and networked with others to help me land a communications or marketing job. I applied for many jobs for which I felt very qualified. Not getting the chance to even interview for a position was very frustrating. Even though interviewing for jobs and then not getting hired was equally frustrating, I would have appreciated the opportunity to interview and improve upon how I was positioning my value to prospective employers.

Nonetheless, I continued searching, fine-tuning my resume, networking, and searching.

To showcase my writing abilities and to share my perspectives on various marketing and communications topics, I had created a blog: The Marketplace Conversation. While researching best practices for promoting my blog, I discovered the role web analytics played in the Google-dominated world of search engine optimization (SEO). Google Analytics is a tool used for tracking and reporting web traffic and user activity on a website. It helps to measure what people are clicking on when they visit a website, how long they stay on the website, where they visit the site from, and much more. Such metrics help the website owner make relevant content or user-experience decisions. I learned about Google Analytics and SEO through self-guided online courses, and even earned a certification. My Google Analytics certification, which demonstrated my expertise in installing and tracking metrics on websites, was a major factor in landing my next job.

That next job was a temporary position with the competitive intelligence team at a consumer and packaged goods company with one of their main offices in Columbus. My job involved helping to compile market research information and making the information available to the company's employees through a web-based system. Measuring and monitoring how the users were accessing and consuming the content on the website was a key part of my job. My manager at the time was fond of saying, "You cannot manage something you cannot measure." My web analytics skillset was a welcome addition to the team, among other skills I brought to the table. My job also involved helping to promote user adoption of the database.

A year and a half later, it was time to make another move. Not only was the new position going to be a permanent role with a benefits package, but it was also going to help buttress my communications experience with work in a traditional communications role in a large corporation. So, in late July 2012, I joined a bank as a communications specialist developing various types of communications to keep employees informed and motivated.

During my more-than-nine years at the bank, I had the opportunity to put my skills to use in ways that delivered significant value to the organization. The professional development I experienced during my time there brought me fulfillment. I benefitted from the insights of colleagues, enjoyed the support of managers, and owned my career by looking for opportunities to solve problems and to make situations better than I found them. In the process, I also had the opportunity to guide others to own their careers.

Highlighting my evolution into a well-rounded professional and business leader were two recognitions I received during my time at the bank: a promotion to Internal Communications Manager, and a subsequent promotion to Assistant Vice President (AVP). As is customary with an AVP promotion, I received a congratulatory letter from the CEO. I handed that letter to my daughter to read it.

The smile that beamed from her face as she read the letter was priceless. And then she said, "This is really cool!"

I nodded and replied, "Yes, it is. It is really cool!"

Following my promotions, I took on additional responsibilities, which gave me more opportunities to add value to the organization.

What I am doing with my career at this point feels like what I would have had in mind for my future at the time I was entering college in 1997, if only I knew as much then as I know now. My path has been a meandering road that involved some thoughtful choices and some events outside of my control.

It took a while but eventually, I made it to a place in my career where I feel like my passion, my natural abilities, and my purpose have all converged.

So, on most days, Steve Jobs' words about loving what you do in order to do great work rings true for me. Whether I'm helping someone figure out the most effective way to communicate a message, or telling a story to inspire others, or helping a client develop a plan for a major initiative, I usually do great work because I love what I do.

With gratitude, I look back on my decision to change careers. I am grateful that I trusted my instincts and did not let the fear of failure hold me in place. Nationwide Insurance is an excellent organization, and I loved the company culture and the people but not the kind of work I did. The years that have passed since I left the company could have gone by with me still doing work that I did not find engaging or fulfilling. Rather, taking that leap of faith gave me better control over my professional destiny, and put me in position to be the best I can be and to love what I do.

I am excited about where my career could go from here. I have options, and I have room to grow. Whether I continue to work in the corporate setting as an employee or pursue entrepreneurship, or do something I have not thought of yet, all the lessons I have learned about work and happiness will guide my next steps.

My aim, in whatever work I choose, will always be to do great work. I will, therefore, aim to do work that I love. In doing that, I hope to find fulfillment and happiness, and work will not just be the thing I do to make a living but rather a worthwhile investment of my time that creates value for me and for the people I serve.

• NINE •

FELT THE FEAR BUT DID IT ANYWAY

"The fears we don't face become our limits."
- Robin Sharma, author and leadership coach

I used to be afraid of ghosts when I was a young boy. Whenever someone died in my neighborhood, I refused to walk into a dark room or even into a well-lit room by myself. There was always the possibility, I told myself, that the ghost of the dead person was lurking around in the neighborhood and could snatch me. As silly as that thought sounds now, I was not alone in that way of thinking. My siblings and many children in my neighborhood were as scared as I was about going into rooms by themselves for fear of ghosts.

I have reason to believe that most people who grew up in Ghana in the same era as I did can relate to this fear of ghosts. Superstitions about ghosts tormenting people are very common in Ghanaian folklore. That fueled my irrational fear.

It sounds silly to think that the ghost of a dead person could appear in my room, let alone snatch me. But that fear was real for me as a boy, especially at the moment immediately following my awareness of a person's death.

On the flip side, children born to Ghanaian parents in America, like my daughter and many of the children I know, appear to have no fear of the dead or ghosts. I have seen many children walk by caskets, stare at dead bodies nonchalantly, and show no fear. Although their parents and I know that the dead body is a piece of clay, most of us would feel a jolt of fear and quickly scan the room for the nearest exit if the casket should accidentally tip over and the dead body fall out of the casket.

Before we hastily conclude that African children born in America have no irrational fears, check out what happens when a bug such as a bee enters a room full of such kids. The fear and trepidation that leads these kids to flee hysterically from the tiny bug is often a sight to behold. While I think their fear of a bug is irrational or at best exaggerated, that fear is real for them.

It is true that many of the things that we're afraid of don't exist, and even if they did, they may not be as enormous as we think they are. Some of the fears we feel as humans, regardless of where we grew up, are inspired by stories we hear over and over again. Just as a lie told often enough begins to sound like truth, a myth heard often enough tends to sound like a true story. Thus, stories about both good and bad ghosts lurking around the neighborhood after the person's death sounds believable to many Ghanaian ears.

Other fears are fueled by our human tendency to exaggerate our emotions to the point of believing things are worse than they really are.

For many years, my fear of failure immobilized me even before I took the first step towards some big initiatives. Fear made me talk myself out of doing those things, and I disguised my fear of failure in procrastination.

The kind of failure I often feared was not the fear of complete failure but rather the fear that the outcome may not be as exceptional as I would have liked. At other times, it was merely a fear of the unknown. Some of these fears were real, not only in my mind but also in real life since the things I feared had real-life consequences. Getting past these fears, real or imagined, had to start in my mind.

In order to address my fears, both the rational and irrational ones, I had to examine my perceptions, my thoughts, and the things I focused on. For example, I had known for months that I needed to leave my job at Nationwide Insurance and go do something else. I knew I was not using my talents and abilities the way I could, and that I wasn't fulfilled in the work I was doing. I knew I was not going to be able to continue with the semi-passive approach I was using on most days. I also knew of the realities of being unemployed with bills waiting to be paid. That fear was real, so it was important to me to preserve the way things were, even though I knew there could be more out there for me. I was afraid of the unknown.

I focused on the income and other employment benefits I would lose and not on what would happen if I found a job that engaged me and possibly paid more money. When I considered leaving my job to pursue acting and filmmaking, the fear I faced was real. There was a greater chance of failure, judging by the available statistics; I was focused on that chance of failure. I was not focused on the fact that I had a unique set of skills that I could develop and be able to rub shoulders with the best in the field. I was also focused on the immediate outcome and was not being kind enough to myself about the fact that success takes preparation, effort, and time. I kept reminding myself that if those fears came true, I would be a broke actor who couldn't take care of his family.

I feared I would become known as the guy who could have been a CPA or could have had a good job in one of the downtown office buildings but instead decided to become an actor and filmmaker, ending up as a "Mr. Nobody." I focused on my fears, not on what would happen if my fears did not come true.

Likewise, for a very long time, I was so afraid of being turned down by a girl I was interested in that I often ended up in the "friend zone." I have often been good at initiating conversations or getting acquainted with strangers, and that skill made it effortlessly easy for me to befriend people from all walks of life. However, in romantic situations, I found myself locking up on the inside when I involuntarily began processing the possible unfavorable outcomes of telling my love interest how I felt about her.

I would often overanalyze the situation, and wonder what she would think of me if she didn't think I was her type or if she didn't feel the same way about me as I did about her. I would wonder who else she would discuss me with. I would wonder how awkward our relationship could become if I didn't say the right words or if my perfectly arranged words were not enough to convey the great love story I had imagined for the two of us. Those fears overshadowed the fact that I might be her type, or that whatever she discussed with someone else should be the least of my concerns, or that any awkwardness between us would be temporary. I focused only on my fears, and not on what could happen if my fears did not come true.

In another fear-laden scenario, I needed to inform my manager at the time about a job opportunity I planned on pursuing. For internal job applications, the company policy required consent from my manager and that was going to be the third of such consents I would be requesting within 12 months. Additionally, my relationship with my manager held the potential of becoming awkward if that new opportunity didn't pan out. I was worried that my manager and other managers would view me as not being fully committed to the team, so that concern weighed on my mind. I feared that I would be stigmatized and become a target for elimination if the department needed to eliminate positions, being that I had explicitly expressed my interest in leaving the team for something else.

I was not looking deeply enough into my fear to realize that conversations about leaving a manager who valued my work would almost always be awkward. Most managers would rather not lose a valuable employee, no matter how invested that manager may be in that employee's career mobility; so that conversation could feel awkward for both parties. I also was ignoring the fact that I was very qualified for the position I was considering, and that it was very likely to pan out. I was unconsciously placing the power of decision-making about my career into the hands of my manager instead of owning my career with thoughtful actions. I was wrongly focusing on my fears about what could go wrong, and not on what would happen if my fears did not come true.

Fear, as I have come to realize, is often a signal that I may not have gathered enough information about the situation, prepared enough, or tapped the appropriate resources needed to accomplish what I'm setting out to do.

When I can isolate the cause of the fear, I am often able to face that fear. And when I face that fear, I often find out that the man behind the curtain is "just a very bad wizard."

The wizard in "The Wizard of Oz" is a terrifying creature, but you have to see the movie to understand why it is not to be feared. Spoiler alert: Once you know what's behind the curtain, your fear will likely disappear. Just as it did for the characters in the movie, learning more about the things we are afraid of and addressing why that fear exists is an important step in facing our fears.

I have also come to realize that fear is sometimes an indication to me that what I'm thinking about doing is simply a dumb idea. With that said, I acknowledge that all fears are not created equal. There is good fear and then there is bad fear. Fear that prompts me to not take things for granted or to not take reckless actions count as good fear. Fear that cripples me into inaction is bad fear. I had to learn to separate the bad, irrational fears from good, cautionary fears. It took time to gain this awareness, and I'm still a working on getting better at examining my fears.

John Mayer, in his song "The Heart of Life" said that, "Fear is often a friend that is misunderstood." Good fear is a good, wise friend. Good fear is an internal control for guarding against reckless risk-taking. Bad and irrational fears are often fueled by superstition and the opinions of people projecting their fears onto others. So, fear can serve a useful purpose when it does not cripple a person from taking necessary or beneficial actions.

In the case of my leaving Nationwide, my fear did not suddenly disappear. It took a thoughtful assessment of the situation, a confluence of events, and the discovery that failure was not final, to push me over the hump. I eventually landed a fulfilling job that engaged me more and paid more money.

Even though I ended up not going to New York to pursue acting and filmmaking, I got rid of most of the fear that held me back from seriously considering that career option. Confronting those fears helped me comfortably defer those dreams and not simply shrink away from them.

Regarding my romantic interests, I have had my share of successes and failures with facing my fears. I have had situations where I later found out that my romantic interest had been quietly hoping that I would pursue her, but I had been waiting around in fear. I have also been in situations that turned awkward because I made assumptions. Even when the situation did not turn out as I had hoped, life went on, and the awkwardness was not as devastating as I had imagined. With that lesson learned, I went on to subsequent situations with better control over my fear. I will be lying to you if I said that specific type of fear has been totally eradicated. It pops up sometimes. One way I manage that fear is to tactfully ask direct questions to assess the situation. The more I know about how my love interest feels about the situation, the more control I have over my fears.

As for the career conversation that I dreaded having with my manager about the job opportunity, our conversation ended up not being as tense as I thought it was going to be. Suffice it to say, that conversation led to a win-win situation for both parties.

As I write this book, I'm confronting some real fears: that I may not be as happy with the final product, that I may end up with a typographical error somewhere in the final print, that someone I respect will disagree with what I think, that people other than those who already know me might not care for what I think. These are real fears, and I am facing them head-on. I feel the fear, but I am writing anyway.

To make sure that I convey my thoughts as clearly and concisely as possible, I have sought feedback from people who are honest enough to tell me the truth about what I am doing well and what needs rethinking. I am marshaling the necessary resources to help me catch errors and communicate as concisely as possible. Please forgive me if there are any typos; these are a lot of pages and I did my best to catch them all. And will everyone agree with everything I say? Of course, they will not. But I have encouraged myself with the idea that most reasonable people will respect my opinion even if they disagree with me. As for strangers caring about what I think, it might not happen overnight, but they will eventually, if they find this book useful. The book's future will take care of itself if I take care of its present. That is what I focused on as I read and reread, and read again.

Facing my fears also mean taking risks. Risks come with opportunities and rewards.

There are opportunities behind every fear. In most cases, the opportunities are opportunities to succeed. In some cases, the opportunities are opportunities to fail. Even when they are opportunities to fail, they are still opportunities. Sometimes, all I have needed was an opportunity to fail. By giving myself permission to venture out, with the consolation that there would be a useful lesson in the failure even if I failed, my fear often subsided. Failing, after you've made a good faith effort, is more valuable than not venturing out at all.

At a 2016 TEDx event in Columbus, one speaker brilliantly highlighted this idea of "opportunities to fail" as part of his story about taking risks. He was a charter school leader whose team focused on enrolling students who were struggling and who also came from poor neighborhoods. The school believed that most kids can be successful when given the appropriate support and affirmation. He attributed the students' success to the environment they created where failure was not a death sentence, but a part of learning.

In the grand scheme of things, failure is not a death sentence but because failure has consequences, failure can feel like a death sentence. Even when failure is a death sentence, a death sentence is not the same thing as death. German philosopher Friedrich Nietzsche said, and Kanye West said it also: "That which does not kill us, makes us stronger." A death sentence will not necessarily kill you; chances are that it will make you stronger.

Patrick Awuah, the founder of Ashesi University in Ghana, is another risk taker whose story comes to mind when I think of feeling the fear but doing it anyway. This Ghanaian engineer and former Microsoft employee set out in 2002 to use his own money to develop a new generation of African leaders. His approach to helping end malpractices such as corruption and apathy, which tend to be major problems in business and society in Africa, was to develop enlightened leaders for the continent.

He was inspired by a quote from Goethe that says, "If there's anything you can do or dream you can, begin it. Boldness has genius, power, and magic." Awuah left Microsoft after about a decade to go to the Haas School of Business at UC Berkeley. This is where he developed his business plan for creating a self-sustaining liberal arts university to contribute to long-term solutions on the African continent. He's been successful at developing ethical leaders who are critical thinkers and problem solvers.

Felt the Fear But Did it Anyway

You could say that his success is because he had a lot of money, or that he's passionate about his mission. No question about that. What is also likely is that setting out to create a privately funded self-sustaining liberal arts university in Ghana was one of the most significant risks he had taken in his life.

It is also very likely that it crossed his mind more than once that he could fail. The challenge of "confronting the problem of leadership and apathy in a country of nearly 29 million, where most of the citizens have a much more significant sense of entitlement than a sense of responsibility," was not lost on him. He acknowledged that in his 2007 TED Talk in Arusha, Tanzania.

To me, that problem he set out to address is akin to looking for a cure for Alzheimer's disease - the prospect of succeeding is currently slim but certainly a worthwhile endeavor.

There was a mountain of evidence that suggested that he was going to fail. He's been successful in making dents in some of the fundamental problems plaguing the continent, and he continues to inspire thousands of people to dream, prepare, and take action. By putting his money and reputation on the line to confront such a challenge, Awuah took a risk that many people would not take. He must have felt the fear but did it anyway, by preparing and preparing adequately.

I draw inspiration from the stories of risk takers, paying particular attention to their methods and not their hype. I'm interested in learning from the truths they tell about their fears, and how they faced those fears. And I'm interested in what people learned from taking risks, regardless of the outcome.

All the celebrated inventors and pioneers in any field of endeavor had to have been risk-takers, and they had to have felt fear at a point. They felt the fear but did it anyway.

So the question begs asking: "What would you attempt to do if you knew you could not fail?"

That is the question on a fridge magnet I keep to remind me of the opportunities that come from facing my fears. When a fear stares me in the face, I often ask myself my version of that question: "What would I do if I felt the fear but did it anyway?"

Just like it was in the movie "The Wizard of Oz," the only way to know what's behind the curtain of the things we fear is to face what's behind that curtain - face the fear.

"The fears we don't face," Robin Sharma said, "will become limitations."

I prefer possibilities to limitations, so I am facing my fears. There are many things, real and imagined, which I've feared. If anything was worth doing, I felt the fear but did it anyway.

· TEN ·

SELF-AWARENESS AND PERSONAL POWER

"He who knows others is wise. He who knows himself is enlightened."
- Lao Tzu, philosopher and writer

Muhammad Ali is one of the greatest athletes of all-time. He died in June 2016 at the age of 74. On the day of his memorial, I was driving from Chicago to Columbus, and listened to a broadcast of the event on National Public Radio (NPR) during my six-hour drive. A moving tribute was delivered on President Barack Obama's behalf. President Bill Clinton delivered a eulogy in person. So did Senator Orin Hatch. His widow Lonnie Ali, comedian Billy Crystal, Jewish rabbis, Muslim imams, Christian ministers, and dignitaries from around the world also offered glowing eulogies. Many TV Stations also televised the event.

Many of the tributes highlighted Ali's courage in the face of federal prosecution for refusing to serve in the Vietnam War, his unshaken resolve when he was stripped of his title, his sense of community in embracing people from all walks of life, and his larger-than-life personality which was a perfect combination of wit and charisma. Among the speakers at the memorial, most of who knew him well privately and publicly, there was a consensus that Ali's quick-witted, self-confident and assertive personality, which many of us came to admire, was a result of his acute self-awareness. They spoke of his uncanny sense of his strengths and weaknesses, and how that awareness made him a great athlete and a brilliant human being. Judging by his actions and words documented in the thousands of videos available on YouTube, Ali seemed very mindful of his influence and also comfortable with the decisions he made during his lifetime.

I spent the rest of my drive to Columbus reflecting on the idea of self-awareness, and how an honest assessment of my strengths and shortcomings is necessary for becoming a better version of myself. Ali's self-awareness, as echoed by the event's speakers and the NPR commentators, offered an inspiring backdrop for my reflection. Some of my experiences and lessons over the years, which have contributed to my self-awareness, flashed through my mind. I thought about my self-awareness journey and how well I was applying that awareness.

In the five years leading up to that moment in 2016, I had learned many things about myself. I learned from my observations of my repeated actions and from the feedback I received from others. I had also learned from structured assessments such as Myers-Briggs Type Indicator, StrengthsFinder, and a 360-degree feedback exercise.

Myers-Briggs Type Indicator is a psychometric questionnaire designed to measure psychological preferences in how a person perceives the world and makes decisions. StrengthsFinder helps a person discover the top five strengths they possess and can harness towards building better, more fulfilling careers. A 360-degree feedback exercise involves confidential, anonymous feedback from others regarding a person's strengths and weaknesses are, and what areas of improvement there are for that person's development.

These different ways of learning about myself have contributed to my clearer perception of my strengths, shortcomings, thoughts, beliefs, and emotions. They've also helped me to understand how I perceive myself, how others perceive me, and how to efficiently manage my relationships with others.

In mid-2011, I was in a place in my life where I wanted to do things differently from the way I had in the past. I was starting over following the end of a complicated on-again-off-again romantic relationship. I was emerging from the consequences of an illegitimate romantic relationship that had caused me public and private embarrassment. I was jump-starting my career after having been laid off for several months. I was in a place where I knew life could and should be better, and believed it was going to get better. I did not know precisely the best way to proceed.

This was when I paid attention to Anthony (Tony) Robbins, an individual who brought the idea of self-awareness into sharper focus for me.

When I first saw Tony Robbins on TV in the late 1990s, I was not fond of him. He seemed to me an overly zealous salesman trying to sell me something I did not need, like a pitchman in an infomercial. Years later, in 2011, when I saw an audio version of his book *Awaken the Giant Within* sitting on a shelf of a FedEx Copy Center, I was intrigued by the title. For $10, the audiobook

Self-Awareness and Personal Power

seemed like a fair price to figure out if Robbins was the real deal or just full of hot air.

The book *Awaken the Giant Within* is about taking control of your mental, emotional, physical and financial destiny. He explained that our beliefs are what we perceive to be true about people, things, and ideas, and beliefs can empower or disempower a person towards whatever his or her destiny is.

Robbins' book covers a range of topics from goal setting to personal finance. It talks about the power of decisions and belief systems, and it offers helpful strategies for making positive changes in one's life. I listened to the audiobook more than once, and learned principles that helped me change my way of interpreting situations. I also realized that he is a smart and sincere man who knows what he's talking about.

According to Robbins, the one thing that impacts everything anyone seeks or does in life boils down to decisions. And the three important types of decisions to pay attention to are: the decisions about what things mean; the decisions about what to focus on; and the decisions about what actions to take. These decisions inform how much power we give ourselves or to others over our respective actions and the outcomes in our lives. These ideas struck a chord with me.

Looking back at the way I had lived my life until that point in 2011, I realized I had made many decisions without focusing on the most important things or without thoughtfully evaluating what things meant. I had made many decisions that were unduly influenced by other people. I had been passive about important decisions that concerned my relationships with others. I had left important decisions in the hands of other people. But when Robbins pointed out that the power to make those decisions were mine, the concept of "personal power" took on a whole new meaning for me. Just as my nose is mine, or my hand is mine, the power to make these important decisions about my life was mine, too. And just as I cannot give my nose or my hand to another person to use for my benefit, I could not give my decision-making power to another person for that person to decide what was in my best interest.

But unfortunately, what I had been doing all along was giving my decision-making power to other people for them to decide what was in my best interest, and that had not served me well. I had relinquished my personal power by not making decisions about what things to focus on, so I focused on fears instead of strengths, and on excuses instead of reasons. I had relinquished my personal power by not making decisions about what things meant, so I often endorsed others' opinions instead of turning to facts and common sense. I had relinquished my personal power by not making decisions about what actions to take, so I made many convenient but poor choices. I was unaware that was what I had been doing all along.

The "giant" inside of me had been asleep all this while because, consciously and unconsciously, I made weak decisions and neglected to make several important decisions. That "giant" inside me was going to have to be awakened if my life was going to take a different course. If I wanted different outcomes, I was going to have to deliberately practice the skill of decision-making, and learn to make empowering decisions.

As a result of the insights from this and other books by Tony Robbins, I reached out for more insights from other people who knew something about self-awareness and personal power. From their books and videos, people like Les Brown, Wayne Dyer, Lisa

Nichols, and my friend Chris McAlister helped me focus on my decision-making framework, reform the way I perceived people and situations, and take thoughtful actions. I became better at making decisions, and also learned to minimize the enormous influence others often had over my decisions. I became better at deciding on what things meant, what to focus on, and what actions to take.

In a 2009 NPR essay, Ali shared a personal philosophy on how the things we focus on affect our outcomes, saying:

"I never thought of [or focused on] the possibility of failure; only of the fame and glory I was going to get when I won. I could see it. I could almost feel it. When I proclaimed that I was the greatest of all time, I believed in myself, and I still do."

On that June afternoon of Muhammad Ali's memorial, as I reflected on my self-awareness and my personal power journey, I recognized that I had come a long way from where I was at the start of 2011. I had made tremendous progress in the decision-making department, and I celebrated that. I'm still a work in progress, and I admit that.

I am still a nice guy who can be naively nice, and allow people to take advantage of my niceness. I still get impatient with people when they act incompetently in doing things I can easily do for myself. I still tend to postpone tedious tasks and push myself close to deadlines. I am still likely to avoid confrontations and awkward conversations. I know these things about myself, and I recognize it when I begin slipping back into my old ways.

Self-awareness reduces the chance of my being blindsided by my shortcomings. My self-awareness highlighted my strengths.

The more attention I paid to the comprehensive inventory of the things I had learned about myself, the more I realized my strengths, too. In addition to my tendency to postpone deadlines, my impatience with incompetence, and my tendency to avoid confrontations, I have an unlimited enthusiasm for life, an even-tempered personality on most days, and a respectable track record of good decisions. Focusing on my strengths helps me to not second-guess myself as much, but rather make better-quality decisions and flush out self-sabotage. Likewise, knowing the unflattering characteristics about me helps me recognize when I inadvertently put myself in a position that robs me of my personal power.

Muhammad Ali is famous for saying, "I am the greatest, and I said it even before I knew I was." Ali is "The Greatest" when it comes to sports. He had greatness inside of him, and he felt that. He told it to himself and repeated that to the world even before he knew the magnitude of what he was talking about.

I am convinced that when it comes to living our respective lives, there is "greatness" inside each of us, as Les Brown often says. Nurturing that greatness – awakening the giant within – is a process to which I committed myself. Nurturing that greatness involves maintaining my awareness of self and paying attention to the three types of decisions Tony Robbins talked about.

Ali is "The Greatest" when it comes to sports, and I am the "The Greatest" when it comes to my life. Every decision I make contributes to my greatness. Every decision-making opportunity is an opportunity to practice decision-making that will make me "The Greatest" in my life.

As I thoughtfully assess the ideas that inform my beliefs, I am putting myself in a position to make better decisions. And as I continue to practice informed decision-making, instead of passively existing, I am nurturing the greatness inside of me.

Self-Awareness and Personal Power

Muhammad Ali made his mark on the world by believing certain things about himself, by deciding what things meant, by deciding what to focus on, and by deciding what actions to take. Ali was not a man without fault but he was a self-aware man.

And as long as I keep the "giant" inside of me awake, I am confident that I will "float like a butterfly and sting like a bee," and use my personal power to impact my world.

Just as Ali did.

· ELEVEN ·

WHAT MATTERS MOST

"Most people fail in life because they major in minor things!"
- Tony Robbins, life coach and entrepreneur

The most efficient way of transporting a dining table is in the back of a truck. I didn't have a truck for the table I purchased on Craigslist, so I tied it to the roof of my sedan car and hauled it home. I successfully made the 15-minute drive, and single-handedly proceeded to move the table into the house. I could have detached the table's legs, carry the pieces into the house, and then reattached the legs. But I didn't. I dragged the entire table and broke one of its legs in the process. I was able to stand the table up even with one of the legs broken. It looked fine, but I knew it was not going to withstand much pressure. It would fall apart if someone placed any heavy load on it.

My experience with the table struck me as a metaphor for what matters most in life. A table's legs hold the table up for the table to serve its purpose. A table becomes vulnerable when one or more of its legs are broken. Likewise, if we were to think of our respective lives as tables, the legs of the table would represent the things that matter most to each individual. In my example, the table had four legs, so I wondered what four things mattered to me the most.

At this stage in my life, the four legs of my figurative table are family, faith, finances, and vocation.

Family has to do with the healthy relationships I have with my biological and non-biological relatives, as well as with close friends. Finances has to do with earning, spending, and living with money. Faith is my capacity to focus beyond my limitations. And vocation is the fulfilling career that aligns with my purpose.

Family, finances, faith, and vocation matter to me the most because these are the things I think about the most on any given day. Some of these represent my refuge in times of adversity. Some of these represent the factors that help me make the most of opportunities. Some of these represent my reasons for how and where I spend my time.

The legs of each person's table may vary, and will also depend on the person's stage in life. For some people, there is likely to be more than four things. For example, good health is becoming increasingly important to me as I discover the physical limitations of my older self. I would like to include that in my list of what matters most. But sticking with four legs for the purpose of this conversation, health at this time is the fifth leg of my table and we can discuss that on another day. I say this to say that while the four things require most of my focus, there are other things that matter as well, and should not be ignored.

For me right now, family, faith, finances, and vocation are the four legs of my metaphorical table.

FAMILY

In the movie "Up in the Air" starring George Clooney, the relationship-averse Ryan Bingham teaches his audience that some animals were not meant to carry each other or live symbiotically. He uses a backpack metaphor with which he illustrates the idea that if you want to live a happy life, "travel light." Travel light in the sense that there are so many unnecessary items travelers pack into their backpacks that weigh them down. He implied relationships generally in his list of "excess luggage" items, but what I think he meant was unfruitful relationships. As we come to find out later in the movie, he had inadvertently "packed a relationship into his backpack" only to find out that ... well, you'll find out for yourself when you watch the movie.

Human beings are naturally creatures of interdependence. Aristotle said man is by nature a social animal, and that anyone who cannot lead the common life or is so self-sufficient as not to need to and therefore does not partake of society, is either a beast or a god. And as a social animal, I need other people. The challenge, however, is to not tag along with just anybody just because I don't want to walk alone.

Family comprises the relationships I share with others, by blood and by our shared, strong social bond. My experience of family of both kinds has been mostly positive, informing my outlook on the importance of family. As a father, son, brother, husband, and close friend, these relationships constitute a community that I depend on, and vice versa.

Family, as it is the case for most people, has not always been a perfect group of people getting along with each other all the time. However, family tends to be the one fixture of stability and dependability in most people's lives. It has been in my case, both as a child and as an adult.

My inspiration for valuing family as much as I do is from my maternal grandfather, John Wilson Afriyiye. He did a fine job demonstrating the essence of family. He was adamant about family gatherings and frequently checked on how his children and grandchildren were doing. He died in 1993, but I wish he had lived longer. His legacy, without a doubt, would be defined by two words – discipline and family.

I knew from a very early age that I belonged to a close-knit group of people led by a patriarch who emphasized discipline and family above everything else. As a result of how much of a priority my grandfather made family social gatherings, these family gatherings, which brought all his children and their children together at his house every New Year's Day, have continued long after his death. My relationships as a grandchild, nephew, cousin, brother, and son with the people in my family have at their core a shared kinship as members of the Afriyiye clan.

Being part of family gatherings is typical for a young child growing up in Ghana, but the sense of belonging that breeds a commitment to the group does not happen automatically. It takes active nurturing, and my grandfather showed the way by his actions. His children followed his lead and nurtured that sense of community that manifests in how we've looked out for each other through the years.

During the my years of living far away from most of my blood relatives, some strangers and friends have welcomed me into their homes regularly, served me meals, lent me money, given me a place to sleep, and looked out for me. These people have become my family, too. A quotation on one of the walls inside a Bob Evans restaurant in Columbus reads, "We treat strangers like they are friends and friends like they are family." That statement rings true about how most close friends have treated me, and vice versa.

Granted that not all the people in my family or anyone's family can be counted on equally (and vice versa), the system of interdependence creates a stable base for me. The people I consider family are those most likely to provide a cover for my blind spots, love me unconditionally, and create opportunities for me.

Family, for me, is the bottom that holds when all else fall out.

FAITH

In my interaction with circumstances I can neither see nor have any control over, I've had to focus beyond my limitations. Be it with the supernatural world that surrounds me in the present or the unknown physical future which is yet to come, faith has been a key resource I count on to block out the distractions.

My idea of faith consists of two parts: confidence in the fact that there's a supernatural force that sustains me, and confidence in my capacity to learn, grow, and deliver results.

I subscribe to the idea that there is a power that sustains the universe and all that's in it. Some people call this power "God," some refer to it as nature, and some refer to it by other names. This supernatural power sustains me in spite of me. I have complete confidence in this power as being capable of nurturing, directing, and protecting my existence on Earth. This confidence informs my fundamental belief that the heart of life is good, and that everything, even the circumstances beyond my human comprehension, will all work out just fine.

While it is true that supernatural events can interfere with the natural world, most of the outcomes we experience in life are subject to physical laws. Therefore, my capacity to learn and to grow is essential to thriving in this physical world. That learning capacity is what reinforces my faith in myself. That capacity also informs my confidence in the fact that as long as I earnestly learn, grow, and apply myself to the principles that govern the circumstances of my physical world, I have almost nothing to worry about concerning the unknown future.

I was standing in line in a store one morning when a man struck up a conversation with the salesman, beginning with what sounded like a rhetorical question: "I wonder why anyone throws up their hands in the air and say there's no work while there's so much work if only you looked." He was reacting to a sign in the window advertising a delivery job. The man talked about once losing everything he owned, becoming homeless, but working his way back to now owning a business and making steady progress in life. He said he was able to do that because he stayed focused on where he was trying to go, and beyond his limitations. He also added that he believed God was on his side, and that what he focused on was bigger and more desirable than his circumstance at the time.

What that conversation affirmed for me was that focusing on something bigger than one's limitations breeds faith, and that faith is strong enough to sustain a person and keep him or her to press on towards his or her goals and dreams.

Faith allows me to envision circumstances in the future, and then work towards them.

My hyperactive imagination, however, sometimes accelerates the due date for the things I desire. During times when my plans or desires have not panned out the way I had hoped, I thought I had a phenomenal power to jinx what I desired. My alleged power to jinx my desired outcomes drove me nuts for many years until I discovered that I had no such power. The things I thought I had jinxed with my vivid imagination almost always happened eventually. If what I imagined happening did not happen, a more suitable alternative came my way eventually.

The hardest part about faith is choosing what to focus on, especially during tough times. Sometimes, I have focused on my confidence in God's nurturing, direction, and protection. Many times, I have focused on my capacity to figure things out by learning, thinking, and doing. Most times, I have done both to varying degrees. Faith, in God and in myself, has been necessary in navigating decisions and situations.

I have learned to identify circumstances within my control, and focus on what I can do to change those. With the things outside of my control, I have learned to trust the supernatural power at work in the universe. My faith in God and in myself is what informs my optimism about the present and the future.

FINANCES

My experience with money has taught me that money isn't everything but money can help meet most needs in life. The ability to earn money is a necessary life skill that I learned early in life. On the other hand, developing a sound temperament for living with money took a while. As part of developing that sound temperament, I learned from my experiences as well as from watching others. I have learned that winning at the money game is as much about earning as it is about spending.

I have made my share of costly mistakes with money, making unnecessary purchases or getting involved in financial commitments that drained my coffers. I kept falling into the traps that keep people poor. For example, using credit cards for non-essential purchases, making only minimum payments on credit card balances, or overestimating my ability to afford certain lifestyle choices. I tried to avoid late fees and excessive interest payments on loans and credit cards, but those efforts amounted to nothing. I knew I should be making smarter decisions, but my actions were out of sync with what I knew. I lacked the focus and discipline necessary until I did the math on how much money I was "donating" to my credit card companies in fees and interest.

Undoubtedly, getting better control of my finances started with financial literacy, but the knowledge did not automatically translate into actions. It was my desire to have a better quality of life that caused me to wake up from unintentionally throwing away money I was earning.

To help me stay on track with my commitment to making better financial decisions, I went looking for podcasts and found Dave Ramsey and his Total Money Makeover program. He is one of the best at what he does - guiding people away from debt and into financial freedom. For a person who made millions by the time he was 26 years old, lost most of it through what he calls dumb decisions, and eventually recovering and spending nearly three decades building his multi-million personal finance business empire, you can bet he knows a lot about money.

Crawling my way back from being deep in debt on more than one occasion, I needed to make a fundamental shift in my relationship with money. I found Ramsey's approach helpful. Even though he can be controversial and heavy-handed at times, you cannot fault him for his tactics, considering that breaking bad habits require tough love.

The phases of the Total Money Makeover program are referred to as "Baby Steps to Financial Peace." Step 1 is saving $1,000 in an emergency fund. Step 2 involves using the debt snowball method to pay off all debt except the mortgage. Step 3 is a fully-funded emergency fund of three-to-six months of expenses. Step 4 is investing 15% of your household income into a 401(k) retirement. Step 5 is putting away money for your children's college education. Step 6 is paying off your home early, and Step 7 is building wealth and giving generously.

From watching hundreds of hours of his YouTube videos and eventually taking his 10-week course, I became more diligent at tracking my income and expenses. I developed better mastery over my finances, even though I have relapsed occasionally. The more competent I became with managing money, the more in control I felt about my life.

Many of the decisions related to work and life are tied to finances. When I can make decisions about the work and life without the undue pressure of financial obligations, I tend to enjoy the resulting experiences much more. Having better control over my finances as well as making thoughtful decisions about money help me keep my income, expenses, savings, and investments in a healthy balance. Having better control also enables me to help others and support worthy charitable causes.

Rethinking my relationship with money is an ongoing process. I'm still learning to guiltlessly enjoy the fruits of my labor. I'm still learning to balance being frugal and being lavish. My goal is to continuously get better at earning and managing resources wisely.

Money is a tool, and like any tool, knowing how to use it skillfully is essential for getting the most out of it. While the love of money is said to be the root of all evil, the ignorance of money management is the root of a lot of pain and suffering. Thus, in the immortal words of Snoop Dogg and Dr. Dre, I'm rolling down the street of life "with my mind on my money, and my money on my mind" because it's that important to me.

VOCATION

The word vocation comes from the Latin *vocātiō*, and it means "a calling or a summons," referring to work to which a person is especially drawn or called. The idea here is that each person has natural talents and interests that are suited for a specific purpose. When my interests and purpose eventually aligned with where I dedicated most of my time and effort, I was in a place of peace about work.

Work is key to making a living as an independent and responsible adult. Work provides an avenue for us to exchange our time and talents for money or other things of value. With my work, I create value for others and receive value in exchange. Sometimes the value is tangible, as in getting paid with money. At other times, the value I get in return is in the fulfillment I find in making a difference in the lives of others. When I find both in one place, by getting paid well while making a noticeable difference in the lives of others, I am always in a happy place.

For many people, choosing work based on passion and purpose may not always be an option, especially in the short term. Sometimes a person takes a job simply to make a living. Sometimes, a person takes a job as a stepping-stone to the job that matches his or her purpose and passion. As a short-term measure, either approach is fine.

For the long term, work or vocation ought to be inspired by passion and purpose rather than by the need for money. Ironically, one of the reasons it is difficult for many of us to make the shift and pursue our true vocation is because of the need for money to take care of our many financial commitments. That need then requires us to keep working on jobs that may not necessarily match our passions or purpose.

It took me a while to find that sweet spot, where the work I do felt less like a chore and more like something that makes me feel alive. On average, I spend one-third of my days working. That is one-third of my adult lifetime. That is a lot of the prime years of my life, and that's why I want to do work that is meaningful. Although money is important to me, it is more important to me that I am spending my time doing work that pays me well and also aligns with my purpose.

FAMILY, FAITH, FINANCES, AND VOCATION

A four-legged table is most stable with all four legs intact. Many kinds of pressure could be exerted onto such a table and it will still stand. For every leg that the table loses, the less pressure the table can withstand, and the less useful the table will become.

Ideally, I would like all four legs of my figurative table to be always intact. However, being the imperfect human being that I am, I sometimes fall short in one area or another. I, therefore, take comfort in the fact that even though four legs are great, a fourth leg may break sometimes. When that happens, having a healthy combination of any of the three other legs of my figurative table would keep me on track while I worked on restoring the fourth leg.

Most things are important but most things do not matter. Focusing on what matters most helps me devote my resources to the areas that need my time and attention the most. Family, faith, finances, and vocation are the important things that matter to me now. These are the major things I try to focus on.

The minor things will take care of themselves if I take care of the major things.

• TWELVE •

THIS I BELIEVE

"It is this belief in a power larger than myself and other than myself which allows me to venture into the unknown and even the unknowable."

- Maya Angelou, author and teacher

My daughter was about seven years old when she asked the question of whether Jews were going to hell. She had heard in church that anyone who didn't believe in Jesus as his or her personal savior was going to hell after he or she died. My daughter had also learned that one of her friends from school was Jewish which meant that her friend was destined for eternal damnation, according to the Sunday School lessons. So, with the sincerity of a child, she wanted to know what the deal was about heaven and hell, and who was in and who was out.

I told her that some people believe there is a place called hell, and unless a person believes in Jesus Christ and follows all of the Bible's rules the right way, that person is going to hell. I added that when it comes to beliefs about heaven and hell, there's still a lot of debate out there, even among the people who believe in Jesus as the only way to God. I then concluded that everyone believes what they believe, and some people believe they're right and everyone else is wrong, but nobody really knows – we all simply believe.

As seriously as I take my responsibility as a parent to diligently point my daughter towards objective truth, I was aware that my answers would be contributing to her beliefs. I had to be as objective, sincere and transparent as possible with my response to what is a complicated question. Thus, I shared with her some of what I believe.

As she's grown older, I've shared with her more of what I believe, and I suspect that she will, like most of us, work her way through these ideas for most of her adult years and eventually come to terms with what she believes. Whatever she comes to believe, my only hope is that her beliefs empower her towards becoming a better version of herself.

Belief, in the general sense, is what we perceive to be true about people, things, and ideas. Our opinions about small and big things inform our respective worldviews, and our worldviews inform our beliefs. Hell is very popular in Christianity, and is believed by many to be the place of eternal damnation that God has reserved in the afterlife for people who do not profess Jesus Christ as their personal savior.

I believe in God with absolute certainty. There are some ideas that I am agnostic about, like whether unicorns are real or not, or whether knocking on wood would stave off bad luck. But one thing I don't have any doubt about is the idea of a creator who initiated and sustains all that is alive. I refer to this creator as God and He goes by several other names in the different cultures.

I do not understand everything about the nature and characteristics of God, but the evidence of life and the sophistication of creation convinces me that there's an intelligent designer. The universe and human beings are too intentional to have been the product of randomness. While Creationism makes more sense to me than the Big Bang Theory, that does not mean the evolution ought to be dismissed. Both ideas have a place in explaining the creation and ongoing creation of our natural world.

I subscribe to the idea that religion is a sincere attempt on the part of humans to fulfill our innate desire to connect with something larger and other than ourselves. For many traditions throughout history, this something larger and other than us has been God. Therefore, people have invented routines and rituals to help nurture that connection. Over the years, this basic idea of maintaining a relationship with the creator of the universe has replicated itself into various world religions, with different but similar rituals and belief systems.

I was born into a Protestant Christian family, and Christianity made sense to me as I entered young adulthood, so I kept faith with it. Over the years, I have had many questions, figured out some of the answers, have had others explain things to me, and forgot some of the questions. I've also gotten comfortable with the idea that there are some questions to which I will never know the answers, so I simply believe. I continue to identify myself as a Christian, and my faith has evolved because of my deeper appreciation of the nature of God and because of my learning more about church history and human behavior. My views on the existence of hell and who's going there, the Bible as the inerrant word of God, and Jesus as the only way to having a relationship with God have evolved through the years.

Christianity has a long history that dates back to shortly after Jesus' death more than 2000 years ago, borrowing from the Jewish tradition and shaped predominantly by the Romans. For many years, the Roman Catholic Church was the only authority on Christianity until the Protestant Reformation, which was initiated by Martin Luther and others like him who challenged the status quo. This was in 16th-century Europe. The Reformation set into motion much of the religious diversity we enjoy today.

The sacred scripture of the Christian religion is the Bible. Written in the 16th century by more than forty different authors, the Bible has a theme of affirming God's purpose for humans. The Protestant version of the bible is made up of 66 different books comprising history, proverbs, songs, prophecies, and letters. The Catholic version has 73 different books (all of the books in the Protestant version and seven more). The widely-available English language version of the Bible was translated from mainly Hebrew and Greek.

The Bible mentions hell several times, with one example being in the Matthew 25 verse 41 where Jesus is quoted as saying, "Then he will say to those on his left, 'Depart from me, you who are cursed, into the eternal fire prepared for the devil and his angels.'"

A torturous hellfire, which is supposed to be the eternal destination for the "unbelievers" or people who don't believe in or faithfully practice the God-approved version of Christianity, reflects more of the retaliatory nature of a man-made God than it reflects the essence of a loving, creative God.

The idea that God who created the universe and all that is in it is so consumed with people worshiping him that he has also created a lake of fire to eternally torture some of the people he created has never made sense to me, even though I used to believe in it out of fear. As I have become older and gained a better understanding of the nature of God, that fear has lost its grip.

The idea of hell may serve a purpose for some. Maybe, the idea of hell compels some people to do the right thing. Somebody once said that many people are Christians because they're trying to avoid hell. I think there is a lot of truth to that statement.

Punishment is a very useful deterrent to bad behavior for many human beings. That is likely why the idea of hell has traditionally been so prominent in Christianity and in the other major religions of the world. The founders of the various religions probably knew that when dealing with human beings, consequences are often necessary to have most people conform to expectations.

Even though the idea of heaven makes more sense to me than the concept of hell, I acknowledge the binary thinking that suggests that there has to be a hell if there is a heaven.

I think life continues in some form after a person dies a physical death. Maybe our memory is wiped, and we take on new physical bodies and are reborn into this physical world as babies. Maybe the non-physical part of who we are will continue living in a non-physical realm. Maybe it is one of the hundreds of scenarios believed by followers of the various world religions. Maybe it is one of the ideas portrayed in movies and novels. Maybe it is none of the above. Since no person has been truly dead and returned to the physical world with any evidence about the existence of heaven or hell, all we can do is to believe what we choose to believe.

I choose to believe in a post-physical-death experience that reflects a father welcoming all his children home, as Jesus taught in the Parable of the Lost Sheep or in the Parable of the Lost Coin or in the Parable of the Prodigal Son. In each of these parables, Jesus emphasized the idea of redemption even for the ones who stray so far off that it is inconceivable to the righteous among us that God would want to have anything to do with them.

The idea of heaven provides a comforting explanation for what happens when the people we love die, and the idea of hell offers a somewhat comforting explanation to what happens to very bad people when they die, too. So, when a good and influential Christian priest dies, the idea that he is in heaven is more comforting than one that suggests he's merely expired and has been buried in the ground to rot away. On the other hand, to think that there is no consequence for people like Adolf Hitler or the 9/11 hijackers or Timothy McVeigh for the terror they visited on innocent people doesn't sit well with most people.

Those extremes of who is going to heaven or hell are easy for most people to agree on. Where the divergence begins is with regards to the fate of the overwhelming majority of people who are neither pious clergymen nor brazen murderers. Without a doubt, the idea of hell satisfies, for most people, the human concepts of ultimate judgment and punishment. The idea of heaven, on the other hand, satisfies our concept of a never-ending life in a more perfect world.

In a 2014 Pew Research Center Study, 72% of Americans believed in heaven defined as a place "where people who have led good lives are eternally rewarded." In the same study, 58% of US adults also believe in hell defined as a place "where people who have led bad lives and died without being sorry are eternally punished." Strikingly, there were 14% of the respondents who seem to believe in heaven but not in hell.

Life In Progress: Winning Where It Matters

Among Christians who believe that only people who accept Jesus Christ as their personal savior are going to heaven, and everyone else is going to hell, there is disagreement on whether a person can lose his or her salvation, and as a result end up in hell. When you ask the question of a random sample of Christians, you're most likely to get a three-way split: one group with a firm position on the exact point you could lose your salvation, one group who maintain that once saved you're forever saved, and one group who admit that they don't know for sure.

Even though they are reading from the same Bible, some evangelicals believe one thing while other evangelicals believe another; Catholics believe one thing and Protestants believe another; Jehovah's Witnesses believe one thing while Seventh Day Adventists believe yet another. Judging by the exclusiveness with which each of these Christian faiths claims to have THE truth, it is very likely that one of these groups has it right and the rest have it wrong, or that they all have it wrong.

Carlton Pearson became a pariah in the evangelical Christian community for a theology that many Christians deemed as heresy. In the early 2000s, this once-fiery evangelical preacher with a 5,000-member congregation lost it all when he adopted what he called the Gospel of Inclusion, a belief that all people will eventually be saved and go to heaven. No hell. He argued that there is no hell like traditional Christianity taught, and that humans create their own hell on Earth. He also questioned the infallibility of the Bible, pointing out glaring discrepancies in translations. Pearson has since fully embraced the Unitarian theology, and maintains that people who believe in hell create it for themselves and others. He adds that we may go through "hell," but nobody goes to hell.

Rob Bell is another evangelical Christian leader who has interesting ideas that probe a rethinking of many of the religious beliefs that form the foundation of the Christian religion. Bell founded the Mars Hill Bible Church in Grand Rapids, Michigan; he grew it to about 10,000 members and served as its lead pastor. In 2011, he stirred up controversy with his book *Love Wins* that questioned the nature of heaven, hell, and salvation. Just as was done to Carlton Pearson, many Christian leaders have condemned Rob Bell as a modern-day heretic for challenging the traditional beliefs that Christianity has held onto for more than 2,000 years.

I have listened to what both of these men have to say about God, human beings, the purpose of life, and religion, and they make sense to me. I recognize that the teachings of people like Carlton Pearson and Rob Bell disturb the faith of many who subscribe to traditional Christianity. This is nothing new. Martin Luther and other Protestant leaders disturbed the faith of many Roman Catholics when they started the Protestant movement. The fact that these men's views on long-held ideas challenge the status quo is probably good for the future of Christianity, just like the views of Martin Luther and his Reformation peers did for Christians of today.

Some people who believe in the idea of hell have expressed a genuine internal conflict about good people ending up in hell with thieves, murderers, and other bad people, merely because they chose a different faith. That conflict, I imagine, stems from trying to reconcile what such people know to be true with what their respective doctrines have taught them to believe.

My maternal grandfather was a Christian for many years of his adult life. He converted to Buddhism, subscribing to the ideas that leading a moral life, being mindful of his thoughts and actions, and developing wisdom and understanding was a way of life that leads to happiness. Until his death, he was so devout that he held prayer meetings several times a week in his house with about 10-to-15 men in his living room, burning incense and chanting *"nam myoho renge kyo,"* a core Buddhist practice. I was fascinated by their chants. My grandmother, mother, uncles, and aunts dismissed the practice as idol worship. My grandfather, who was very set in his ways, was unfazed by what his family thought of his path to enlightenment.

In discussions with some members of my extended family about heaven and hell, I've asked them whether they think the man we all knew as Paapa is in heaven or hell. My extended family is mostly Christian, some being more devout than others. The majority of them believes he is in hell, but they would often absolve themselves of that indictment by adding, "Yes, he was a good man, but it is the Bible, and not me, that says you're going to hell if you don't accept Jesus as your personal savior."

My mother's grandfather was a Moslem. I never met him and learned this fact only through a picture of my grandmother with his father. I am yet to ask the question of my grandmother if she believes her father is in hell. I think I know what her answer will be, so I will spare her the uncomfortable conversation. My mother, who is a devout Christian, believes that there is a heaven and a hell but the answer to the question of who goes where is better left to God; rather, we should focus on doing God's will.

The idea of hell does not add to my relationship with God, and therefore I don't subscribe to it. I focus on the loving, redemptive relationship a father would want with all his children. The idea of hell is inconsistent with my idea of God.

When Afriyie asked her question about hell, it would have been convenient for me to dismiss her curiosity, but that would have been a disservice to her. She is learning about the Bible's stories, characters, and lessons.

We've had conversations about God and Christianity, and I have sincerely pointed out when I do not know something and encouraged her not to believe something just because I, or her mother, or other people she loves and respects believe that.

I believe what I believe because I choose to believe that. If my neighbor doesn't subscribe to the same ideas, I don't think of them as being wrong. I just think we're on different paths on our respective journeys.

It is good when we can suspend our disagreements about heaven and hell, and who is going to hell or heaven; and instead build thriving communities where our respective faiths inform our fair and empathetic treatment of one another.

Rather than focusing on the doctrines and beliefs that divide and distract us from building healthy communities that allow us to thrive, I have committed myself to contributing to creating a "heaven" here on Earth. I do that by serving the people around me, and making myself useful and relevant.

As to what happens when I die, I'll find out when I die. We will all find out when we die.

There may indeed be pearly gates somewhere in the sky with St. Peter sitting there and inspecting visas into heaven. If there is indeed such a gate, there will very likely be many groups of people at that gate arguing with him about the entry requirements.

I will continue to tap wisdom from religion (and from anywhere else) and let my beliefs guide me towards caring about my neighbors, serving humanity, and making my time on Earth count, rather than counting down to when I get out of here for an unknown destination. If that unknown destination is heaven, great. If that destination is hell, so be it.

When it comes to matters of heaven and hell, faith, God, and life after death, nobody knows; however, we all simply believe in what we think should be the right thing to believe.

· THIRTEEN ·

MAKING SENSE OF GOD

"When you change the way you look at things, the things you look at change."

- Wayne Dyer, author

I was sitting in the office of a car dealership several years ago, with a pen in hand ready to sign a purchase agreement and then drive off with a used car. The purchase agreement showed a total price that included the price of the car, sales taxes, fees for tags and title, and then a $250 documentation fee. Even though I was excited about the purchase, I couldn't get rid of the lingering feeling that the official-sounding item labeled Documentation Fee didn't make any sense, so I asked why I had to pay that.

The salesman answered that it was for all the paperwork related to getting the car ready for me to purchase. And he added, almost conclusively, that it is a fee everyone pays, leaned back in his chair and folded his arms across his chest. He stared at me waited for my response, and I thought about what he had just said.

The fact that everyone paid a fee didn't mean I had to pay it, too. After several minutes of back-and-forth with me, and also with his manager, they waived the fee. I thanked them, finished the deal, and then drove off.

The lesson I took with me from the dealership that day was that there's an additional price most of us pay, whether in buying cars or other things, simply because we do not read carefully enough or ask questions. I may have paid a documentation fee in the past. I am not sure. But on that day, I did not pay a documentation fee, and I didn't have to.

Believing ideas about God simply because that's what most people believe is equivalent to paying a documentation fee, not because it's a valid charge, but rather because "that is a fee everyone pays."

There is a myriad of contradicting ideas about God that are promoted by well-intentioned individuals and groups, and many people have accepted these ideas without any questions. I have believed ideas about God from people I trusted, who were told by people they trusted. Based on answers I've received to my questions about God and from my own experience of God, I have updated what I believe about God.

In almost all religions, there are obvious mischaracterizations of God that have led some to use religion as a tool for manipulating other people. Instead of using religion as a means for good, many self-styled pastors, priests, and prophets have used religion and the name of God to control and harm others.

For many years, I wondered why I could not simply believe most things about God and my Christian religion like everyone else I knew. With time, I came to realize that my inquiring mind is a gift, and that it is all right that I have questions. It is all right that I have questioned the things I have been taught about God.

I have never questioned the idea of God itself. It is the descriptions of God, the characteristics of God, the expectations God is believed to have of human beings, what is or what is not God's words, the idea that a person has to be in an exclusive group in order to be in good standing with God; these are the things I have had questions about. I have received answers to some of those questions. Some of those answers I also have questions about, and I have filed some of the questions away as mysteries that were meant to be marveled at.

There are persuasive arguments on the subject of God that could be made, and have been made by people from all walks of life. I contend that God is bigger than any human mind can conceive, and therefore, no single religion knows all there is to be known about God. There are ideas about God that we can all agree on, and there are others on which we can agree to disagree.

The story is told of a group of seven blind men who went to see an elephant for the first time. The man who touched its leg concluded that the elephant is like a tree. The man who touched the tail argued that the elephant is like a rope. And then another said it is like a fan after he touched the elephant's ear. Another said it is like a wall after he touched the elephant's belly. The man who touched its trunk said it is like a big snake. "Oh, no! It is a spear," said another man who touched the tusk of the elephant.

Each of these men had an idea of what an elephant looks like based on the body part they touched. They each had an idea of what that part of an elephant is, which was true to their experience. But that idea was not complete. It is presumptuous of any of the blind men to claim to know what an elephant is simply based on his limited experience.

With the moral of this story in mind, I am humbly making sense of God and acknowledging that my preferred religion may not have all the answers to my questions about God. I also recognize that others with different points of view about God may have something to add to my understanding of God, so I welcome healthy conversations about the subject and shy away from contentious debates.

Imagine the seven blind men debating whose idea of the elephant is more complete, and each of them claiming to know for sure what the elephant looks like. That's a debate no one is going to win. Furthermore, imagine their going back to their respective communities to spread their ideas about the elephant. Each man will convince his people of what he had experienced. It is very likely that you imagined a world where each community becomes so entrenched in their idea of the elephant that if an elephant one day wanders into town, no one would know what it is.

I wished the blind men had talked to one another. Perhaps they would have been able to pool their ideas together to provide a more accurate description of the elephant. Maybe they did not confer with one another because none of them recognized that they were all limited by their blindness. Or maybe none of them knew each of them was blind and each pretended to have sight.

The idea of God is a big one, and it forms the foundations of many of the world's monotheistic religions, that is, religions that believe there is only one God. I believe there is one God who is all-knowing, all-powerful and always-present. That belief is sufficient for my interpretation of creation and my relationship with the Creator. Those who have different beliefs about God are not wrong; they just have a different interpretation of the same idea. It is possible that they are right and I am wrong, even though my preference for what I believe makes me downplay the possibility that I could be wrong. And it is also possible that all of us could be wrong in what we believe about God.

The idea of a Creator, which is expressed in the different creation stories of cultures around the world, makes sense to me, although the answer to the question of who created the Creator will remain a mystery. While the Big Bang Theory does not convince me as the explanation for the beginning of the universe, science and religion together help me appreciate God more.

I like what Martin Luther King Jr. said when he said, "Science investigates; religion interprets. Science gives man knowledge, which is power; religion gives man wisdom, which is control. Science deals mainly with facts; religion deals mainly with values. The two are not rivals."

I subscribe to the God of the Bible, and I very well know that the God of the Bible is a construction of the human mind. I recognize that human beings who sought to document their experiences and interaction with God wrote the books of the Bible. As inspired as they would have been to be thorough and accurate, the authors' accounts and interpretations of God were bound to reflect the limitations of their human minds. So, these authors understandably ascribed to God attributes of man because the noblest living creatures they knew were good human beings and gods (who also had been ascribed human characteristics).

My faith in God has grown because of my examining who God is and how he operates. And by the way, I refer to God as

"He" for simplicity. I suppose God is genderless and would not be upset if I referred to Him as "She."

Even though I recognize that the idea of God is bigger than any one Holy Book can detail, the God of the Bible often suffices for me as a starting point.

Others dismiss the existence of God, and I think they are entitled to that opinion. Comedian George Carlin has a funny bit on religion and God. He points out a fundamental contradiction in Christian doctrine. The contradiction also underscores Carlin's point that the God of the Bible is a creature invented by human thinking. He says:

"Religion has actually convinced people that there is an invisible man living in the sky. Who watches everything you do – every minute of every day. The invisible man has a list of ten things he does not want you to do. And if you do any of these ten things, he has a special place full of fire and burning, and smoke, and torture, and anguish, and will send you to live and suffer and burn and choke and scream and cry forever and ever; until the end of time. But he loves you."

He goes on for another seven or so more minutes, and talks about religion's persistent claim that God needs our money, the unjust events around us being evidence of either incompetence or apathy on God's part, and the fact that praying to God on His day off (Sunday) is an inconsiderate thing to do. I get the humor in his routine and his atheistic point of view. What I find fascinating about the routine is that even though he and I disagree on the fundamental question of the existence of a God, I agree with him on the contradiction of the religious doctrines that portrays a very angry, needy God who is also very loving.

I discussed my views on the first part of Carlin's commentary in the *This I Believe* chapter. Suffice it to say that I believe hell is an idea invented by religion to encourage compliance with the church's doctrine, and has endured through time because it is an effective scare tactic. However, it is inconsistent with the loving nature of God, which inspires hope and advocates redemption.

The concept of God's love has become more relatable through my experience as a father. My relationship with my daughter is a physical version of my relationship with my invisible father, God. Just like I do for my daughter, God wants the very best for me. I believe God loves me unconditionally, so I cannot earn his love nor do I have to prove my love to him. I do not need my daughter to continually remind me of how much she loves me in an effort to prove her love for me. And if my daughter wants something from me, I would expect that she would ask me directly and politely, and not coerce me with long, enticing words.

My relationship with God is also a parallel of my human parental relationships as a son to my mother. My mother has always wanted the best for me and embraces me as one of her beloved children no matter the error of my ways.

My mother does not need money from me, even though she'll welcome a kind gift from time to time. She will certainly not claim that I am robbing her for not giving her a tenth of my income. Not having to prove anything to my mother allows me to honor her wholeheartedly, and not out of obligation. And therefore, I give money to the Church or to charity out of generosity and from my appreciation of the role that particular organization plays within the community, and not out of obligation or as an attempt to avoid the wrath of God.

My daughter is my daughter not because she is perfect and does the right things all the time. She is my daughter because she is my daughter. On the occasions when she does not do the right thing, and I allow her to suffer the consequences of her actions, it is never intended to create a chasm in our relationship. Instead, it is to help her learn to make better choices as she's learning how to lead a successful, independent life. Even in the improbable event that my daughter does something as horrible as to kill another human being and is thrown into jail, I would not sit by idly and watch her be tortured simply because she did not follow what I taught her – which were for her own good by the way. Likewise, I don't see God ever abandoning me.

There is a Bible verse that quotes Jesus as comparing earthly fathers to God. It's in the book of Matthew where he is believed to have said, "If you, then, though you are evil, know how to give good gifts to your children, how much more will your Father in heaven give good gifts to those who ask him!"

To me, this verse is not about using God as an ATM that provides unlimited cash access to those who pray for money. Instead, Jesus was teaching about the essence of relationships. He was stirring up a paradigm shift away from quid pro quo relationships towards what it means to love another human being.

He was leading to a point about treating people right just because it is the right thing to do. That is probably why he followed that verse with, "**So,** in everything, do to others what you would have them do to you."

He was certainly talking about God wanting more for us than our earthly parents could ever do.

My relationship with my daughter or my relationship with my mother is the lens through which I view my relationship with God. It may be difficult for some people to embrace God's love the way I do because their experiences with their earthly parents may not have been positive, or they have no experiences with loving a child. I would suggest not taking Jesus' words literally but instead substituting earthly father with any relationship that affirms and nourishes you.

I find it comforting to know that God loves me, and everyone else. I am as precious in His eyes as any of the billions of people around the world is. God does not love me any more than he loves the Tibetan kid roaming the streets of China or a Sierra Leonean man who lost his hands in a civil war. I can't explain why that Tibetan kid is orphaned or hungry, or why the innocent Sierra Leonean man had to lose his hands because of the actions of people with hate in their hearts.

I don't know why evil and injustice exist. I don't understand why God doesn't just wave a wand and make the world a better place. But I know God loves me as well as all the people in the world. God loves the poor as well as the rich. God loves the good people as well as the bad people.

Maybe, just maybe, God is looking to you and me to "do unto others what we would have them do unto us." Maybe God is looking to you and me to help others experience His love by how we treat each other.

The Bible is the most popular account of God's relationship with His creation, especially with human beings. Many people, including me, quote the Apostle Paul in referring to the Bible as "inspired by God and is useful to teach us what is true and to make us realize what is wrong in our lives. It corrects us when we are wrong and teaches us to do what is right." It is perfect for that purpose, especially when taken in context. "Inspired" is an important word to remember.

Out of the Bible has come hundreds of Christian denominations and sects, mainly based on the different interpretations of the words contained in the Book. Some people interpret the entire Bible allegorically by drawing on the meaning hidden behind the stories. Others interpret the entire Bible literally by taking the words exactly as they are written. Some people interpret some parts literally and other parts allegorically. Our interpretations of the Bible, whether literally or allegorically, can inform the way we view God and our relationship with Him.

There are many good examples of virtue and love in the Bible, and those examples are useful in teaching us how to treat others. Also in the Bible are many indefensible actions, such as murder and slavery, which God seemingly endorsed. These accounts are presented as approved by God because much of the Bible is a historical account of people behaving in ways that made sense in that era, and then justifying their own ideas with what they believed God was telling them. Just as God would not approve of murder and slavery in today's age, I believe He disapproved of these actions more than 2,000 years ago. But since those actions were acceptable to the people who thought they were acting on God's orders, they wrote about it in the Bible as having been approved by God. This is why the historical context and the worldview of the Bible's characters are important factors in interpreting the Bible.

As a matter of intellectual honesty, I do not view an account of history, which started out as Jewish oral tradition, handed down from generation to generation, and later documented through the process of human writing and editing; selected by a group of church leaders and scholars, and then translated from language to language, as the "inerrant and infallible Word of God." Parts of the Bible, not the entire compilation, could be words from God to a particular group of people (even though anybody can benefit from the lessons the Bible teaches.)

The Bible is a transformative Book with good examples of how to live life well and relate with others. It is as inspired as Neale Donald Walsch's *Conversations with God*. They both teach me valuable lessons about maintaining a relationship with God. They both have elements that leave me scratching my head.

While it would be presumptuous of me, or anyone, to dismiss the Bible as an authority for the purpose of life, I believe that taking such a historical document literally and ignoring the cultural and historical context of the accounts is not helpful either. Therefore, I take the words of the Bible literally where it makes sense to take it literally and take it allegorically where I believe it was meant to be taken as such.

For example, I embrace the wisdom in Verse 5 of Chapter 3 of the book of Proverbs that states, "Trust in the Lord with all your heart and lean not on your own understanding; in all your ways acknowledge Him and He shall direct your paths." But I do not take it literally when David says in Verse 9 of Psalm 91 that, "If you say, 'The Lord is my refuge,' and you make the Most High your dwelling, no harm will overtake you; no disaster will come near your tent. For he will command his angels concerning you to guard you in all your ways; they will lift you up in their hands so that you will not strike your foot against a stone. You will tread on the lion and the cobra; you will trample the great lion and the serpent."

Clearly, those are not God's words but David's, and Jesus did not take Psalm 91 literally when Satan reportedly tempted him and quoted this psalm. Taking the words of this psalm literally would almost always lead to disappointment and eventually lead to blaming God for not honoring His Word. I think this psalm, a hymn or a song, is about trusting in God to be a refuge and comforter in times of hardships if you count on him for divine provision and protection. It is not about literally treading on lions and cobras to prove that God is protecting you.

I embrace the Bible as an important book for guidance on maintaining a relationship with God and for living with others. When it comes to how its ideas inform my life, I quote Rabbi Laura Janner-Klausner in saying the Bible has a vote, not a veto.

Many of the attributes ascribed to God in biblical accounts reflect the cultures and worldviews of the religious leaders of the early Church who curated the "standard list of authorized writings" that have been passed on through various translations, political influences, and several individuals' attempts to make sense of God. They were doing their best to make sense of God. Back then in the biblical times, their worldview was limited.

We know more now about the world than any group of people who ever walked on the face of the Earth. We have access to more information than any people who came before us. With the Bible and other church doctrines being subjected to scholarly scrutiny, some ideas have been left behind. This is why the Roman Catholic Church's interpretation of God is no longer the only interpretation available. This is also why churches that used to insist on women covering their heads with a scarf when in church - or men and women sitting in seperate sections during service - no longer practice or enforce such doctrines.

After many years of holding a firm grip and an exclusive right to the Bible, many of the Catholic Church's practices (that were supposedly authorized by God) were challenged and abandoned by Protestants. Evangelicals and Charismatics abandoned some ideas Protestants still hold dear and live by. As the evolution of the Church continues, every new wave of Christianity abandons some ideas of their predecessors even though they're all reading from the same Book. That is because our interpretations of God and of the Bible continues to evolve.

The Catholic Church, to her credit, has evolved somewhat. It is not the same church it was in the 14th century. It is not the same church that would declare someone like John Wycliffe a heretic and burn his works, exhume and burn his corpse, and throw his ashes into a river. His crime? He had a long history of rightly challenging the excesses and privileged life of the clergy.

He translated the Bible from Latin into English, arguing that every Christian who wanted to read the Bible should have access to it. In Wycliffe's time, only Latin translations were authorized and available, and most people could not read Latin. The Catholic Church opposed him, arguing "By this translation, the Scriptures have become vulgar, and they are more available to lay, and even to women who can read than they were to the learned scholars, who have a high intelligence. So the pearl of the gospel is scattered and trodden underfoot by swine." Those are some disturbing words, but a reflection of the worldview of the leaders of the church in that era.

Like the Catholic Church, other Christian denominations have gone through their own reformation but much more change is needed. Some churches have left behind doctrines that discriminate against other people. Others, unfortunately, still hold on to ideas that systemically discriminate against women as well as other ideas that concentrate power in the hands of a select few. I am hopeful that the reformation of the Church at large will continue, and that those of us who have experienced the grace and love of God will be more willing to extend it to others.

Speaking of the Roman Catholic Church, its 266th leader, Pope Francis, is a fascinating man. He is possibly the most influential religious leader in the world, judging by the size and reach of his influence. I like him for several reasons, including his humility and his emphasis on God's love and mercy. He is understandably expected by his faithful followers to have definitive answers to the difficult questions concerning man's relationship with God. Sometimes, his honesty slips past the long-standing doctrines of the church; some of those have stirred up controversy and led the Catholic Church to have to clarify when the Pope speaks for himself and when his words imply doctrinal direction.

All the same, it is refreshing to learn from the man (who is expected to hear from God on behalf of nearly 300 million people around the world) that he is also wrestling with some of the difficult questions most people are wrestling with.

Pope Francis, after acknowledging in 2016 that everyone, including him, at times, experience doubts about their faith, he said the following at one of his weekly general audiences:

"Such doubts can be a sign that we want to know God better and more deeply. We do not need to be afraid of questions and doubts because they are the beginning of a path of knowledge and going deeper; one who does not ask questions cannot progress either in knowledge or faith."

I make room for doubt as I partake in the rituals and routines of Christianity. While God is unchanging, human ideas about God have changed throughout human history. Therefore, I make room for what I may need to learn or unlearn.

With the idea of God being as transcending as it is over what the human mind can conceive, we are no different from the blind men who described an elephant based on what part of its body they touched. Granted that some of the blind men would insist that their descriptions of the elephant ought to be the only and authorized description, the elephant remains an elephant for each blind man to discover more of. So when the blind man who touched the trunk (and believed the elephant is like a snake) also touches the tusk (and realize that it feels like a spear), that blind man will try to make sense of the elephant, acknowledging that there has to be more to the elephant than what he had previously believed.

I am making sense of God through my questions and my sincere pursuit of understanding. I am making sense of God through my experiences with the divine and through my experiences with the people around me.

When I participate in worship services, that makes me feel closer to God and to the people around me. The worship songs remind me of God's goodness; the prayers remind me of God's presence and audience; and the people remind me that we are all connected. That is a cherished experience and a sure reminder to me of God's love.

Above and beyond participating in worship services, I feel God's love most when I see or experience people doing things to make others' lives and the world better.

Regardless of the path each of us chooses for maintaining a relationship with God, what matters most is that we each seek to be instruments of God's love on Earth.

Just as St. Francis of Assisi prayed, I hope that we all seek to "sow love where there is hatred, pardon where there is injury, truth where there is error, faith where there is doubt, hope where there is despair, light where there is darkness, and joy where there is sadness."

And may the peace, and love, of God be with us all.

· FOURTEEN ·

MY OBITUARY

"You only live once, but if you do it right, once is enough."
- Mae West, actress and writer

In a commencement address at Stanford University in 2005, Steve Jobs, the iconic founder of Apple and the man whose visionary leadership brought us the iPod, iPhone and other iDevices, said the following:

"When I was 17, I read a quote that went something like, 'If you live each day as if it was your last, someday you'll most certainly be right.'

It made an impression on me, and since then, for the past thirty-three years, I've looked in the mirror every morning and asked myself if today were the last day of my life, would I want to do what I'm about to do today? And whenever the answer has been 'No' for too many days in a row, I knew I needed to change something.

My Obituary

Remembering that I'll be dead soon is the most important tool I ever encountered to help me make the big choices in life. Because almost everything - all external expectations, all pride, all fear of embarrassment or failure - these things just fall away in the face of death, leaving only what is truly important.

Remembering that you are going to die is the best way I know to avoid the trap of thinking you have something to lose. You are already naked. There is no reason not to follow your heart."

Jobs died in 2011, and he was 56 years old. Even though I wish we had him here a little longer, I am grateful for what his insight about death teaches me about making my presence on Earth count.

One thing that was clear about the way he lived his life was that he lived with conviction, and took risks most people would be too afraid to take. His Type A personality certainly helped him navigate the uncharted territories that marked his early success, failures, attempts at restarting, and eventual return to the top as king of the world. He knew he would be dead someday, so he lived a driven life while he lived. His authorized biography by Walter Isaacson is a good read, as is *The Steve Jobs Way: Leadership for a New Generation* by Jay Elliot, a former Senior Vice President of Apple Computer and close colleague of Steve Jobs.

My awareness of my mortality is the reason I purchased a life insurance policy because if I die before my daughter is old and independent enough, I would like for there to be enough money to help take care of her. This same awareness of my mortality is what keeps me thankful that I get to be here and enjoy the remarkable people and places around me. Usually happy, healthy and hopeful, I have almost always felt like I would live forever. But the truth is that I could be here for another 50 years or only the next 50 minutes.

While I prefer having 50 healthy years to expiring 50 minutes from now, the length of time continues to be less relevant to me. What I do with my time on Earth, however long it turns out to be, has become more important to me as I have gotten older. I believe I have impacted the lives of other people in small and big ways, and I hope to continue to do so as long as I have breath and good health. More than that, I hope to die as empty as possible.

This idea of dying as empty as possible was affirmed for me by the simple truth in the poem, "The Dash". It speaks of the dash that exists in between the date of a person's birth and the date of the person's death when presented in an obituary or on a tombstone. The poem implies that the time between the two dates, represented by the dash, is what matters most about a person's life on Earth. The poem closes by asking, "So, when your eulogy is being read, with your life's actions to rehash; would you be proud of the things they say about how you spent your dash?"

I have heard many tributes and eulogies read, and I have thought about what is said publicly when a person dies. While most of these tributes are honest attempts by loved ones to honor the memory of the deceased, it never ceases to amaze me how people often become heroes and heroines in their death. As it is the case with the funeral-obsessed aspects of many African cultures, the seriousness with which we mourn and ascribe accolades to the dead is legendary. While these accolades and praise, whether exaggerated or fitting, may serve a ceremonial purpose, the proof of the pudding is in the eating. People who knowingly bear false witness about a dead person are people for whom I have very little patience.

When I die, I am pretty sure some people will cry. Some people will post kind comments about me on Facebook and Instagram or on whatever popular social media platforms there will be at the time. It is also possible that some people might shrug at the news of my death, and that will be perfectly fine. Trust me, how people react to news of my death will not hurt my feelings. I will be dead.

But hopefully, the kind words some will say about me when I'm dead will be a source of comfort to those who will be grieving. I hope my death would be an occasion for people who know me to reminisce about the memories we've shared. To that end, I am making every effort to live my life purposefully and sincerely enough that people who care about me would not have to exaggerate stories or make up new stories in offering what they deem to be a fitting eulogy.

Of all the things that would be said about me when I'm gone, it is the objective obituary that I'm writing in the hearts and minds of people that will matter most to me. It will not matter to me then (because I will be dead), but it matters to me now. It matters to me that I spend the rest of my days in such a way that leaves an imprint on their hearts and minds.

My father died in January 2018. He was 80 years old. He never seemed intimidated by the idea of dying. As far back as before I was a teenager, my father would sometimes talk about the inevitability of his own death. When someone we knew died, my father would often empathize and then add that, "Oh well, we'll all die someday."

When my brother told me of the news, my first thought was that "someday" had finally come for my father. We discussed the facts he knew at the time about the incident, and then reminisced about some of the fond moments we shared with him.

Ɔsaman is the Twi word for ghost. It was my father who explained to me that ɔsaman is a condensed form of the sentence "w'asa wɔ ɔman mu" (translation: he's finished in the world), and that ghosts are not real but figments of our imagination. That was how my father helped me conquer my irrational fear of ghosts.

Ghanaian musician Kojo Antwi, in his song "Ɔsaman," talks of someday when he'll shut his mouth, never to speak again; be laid in a box, never to be seen again; clench his teeth, never to laugh again; his hands rested on his chest, never to wave again at anyone; that someday is when he'll become an ɔsaman. My father's "someday" had come. He is now an ɔsaman, and has moved out of this world.

As I cherish the memories I have of my father, I have also grappled with the reality of his being gone. I was scheduled to visit Ghana in July 2018, and planned to have a series of conversations with him on various topics. This was going to be part of a book, *Conversations with My Father*, which I envisioned as capturing my father's life experiences, his reflections on life and the wisdom he wished to pass on to others. Even though that book will not happen in the form I envisioned it, the current version of my memories of him will always be with me. Those memories make up the version of his obituary which he wrote in my heart and mind.

Like my father, I am not intimidated by the idea of dying. I have wondered, though, what it means to die, and what my death would mean to me. Will it be an out of body experience where I walk towards a tunnel of light and see all the loved ones who've gone before me welcoming me home?

Will I lose all consciousness like in a deep, dreamless sleep? Will I know I'm dead when I'm dead? Will I, or a part of my consciousness, hang around the neighborhood hoping to comfort the people I've left behind? Will a part of me inhabit the body of a foetus and be birthed by another mother, and start this life cycle all over again? Will children remain children after they die or the part of them that continue on will get older?

I don't know the answers to these questions. Every time I hear of a person's death, the one thought that usually crosses my mind is that the dead person knows for a fact what it means to be dead. The rest of us, I suppose, will have to wait to find out about that when we're dead.

Movies such as "What Dreams May Come True," "Ghost," "City of Angels," and "Five People You Meet in Heaven" give a sense of what happens when people die. While their interpretations of what it means to be dead is a good-faith effort at answering a question no living person knows the answer to, I appreciate the emphasis these movies place on living life well while we have the opportunity to do so.

My biggest takeaway from these movies is the outside-looking-in perspective of how to live so that I have no regrets when I'm dead. Assuming that it is possible to have regrets in death, I don't want to look back and wish I had done things differently.

There is an obituary writing exercise that is sometimes offered as part of some graduate school coursework or personal development workshops. People who have participated in the exercise speak of how it reminded them of what matters most in their lives, and helped them focus on that. This exercise is believed to have been inspired by a story told of Alfred Nobel, the founder of the Nobel Prize.

What most of us know about Alfred Nobel is that his last will directed that the bulk of his fortune be used to establish the Nobel Prize, which honors outstanding achievements in physics, chemistry, medicine, literature, and for work in peace. Had it not been for an obituary of him that was prematurely published in a newspaper, we probably would now know Alfred Nobel for something other than what he thought his life's work was.

As the story goes, he read in a newspaper one morning that he had died, and the obituary was not a flattering one.

"The merchant of death is dead," the obituary declared. "Dr. Alfred Nobel, who became rich by finding ways to kill more people faster than ever before, died yesterday."

It was Alfred Nobel's brother Ludvig who had died, but the newspaper mistook him for Alfred, the famous Swedish scientist who had invented the explosive dynamite used during the Spanish-American war to kill thousands of people. To Nobel's credit, his invention served important uses in the mining and construction industries, where he reportedly made most of his money. The world, however, was going to remember him as "the merchant of death."

Fortunately for him, he had a wake-up call after reading his obituary before his death, and did something about the parts that he wasn't happy with.

When I first heard about the obituary exercise, I understood it as being an exercise about writing down how you want your life story to be told when you are dead. It seemed a little too self-serving, so I didn't pay it any more attention.

My Obituary

A couple of years later, an article from www.Lifehack.com gave me an additional perspective on this exercise. The article challenged me to look at my life now and assess if I would be satisfied with the way I've lived should my life end at that moment. If I were to die today, the article asked, and my obituary was to be written truthfully, without embellishments, would I be satisfied with what it would say?

The main questions from the article were:
- Am I satisfied with the direction in which my life is headed?
- Am I happy with the legacy that I'm creating?
- What's missing from my life?
- What do I need to do for my obituary to be "complete"?

I have answered these questions and do revisit them from time to time to see if there is room for improvement.

By the way, if you thought, by reading the title of this chapter, that you'd be reading the actual words of what I want to be read at my funeral, I'm sorry to disappoint you. You'll have to wait until I'm dead to read it because someone else will write it.

When it is written, I hope my obituary serves as an inspiring reminder to those who read it. I hope it reminds someone to live more purposefully before he or she dies.

My friend Tom Dearing shared with me a poem about how he would like to be remembered when he transitioned out of this life. Tom did not write the poem but was so moved by the words that he printed a copy for me, instead of merely forwarding the email to me.

I met Tom in 2001 through Kofi Owusu-Ansah, who had contacted Tom for a possible job opening at his video production company. Tom didn't have a job for Kofi at the time, but he invited him over for a conversation.

Kofi, who I had collaborated with on a few video projects, described Tom as a very insightful and big-hearted person, so I told him that I would be happy to meet him and engage in conversation.

I had lunch with Tom and shared samples of my past video projects as well as other ideas I had. We had long conversations about what I wished to do with my career, he told great stories about the work he had done, and about the people he had met along the way.

In the years that followed, I worked on various projects for him as a cameraman or a production assistant. He would often have me tag along just because I asked him or because there was someone he thought I would like to meet.

Many times, he encouraged my dreams, and on a few occasions, he became upset with me for not showing up on time for appointments. Many times, he would cook a big meal, and we would sit around his living room table to eat and just talk. I attended several of the annual August parties he held in his backyard, shared several Thanksgiving meals with him and his friends, and went bargain hunting at the second-hand clothing boutiques in Columbus' Clintonville neighborhood. When I was in the middle of a job search, I would bounce ideas off of him. I often walked away from our conversations with more clarity and renewed focus. Tom genuinely cared about people, and there are tons of people with stories similar to my experiences with Tom.

In early September 2017, after I completed the first draft of this book, I shared the table of contents with Tom. "Why don't you email [the book] to me; I'd love to see it," he asked.

My Obituary

I told him I was making edits based on the editorial feedback on the first draft and would get him the improved second draft in about a month. I knew Tom would not only be honored to provide feedback but would also be proud of what I was creating.

I had not been in contact much with Tom in the previous 12 months, except for a few text messages from time to time. When I called him in late September to say hello and to update him on my progress with the book, he sounded like he had a cold. When someone knocked at his door and his dog barked at the same time, he became distracted. He hung up and was going to call me back later.

I did not know that Tom had been sick with cancer for about a year. The following Tuesday, his wife, Laralyn, texted me that Tom had been fighting cancer in his kidney and hip for about a year. Radiation, hip replacement and two rounds of chemotherapy did not stop the disease from spreading. Tom had a short time left, so he had started hospice care at home. Before I could see him, I received word that he was slipping away as his organs began shutting down. Tom passed on shortly after that.

The memories of the moments I had shared with him flashed through my mind, and I was filled with gratitude that I had those moments by which to remember him. I found the poem he gave me years earlier, gave it to Laralyn, and she read it to him before he finally passed on.

The words of "To Remember Me" by Robert N. Test felt more surreal this time. The words were perfect for remembering Tom:

TO REMEMBER ME

The day will come when my body will lie upon a white sheet neatly tucked under four corners of a mattress lo-

cated in a hospital busily occupied with the living and the dying.

At a certain moment, a doctor will determine that my brain has ceased to function and that, for all intents and purposes, my life has stopped.

When that happens, do not attempt to instill artificial life into my body by the use of a machine, and don't call this my deathbed.

Let this be called the bed of life, and let my body be taken from it to help others lead fuller lives.

Give my sight to the man who has never seen a sunrise, a baby's face or love in the eyes of a woman.

Give my heart to a person whose own heart has caused nothing but endless days of pain.

Give my blood to the teenager who was pulled from the wreckage of his car, so that he might live to see his grandchildren play.

Give my kidneys to one who depends on a machine to exist.

Take my bones, every muscle, every fiber and nerve in my body and find a way to make a crippled child walk.

Explore every corner of my brain. Take my cells, if necessary, and let them grow so that someday a speechless boy will shout at the crack of a bat and a deaf girl will hear the sound of rain against her window.

Burn what is left of me and scatter the ashes to the winds to help the flowers grow.

If you must bury something, let it be my faults, my weaknesses and all prejudice against my fellow man.

If by chance you wish to remember me, do it with a kind deed or a word to someone who needs you.

If you do all I have asked, I will live forever.

My Obituary

I also share this poem with you because this is one of the ways I would like you to remember me when I'm gone. When I take my final bow, and there is applause, I hope the applause will be because my time here made someone's life better. I hope your applause will be because of the moments we shared and what my life meant to you.

I am only living once, and I hope to do it well so that once is enough.

· FIFTEEN ·

MY PLAYLIST

"One good thing about music - when it hits, you feel no pain."
- **Bob Marley, musician**

My playlist is a compilation of songs that are the soundtrack to my life. These are songs with which I identify in a special way. These songs have helped me through stressful situations, affirmed a belief, or inspired significant actions. These are also songs that I return to when I need inspiration and affirmation. There are hundreds of songs that serve similar purposes in my life, but these bubble up to the top – the short list, if you will.

In addition to the melody and arrangement that bring the songs to life, I feel like most of these songs' writers wrote these songs specifically for me or had me in mind at the time they wrote them. So highlighting these songs here is my way of saying thanks to their creators. These songwriters and the performers poured their souls on paper, on guitars, and on pianos sharing their gifts with me and the world. I am forever indebted to them for not holding back from expressing these thoughts.

My Playlist

One good thing about music is that when it hits, you feel no pain. Another good thing about music is that when no one seems to understand me, or my most private thoughts seem too bizarre to share with anyone, I can always count on music like a prudent best friend who always has the right words to say.

And it goes without saying that many songs serve this purpose but this is my short list. These reflect my thinking, feelings, inspiration, and aspirations at various times. In no particular order, I share them for your enjoyment and your appreciation.

1. Not the I but the You in Me (Anointed)

I stumbled upon Anointed's album, "The Call," in the 1990s while sampling the latest music at the listening station in a music store in Irvington, New Jersey. The opening track grabbed my attention right away with its funky intro. The lyrics were refreshing and inspiring, and it had a sincerity to which I could relate. The R&B and pop styling of their music closed the deal. Many of their songs conveyed a straightforward connection between my Christian faith and the real-life issues that were swirling around in my young adult head. The words in "Not the I but the You in Me" spoke about God choosing to use me as a vessel, in spite of my imperfections, for the things I get to do.

It reminded me that I am who I am, and God loves me all the same. That was hugely affirming for a young man trying to find his place in the world.

"Every good thing I have done, everything that I've become; everything that's turned out right is because You're in my life. And if I ever teach a child the way, ever learn myself to change; ever become who I want to be, it's not the I but the You in me."

2. Intentional (Travis Greene)

I believe most events in my life are part of a perfect design. The events in my life - those within my control and those outside of my control - all work together ultimately for my good. The word "intentional" captures the essence of what I understand about the nature of God. The song affirms my faith in a Creator of the universe who designed me perfectly for my purpose.

"All things are working for my good; He's intentional [and] never failing ... And although I can't [always] see how, it's working for me."

3. Champion (Kanye West)

Kanye West is a genius. I know he says unexpected things and his ego will not fit in most rooms. But there's no denying that he is one of the most exceptional musical talents of my generation. This song is one of my favorite hype songs. It's often served as a reminder to me that no matter how tough life gets, there is a champion inside of me. The words of the song remind me to keep pressing on against all odds.

"When it feels like living's harder than dying, for me giving up is way harder than trying ... Did you realize that you were a champion in their eyes?"

4. Iris (Goo Goo Dolls)

In the movie "City of Angels," Seth is an angel who appears to those who are close to death and guides them into the next life. Maggie is a surgeon who loses her patient in spite of her best efforts. Seth observes how hard Maggie fights to keep his patients alive, becomes romantically attracted to her, and eventually makes himself visible to her. Until he became fully human in the physical flesh, Seth hoped Maggie would recognize and understand his world. That's the context of the song.

It feels really good when I come across people who think as I do or can relate to my unusual thoughts. This song reminds me not to think I'm crazy in times when most people don't seem to see things from my point of view.

"And I don't want the world to see me 'cause I don't think that they'd understand; when everything's made to be broken, I just want you to know who I am."

5. Su Nkwa (Kojo Antwi)

"*Su Nkwa*" is a phrase in the Twi language from Ghana and it translates into "pray for life." It catalogs the many cherished things a person desires in life, and offers a reminder that all these things mean nothing if you're dead.

Drawing on the idea that life is a gift, this song is a reminder to me that life and good health are the most important things for which to wish and pray. I could use all the fine things in life but I need life, good health, patience, and courage the most. So, every time I sing along to this song, I'm praying for those things that I really need.

"*Ɛnkwa ne ahooden, ɛno nkoa n'ehia me; abotrɛ ne akokoduro, ɛno nkoa n'ehia me…mesu m'afrɛ Nyame, obɛyɛ ama me.*"

Translation: Life and strength, that's all I need; patience and courage, that's all I need … I will call upon God, He will grant them to me.

6. When You Believe (Whitney Houston and Mariah Carey)

This is a simple prayer sang by two of the most beautiful voices I ever heard, and from the movie "The Prince of Egypt." Miracles do happen. Sometimes miracles happens because I put in the work. Sometimes they happen in spite of me. Either way, there's a good reason for me to believe in miracles.

"*Though hope is frail, it's hard to kill; who knows what miracle you can achieve when you believe...*"

7. Ohene (Obrafour featuring Tinny)

Obrafour is one of the pioneers of the hiplife music genre that emerged in Ghana in the late 1990s. With his philosophical ingenuity, his musical aptitude, and his masterful command of the Twi language, Obrafour has earned my endorsement as the linguist of my generation.

In the song "*Ohene*," he declares himself the "king" of the genre and reminds his nemeses that he's on a whole 'nother level. It is for me a perfect silencer to my inner critic, and also the right motivation for summoning my inner strength in the face of any opposition. I remind myself that I am a king and a "monarch of all that I survey."

"*Megyina konkɔn, afei na wooforo...wo ne wo si tenten pɛ a ɔnyɛ w'afɛ...etirey wɔ hɔ a yɛnshɛ kotodwe kyɛ...wo di kan kort a na wondii bim.*"

Translation: I'm at the top of the hill, you're now climbing ... being as tall as your father does not make him your peer ... a hat is meant to be worn on the head and not on the knee ... arriving first in court does not prove your case.

8. The Measure of a Man (4Him)

There are milestones that every growing person is expected to reach. I am fully aware of the key metrics that usually suggest success in life. However, this 1990s contemporary Christian quartet offered me an uplifting perspective on what is the most important metric: the content of my heart.

"... I say the measure of a man is not how tall you stand, how wealthy or intelligent you are; 'cause I've found out the measure of a man, God knows and understands. For He looks inside to the bottom of your heart. And what's in the heart defines the measure of a man."

9. Walk on Water (Blue County)

My daily personal challenge is to be a better version of myself, doing the best I can and doing the right things as often as possible. This song from the soundtrack of the movie "Evan Almighty" is a reminder to me that even though I may not be able to perform miracles (walk on water), living a decent life is enough.

"It's the path you take, the steps you make that make you who you are; it's the life you live, the gifts you give, the love that's in your heart. Just try to do the best you can to be a better man. You don't have to walk on water; it's how you walk on land."

10. The Lord Is My Light (Andre Crouch)

During the 1990s, many times I went to sleep and woke up to songs on Andre Crouch's "Mercy" album. I would have the CD playing on repeat through the night and into the morning. The words of "The Lord is My Light" offered a particular reassurance and waking up to it always put a bright smile on my face.

"I have a secret place where I seek God's face; He gives me peace for my troubled mind. He carries me over mountains high. He comforts me through the valleys low. When I'm going through the storm, I'm protected in His arms. Oh, my father loves me. That's why I say the Lord is my light and my salvation..."

11. The Heart of Life (John Mayer)

No matter how good things get, they could get better, and no matter how good things get, they could also turn bad. Disappointments will occur. Bad things will happen. But in spite of all that, many things in this life make life worth living. The underlying idea is of the song reminds me to see the glass as half-full and look for the silver lining whenever dark clouds appear.

"...No, it won't all go the way it should, but I know the heart of life is good."

12. Seasons of Love (Jonathan Larson)

Multiply the 365 days in a year by the 24 hours in each day, and then by the 60 minutes in each hour; that equals 525,600 minutes. That's one way of measuring a year in the life of a woman or man. Each of those minutes in a person's life could be filled with meaningful and loving moments. We often measure our time on Earth in years but maybe we should measure them in moments. Maybe measuring it that way would highlight the moments that matter the most - hopefully, the moments of love.

From the Broadway musical "Rent," this song puts the value of a year in perspective. How would I live each of the 525,600 minutes, if all I have left to live is only one year? I would seek to create memorable moments for me and for those around me, and strive to fill each of the four seasons with love.

13. Lose Yourself (Eminem)

Eminem's character in the movie "8 Mile" is an amateur rapper trying to launch his career. Based largely on Eminem's real life, his character, the talented-but-anxious Rabbit, had a big moment at a rap battle. His life had been a rough one, and the odds were stacked against him. His talent was going to be his way out of poverty. That rap battle was his chance to make a name for himself. But he froze with inaction in that moment.

He eventually found his self-confidence, and with encouragement from his close friends, he took the stage at another rap battle and annihilated an established rapper. As this song suggests, he lost himself in the music in order to grab the opportunity.

"Lose Yourself" starts with his asking, "Look, if you had one shot or one opportunity to seize everything you ever wanted; in one moment, would you capture it, or just let it slip?"

That's a question that is answered in the song's chorus, and that answer, after swapping "music" for "hustle," is a perfect inspiration for when I need to *carpe diem* or seize a moment:

"*You better lose yourself in the [hustle], the moment; you own it, you better never let it go. You only get one shot; do not miss your chance to blow. This opportunity comes once in a lifetime…*"

14. Forever Young (Mr. Hudson featuring Jay Z)

When my mother was 35 years old, I thought she was old. When I turned 35, it didn't feel like I thought 35 would feel, because I didn't feel old. I felt as young as I had always felt. As the years have gone by, I've lost some of the hair on the top of my head, and I sometimes experience random, unexplained physical pains in my body. Through all of that, I feel much younger than I thought I would feel at my current age. I feel like I might live forever. Yeah, I know that's not possible but that's how I feel, and I will not voluntarily give up this feeling. I hope to never lose the youthful enthusiasm with which I approach life. Jay Z and I have the same idea about the years ahead.

"So we live life like a video, when the sun is always out and you never get old ... just a picture perfect day to last a whole lifetime ... I'm forever young."

And while I'm at it, let me add that my favorite albums of all-time are Cece Winans' "Alone in His Presence" and George Darko's "Highlife Time." I like Cece Winans' for the special place of focus its solemn content takes me, and George Darko's for being a fun, ground-breaking piece of work.

An honorable mention goes out to a young man I've seen grow into an amazing musician - Nana Boamah, who goes by the stage name NanaBcool. His track titled "Dope" is in fact dope (as in awesome), and I raise my glass to his "10,000 Hours." I look forward to his tremendous success in the years ahead.

Danish author Hans Christian Andersen said, "Where words fail, music speaks." Music has always been my friend who always knows just what to say, and is always there when I call. Friedrich Nietzsche noted that without music, life would be a mistake, and I couldn't agree more.

So, let it play on!

Life In Progress: Winning Where It Matters

My first official portrait (1975)

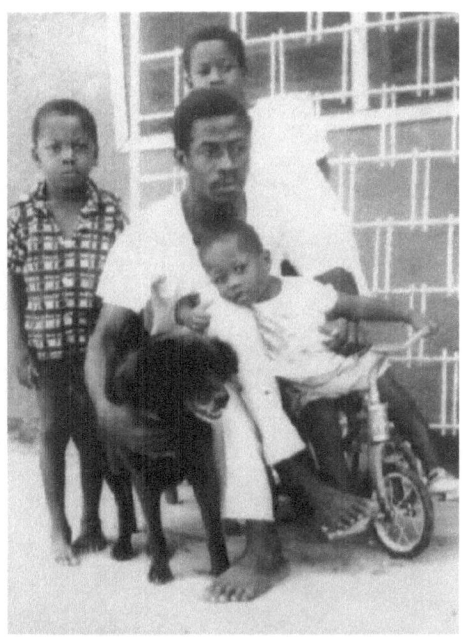

With my brother Joe (left), my father (middle), my sister Barbara (behind my father), and our dog Black Beauty.

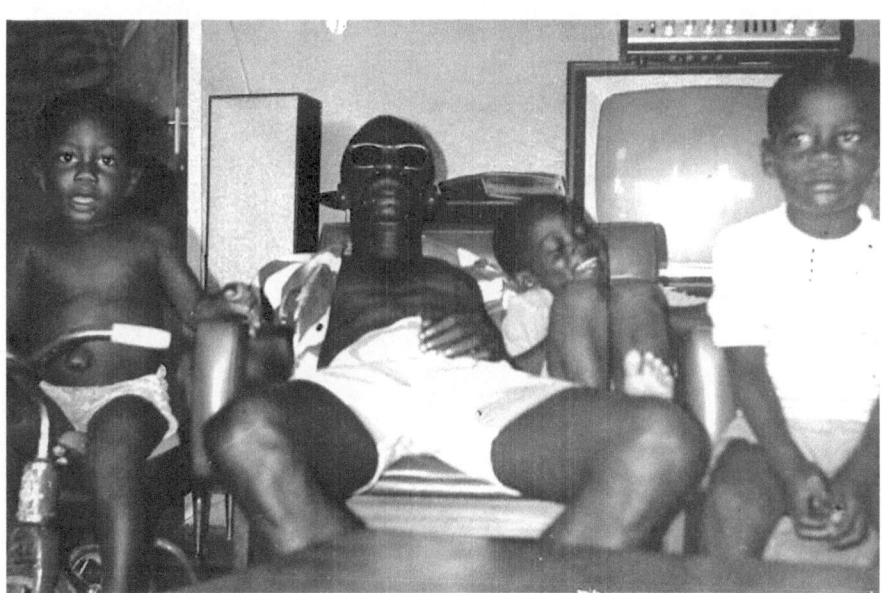

Lounging around with my father (middle-left), Arthur (middle-right) and Oliver (right); me on the tricycle.

Life In Progress: Winning Where It Matters

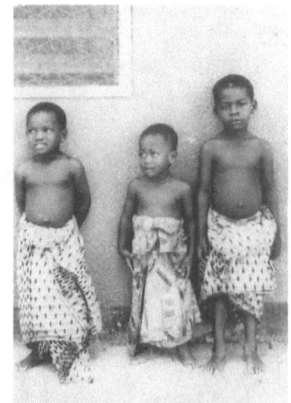

Life In Progress: Winning Where It Matters

LEFT: Top - Me on the tricycle; me heading to preschool; Arthur, me, and Oliver. **Middle** - Oliver, Amponsah, Arthur and me; Arthur, Oliver, me (on right and in my favorite "The Jungle Book" t-shirt), and Obeng. **Bottom** - me on a Sunday afternoon in Accra; Oliver, Arthur, Nana Yaw, me (right), and Obeng.

BOTTOM: **Top-left** - With my grandmother Maame Aso (seated and holding Panin and Kakra), my aunt Mama Julie (behind Maame), my mother (left), and my siblings. **Top-right** - me (left) with Afia Kine, Arthur, Oliver, Panin, Kakra, and Obeng. **Bottom** - At a party (second from left) with Mr. Amoah in cap and Sister Konadu in head gear.

Life In Progress: Winning Where It Matters

TOP: Birthday party for my twin sisters Panin (seated right on the floor) and Kakra (held by my mother); me standing next to Arthur in top row and hiding behind Getty Bediako.
BOTTOM: At a party with Kakra, Arthur, Obeng and Oliver somewhere in Accra.

Life In Progress: Winning Where It Matters

TOP: Left - My grandmother Maame Aso with her father **Right** - My grandfather John Wilson Afriyiye (middle and right) reporting from a location for Ghana Broadcasting Corporation.
BOTTOM: My uncles, aunts, cousins and siblings get together at my grandparents' home at Dansoman each January 1 to celebrate the new year.

Life In Progress: Winning Where It Matters

TOP: With Sammy Fiscian at WASS (1989).

BOTTOM: Second from right at a mock OAU summit (1990) with WASS Pan-African Club members John Ammah-Tagoe, Paa Joe, and Robert Bennett; at center is PRESEC Pan-African Club member Mike Ocquaye.

Life In Progress: Winning Where It Matters

TOP: My WASS Form 5 Science classmates (Standing L-R: Edwin Opare, Asare Darkwa, Richard Ackah, Muftaw Giwa, and me; squatting L-R: Nicholas Nartey, Mark Bekoe Yeboah and Yakubu Kassim)
BOTTOM: Last day at WASS (me fifth from left and with arms raised) after final G.C.E. O-Level exam.

TOP: At my first PRESEC Drama Club meeting; a cold reading of "The Search" script.
BOTTOM: Top - As Casper in "The Search" with Michael Commey and Nii Otu Okunor;
Bottom - Cast and crew of "The Search" after a performance at the Legon Drama Studio.

Life In Progress: Winning Where It Matters

TOP: On Ghana Airways' maiden direct flight to New York, and then to Toledo, OH.
BOTTOM: In the forecourt of the Toledo Zoo with students and chaperons from PRESEC and Toledo Excel.

Life In Progress: Winning Where It Matters

TOP: Ohene Bediako (Oblajay), me, Sasu Bediako (Alaska), and Kwabena Bediako
BOTTOM: Kwabena Bediako and me at a Harvest Gospel Choir concert at the Labadi Beach Hotel; I performed that evening with both the adult and youth choirs.

Life In Progress: Winning Where It Matters

TOP: Phil Acquah (Elsie's brother), Elizabeth Armstrong-Mensah (Elsie's cousin), me, and Elsie Osei-Tutu at Alajo.
BOTTOM: With Susan Prah (seated in middle), a lead teacher (seated on right) and some of our Kotobabi 1 students during my national service.

Life In Progress: Winning Where It Matters

TOP: With Francis Aikins (left) and Obeng (right) on Avon Avenue in Newark, NJ.

MIDDLE: Left - With Eric Amankwah; **Right** - With "Uncle" Ed Mettle

BOTTOM: With Dr. David Yamoah, Mrs. Diana Yamoah, and Afriyie in Union, NJ during Mrs. Yamoah's 60th birthday.

Life In Progress: Winning Where It Matters

TOP: My headshot used for auditions in 1998. Even though I took a few acting lessons after moving to Columbus, my focus shifted to creating content (screenplays) rather being on the screen.

BOTTOM: With Obeng (left) and Eric Amankwah (right) during my graduation from Kean University.

TOP: Left - With Afriyie at about six months old; **Right** - With Afriyie at 13 years old.
BOTTOM: With Trenyce Twumasi, Tryphena Awuah, Afriyie Amoako and Benjamin Ohene during a volunteering event at Dress for Success in Columbus, OH.

TOP: **Left** - With Kwabena Boamah-Acheampong at a Ghana Independence Day flag-raising event; **Right** - With Elder Awuah at the Columbus Picnic. **MIDDLE**: With Kwasi Wiredu, Kenneth Okyere and William (Odo Yewu) Ampadu.

BOTTOM: With Anna, Ache, Sandra, Mansa, Julie, Albert, and Kobe during a March 2018 remembrance service in Columbus in honor of my father.

Life In Progress: Winning Where It Matters

TOP: With my cousins Nana Kwasi Boatey (left) and Daniel Afriyie (right).

MIDDLE: With my sisters Barbara (middle) and Kakra (left).

BOTTOM: With Kakra, Obeng, and my neice Lyric Maame Gyamfuah Gambrah (middle).

TOP: Left - With Kakra (left) and Panin (middle) during my father's funeral; **Right** - With my mother during my father's funeral.

BOTTOM: With Kakra and her children Michelle (left), Manuel (right) and Charisa (middle).

Painting by my friend and colleague, Glen Zehr, to commemorate the completion of this book.

PART III:
TIES THAT BIND

• SIXTEEN •

WHAT'S LOVE GOT TO DO WITH IT?

"Tis better to have loved and lost than never to have loved at all."
- **Alfred Tennyson, poet**

Rightfully, almost everyone has an opinion on love. Many of these opinions regarding romantic relationships have been informed by personal experiences, by accounts of other people's experiences, and by the images portrayed in the media. That has been no different for me.

Most of my opinions about love, especially those formed during my young adult years, were heavily influenced by images portrayed in music and movies. That information shaped my early ideas about love, and informed my idealistic view of what it means to fall in love, and be in love.

I grew up to find out that it is one thing to know about love, but it is another thing to know about love through experience. My experiences have taught me valuable lessons about the subject and deepened my appreciation of what love is, and what it is not.

I will attempt to tell you what I know about love from the information I have gathered, as well as from my experiences. I will try to convey the idea that love is beautiful and perfect, and that it is we the people who screw things up and then blame it on love. I will attempt to share love's potential for making our lives better. And even though I am not an expert on the subject, my experiences give me something to talk about.

The ancient Greeks, who laid the foundations of modern Western civilization and defined many of the ideas modern-day people have about love, thought of love as not just one thing. They had six different words for describing this intense feeling of affection humans usually experience. They had *eros* (sexual passion), *philia* (deep friendship), *ludus* (playful love), *agape* (love for everyone), *pragma* (long-standing love) and *philautia* (love of self).

Romantic love appears to be a combination of the *eros*, *philia* and *ludus* kinds of love. It is worth noting that the ancient Greeks didn't always think of *eros* as fondly as we do today. They thought of it as a dangerous, irrational form of love that could take hold of a person and make that person do irrational things. Instead, they placed a lot more emphasis on *philia* or deep friendships, the kind of bond that breeds loyalty and deep empathy, often leading to one sacrificing for the other and vice versa. According to some accounts, ancient Greeks preached this idea because they needed a strong army for their wars and didn't want their soldiers being distracted by *eros*. It is very likely that if they could be here today, the ancient Greeks would frown on how much attention we pay to the celebration of Valentine's Day.

Most of my romantic relationships have involved a combination of the *eros*, *philia* and *ludus* kinds of love. I prefer that it goes from *ludus* to *philia* and then to *eros*. Sometimes it has followed that sequence and other times it has not. In most instances, I have found *eros* to be more meaningful when *philia* existed. The *philia* and *eros* are certainly enhanced when lots of *ludus* is present. While my experiences with love may have felt like a single emotion, it has been beneficial to know that it is, in fact, a patchwork of several distinct-but-closely-knit emotions.

This awareness has helped me appreciate the composition of my attraction towards another person. It has also helped me identify the elements of love I need to cultivate to create a healthy, fulfilling romantic relationship. Falling in love is a thrilling experience, and it is often a process that involves some *ludus*, *philia* and ultimately *eros*.

The process of my becoming romantically involved with another person has usually started out with my being attracted to the other person, or the other person being attracted to me, or both of us simultaneously being attracted to each other. The attraction may have been due to a single thing I found interesting about the person or a combination of things. And under the right circumstances, the attraction leads to a conversation and then to more and more conversations. The conversations would eventually lead somewhere or go nowhere. When it leads somewhere, I would expect that it leads towards a mutually beneficial friendship, and subsequently into a relationship.

Often, what attracts me to a potential mate is the individual's personality, which is a combination of physical, intellectual and emotional characteristics. The way a person looks matters to me. Life is better when the person you're sitting across from is pleasant to look at. The way a person's mind works also matters to me because life is more interesting when we can discuss ideas and situations ranging from the simple to the sophisticated. And of course, emotional maturity matters to me. Life is always better when each of us can understand and manage our emotions, and be reasonable with each other.

Conversations reveal a lot about a person. Conversations with a potential mate give me the opportunity to assess if the characteristics that are important to me are present in reasonable doses. A potential mate falling short in one of the categories is not necessarily a deal breaker. To sustain my interest and enthusiasm in pursuing a relationship, however, the individual would need to be exceptional in the other two areas. With this not being an exact science, these criteria also apply on a case-by-case basis. Regardless, I have found it to be true that specific early signals of incompatibility prove themselves to be correct with time. I learned some of these lessons the hard way when I ignored red flags and suffered the consequence.

After working my way through the initial stages of infatuation, and making as careful an assessment of my potential mate as I can, and with her completing her evaluation of me, the budding friendship might magically turn into a romantic relationship, if the feeling is mutual. When the feeling is not mutual, it is almost always a good indication to let it go. It is not the easiest thing to let go of a love interest even when the feeling is not mutual, but the persistent pursuit of a person who is not into you would most likely turn out to be a fool's errand.

I'm not sure of the exact point in this process where infatuation or merely liking someone turns into loving the person. I suppose it is different for everyone and it depends on the circumstances. But generally, infatuation is a short-term excitement that is based on limited knowledge about someone. Falling in love, on the other hand, is deeper and often based on knowing significant facts about the person.

Billy Ocean sings, "I used to think that love was just a fairy tale, until that first hello, until that first smile ... Suddenly, life has new meaning to me; there's beauty up above and things we never take notice of. You wake up, and suddenly you're in love."

Mr. Ocean may have fallen in love suddenly - after one hello and one smile - but I'm not sure I believe in the idea of love at first sight. Infatuation at first sight, definitely. Love, to me, takes a little longer than first sight.

Infatuation can linger around for a very long time and even seem like love. Love, the longer-term version, is often informed by more than what meets the eye, often takes time and knowledge about the person. The specific length of time for what will pass as "short term" or "long term" is relative, so what could take one month for two people could take six months or more for another couple. Regardless of how long it takes, going from infatuation to being in love is often marked by going from being consumed by just warm and fuzzy feelings to having a genuine interest in the long-term well-being of the other party. And at that point, it feels more comfortable for me to entrust this love interest with more of my feelings, hopes and fears, and begin factoring this person into more and more of my long-term plans.

While the process of falling in love may predominantly involve pleasant experiences and even cause us to ignore red flags we should be paying attention to, falling in love has real outcomes. For many of us, falling in love leads to fruitful outcomes such as finding a trusted partner with whom to share our dreams, ideas and time. Some people have even reported feeling a sense of completeness from falling in love. Unfortunately for some, the promises of happily-ever-after were never realized, and these individuals were left questioning why they fell in love in the first place.

In the best-case scenario, the short- and long-term plans of the two people work out as expected. The two people want the same things and they live happily ever after. In the worst-case scenario, one or both of the parties involved leave the relationship disappointed.

In the real world, however, a couple's interest in each other may end up being neither the best-case scenario nor the worst-case scenario depicted above. The two people may start out liking each other but may discover they want different things. The two people may start out wanting the same things but discover things about the each other that diminishes one party's (or both parties') interest in moving any further with that budding relationship. Either way, if the process takes its course and the two people can be honest about how they feel about the situation, and what wants and needs are negotiable, and which ones are not, they may or may not find enough common ground to proceed with a relationship.

The potential adverse outcomes of falling in love are probably why the ancient Greeks thought of romantic love as a dangerous, irrational form of love that could take hold of a person and make him or her do irrational things. It is, however, unfair of the ancient Greeks to ignore the good things that come from individuals' falling in love, and to blame love when things go sour. Often when human beings behave irrationally in relationships, they blame it on love. That is not fair.

I have not always made rational decisions when it comes to falling in love. Blaming love for the outcomes of my irrational choices would be like blaming my tongue when I bite it during a delicious meal. It is not my tongue's fault that I enjoyed the food so much and chewed too fast, and bit my tongue. I made that choice, so the responsibility would be mine alone.

Love, like the tongue, facilitates the pleasant and fulfilling experiences that we desire. Without the tongue, we would not be able to experience the sense of taste. Likewise, we would not be able to experience the full essence of romantic relationships without love. The tongue is perfectly placed in between our teeth, but we sometimes chew too fast and bite our tongues. Likewise, love is perfect, but we sometimes get hurt (from falling in love) because we do not always make rational decisions.

Marketing and other media messages have also influenced my definitions and expectations of love, albeit subconsciously. For many of us, such messages affect what we expect to feel, see or think when we hear or talk about love.

A case in point is what happened to me when I drove past a billboard advertising an adult novelty store. The store sells lingerie, adult pleasure gadgets and adult movies. The advertisement had the words "Passion, intimacy and romance" as its tag line. For a brief moment, I was hung up on the fact that nowhere on the billboard did it mention love. My brain quickly went into its hyperactive mode and overanalyzed their choice of words.

This was a week or so before Valentine's Day, so all the talk on the radio may have had me thinking about love, so expected to read about love on that billboard. Furthermore, the overuse of the word "love" during Valentine's season may have primed me to expect the word as part of the message. I assumed that an adult novelty business' mission is to facilitate romantic relationships and that they should have mentioned "love" in the ad.

I concluded that the company might be focusing on a particular kind of love: *eros*. So, they chose the words accordingly. I also concluded that many lovers during the upcoming Valentine's Day would be engaged in various activities to rekindle passion, intimacy, and romance in their relationships, and that the company had done their market research and landed on those words. It turned out that my analysis wasn't in vain. I had realized something noteworthy about sustaining a romantic relationship.

Passion, the compelling and pleasurable desire for another person, sustains enthusiasm in a relationship. Intimacy, the physical and emotional closeness, allows the two people to be naked both literally and figuratively, and not be afraid. And romance, the expression of that physical and emotional attraction, reinforces the desire to connect. Putting all the three together makes us fall in and stay in love. I am sure the purpose of the billboard was not to teach about love but to sell their products. However, I accidentally learned something new.

Music's influence on my opinion about love has come full circle. This time, as a father listening to my teenage daughter happily singing along to Boyz II Men's "End of the Road," New Edition's "I'm Still In Love with You," and similar songs. I couldn't help but wonder, "What do you know about that!?"

Of course, those innocent sing-alongs are what typical teenagers do as they hit puberty and develop an interest in the subject. Music is an excellent means for discovering the language of love. Music sources such as YouTube, Pandora, and Spotify make it so easy these days to find various kinds of songs. It has certainly been amusing to observe my daughter as she comes into her own and approaches the realities of love and romantic relationships.

She discovered these love songs from the 1990s without my prompting. With her going back more than two decades, to an era of music from when her parents were about her age, marked a moment. A part of me relished the fact that she is listening to the kinds of music that shaped my early ideas about love. Another part of me grappled with the idea that she's entering a new phase of her evolution into adulthood. I appreciate the range of love perspectives that most love songs offer, and the fact that she is getting exposed to some of these ideas in a relatively safe, no-pressure manner.

Most love songs inspire a range of scenarios about romantic relationships, by highlighting two extremes or the various in-betweens of this intense emotion. On one end, love songs talk about the perfect love that will go on forever. On the other end, they talk about the disappointment that can cause a lot of hurt and pain. In between those extremes are various forms of love scenarios that even I, as an adult, have not experienced, let alone a fresh teenager. For now, I am sure it's all rainbows and butterflies when my daughter thinks of love. But the time will come, and it appears that time is not that far off, when she will have to navigate the sometimes-complex world of relationships. I am sure she'll develop her own ideas about love from these songs and from her own experiences. And those ideas, I hope, help her put things in perspective.

There's a book by relationship and family life expert Dr. Gary Chapman called "The 5 Love Languages." It identifies five preferred ways most people give and receive love: through the giving and receiving of gifts, through words of affirmation, through acts of service, through sharing of quality time, and through physical touch. According to Dr. Chapman, the love languages offer the secret to love that lasts. That notion is based on the premise that if a person receives love in a manner consistent with the way they prefer to receive love, the expression of love will have a stronger and longer-lasting impact.

In romantic relationships, some people show their love by giving gifts, and some people feel loved when they receive gifts. Some people show their love through their encouraging and supportive words, and some people feel loved when they hear those kinds of words. Some people show love by serving others, and some people feel loved when they are served. Some people show their love through the undivided attention they give, and some people feel loved when they feel like they have the unreserved attention of their partner. Some people show their love through physical contact, and some people feel loved when they are often touched.

By completing an introspective questionnaire on the website www.5languages.com, you can discover your love language profile and an explanation of how your primary love language may apply in your relationships.

Of the maximum possible score of 12, my highest scores were 10 and 9 for quality time and words of affirmation, respectively. The author explains that it is common to have two high scores, although one language does have a slight edge for most people. While I was not surprised by the top two, I thought acts of service would come in a close third, but it was a distant third.

As important as each of these love languages are to me, I understandably wished the results of my profile was a five-way tie or that the scores were closer together. Physical touch, which is often an effective way to communicate non-verbally, came in fourth place. Gift giving, which I find very meaningful especially when it's unexpected or when the giver puts some thought into selecting or creating the gift, came in fifth.

The exercise pointed out my foremost preferences when it comes to expressing and receiving love. It also reminded me to pay attention to the preferences of the person I'm directing my love towards. The results explained to me why, for example, being around someone I care about, even if we're not doing anything in particular but just hanging out, feels meaningful to me. The quantity of time is important but the quality of time is more important. Said differently, if I had to choose between quantity and quality, I'll choose quality all-day, everyday. But being the hopeful person that I am, I would like to have both.

In many ways, expressing love is like creating a work of art: it can be simple or complicated. A two-dimensional outline drawing of a box on paper is a work of art. So is a three-dimensional watercolor painting of a box. They are both expressions of the same idea but they come with different degrees of effort, risk and sophistication. Almost anyone with a ruler and a pencil can successfully draw a two dimensional box on paper. Very few people can paint in watercolor a three-dimensional picture of a box, especially on first try.

In some cases, expressing love require the equivalent of the skills required for drawing a two-dimensional box. In many cases, expressing love requires the equivalent of the effort, risk-taking and sophistication required to paint a three-dimensional box. In the latter, acknowledging what it takes and responding well to feedback can be very valuable.

In much the same way as I have embraced the idea that there are uncertainties with creating a non-simple work of art, I have embraced the fact there will always be uncertainties with falling in love or pursuing a romantic relationship. When I set out to paint a picture or write a poem or make a movie, I hope to make a masterpiece. I hope my intended audience appreciates the beauty of what I'm expressing. I, however, do not get distressed when my art doesn't receive any praise. The fact that I set out to create something and did create something is often satisfactory.

There is usually something to be learned from exploring or experiencing a romantic relationship, no matter the eventual outcome. At the least, I almost always learned something about myself and grew from each experience.

Alfred Lord Tennyson has a good answer to the question of "what's love got to do with it?" when he says, "Tis better to have loved and lost than never to have loved at all."

To that same question of what's love got to do with "it," I think love's got a lot to do with "it;" where that "it" is a meaningful relationship that involves sharing our hearts, hopes, and resources with another person.

That question, however, will be best answered on an individual level. When each person finds another person with whom to share their heart, hopes, and resources in ways that suit their respective wants and needs, each person will find a custom-made answer to the question of what's love got to do with "it."

• SEVENTEEN •

LOVE AND MARRIAGE

> "All because two people fell in love…"
> - **Inscription on a wedding invitation**

Many people believe that falling in love must always lead to marriage. Frank Sinatra sings about love and marriage going together like horse and carriage, and that you cannot have one without the other. I've even heard people say of their love interests, "If he loves me, why will he not get married to me?" or "She says she loves me, but she doesn't think it's necessary to get married."

When two people fall in love and decide to maintain a long-term committed relationship, some of them will get married and some of them will not. Many will marry because the benefits they expect from marriage justify the obligations of the marriage institution. Likewise, some will remain unmarried because they don't expect that the benefits of marriage will merit the obligations. Some may have certain needs they believe marriage will help meet, so they will enthusiastically get married. Some may have certain concerns about how marriage may change the nature of the relationship, so they may cautiously approach getting married.

For the two people in love with each other, commitment is often necessary to make it worthwhile for each party to remain in the relationship. Commitment comes in many forms, and marriage is one of the options available to the couple. Marriage, however, is not the only option.

Marriage is an honorable institution because it forms a sound base for the traditional family unit. This union of two individuals with a common goal of sharing their lives with each other has an important place in helping societies thrive. For many years, marriage has been one of the most celebrated rites of passage in cultures around the world. Many people have also embraced the idea as the ultimate sign of commitment to another person. However, marriage is not necessarily the litmus test for love.

From my observation, most people get married for one, two or three of the following primary reasons: to form a bond of companionship they can count on in good and bad times, to have and raise children together, and to create synergy for accomplishing more than each person could by himself or herself.

Love may seem to be the reason most people get married, but love by itself is not enough of a reason to get married.

Without question, love facilitates the success of long-term relationships, and it is often a reliable indicator of a marriage's long-term success. However, love by itself tends not to be enough to sustain a marriage when none of the three primary reasons are present. On the other hand, it is possible for two people to remain married even when they don't necessarily love each other, but share these three primary reasons.

Getting married because of love is like buying a house because you have a good credit score. While a good credit score is a reliable indicator of success with homeownership, no one buys a house primarily because he or she has a good credit score. People buy houses primarily because they need somewhere to live, want more living space or want to invest for the future.

A successful marriage takes work. It takes more work than it takes love. The amount of work it takes to merge minds and resources is not something everyone is able or willing to do. Love, the great facilitator, comes in handy to help the relationship run smoothly, but the work that is required is still required. As long as the people involved are willing to put in the required work, many people around the world have experienced what they will deem successful marriages, even in the absence of love.

I know people who have nurtured successful marriages that began without necessarily loving each other. For example, some arranged marriages start out with two people barely knowing each other, let alone loving each other. Many such marriages have been successful because the two people involved found a way to work together towards their shared goals. Love came later. In some of these cases, love never came.

Marriage, according to almost every definition that I have come across, is the legally and/or culturally-binding union of two people as partners in a personal relationship, which bestows certain obligations and benefits onto the couple.

To protect each party's welfare or stake in the union, a couple could ask an institution such as a civil authority to recognize their love relationship as legally binding. It is this statutory or legal recognition that makes it possible for the individuals to enjoy benefits exclusively available to married couples, such as tax benefits, legal standing to make major decisions on each other's behalf, and inheritance benefits.

It is also this legal recognition that gives the court permission to intervene when the two people cannot agree and need to part ways. For most consenting adults, the benefits and the obligations of this legal recognition have been worth it. For others, it has not. Weighing the costs and the benefits, individuals have the freedom to choose to seek this legal recognition or not.

Without a doubt, marriage also offers economic benefits and synergies that make it possible for many people to experience lifestyles they may otherwise be unable to afford by themselves. Marriage allows many couples to build towards a financially secure future, and be able to be charitable towards others when two people have combined resources. In spite of these very potentially favorable outcomes, marriage remains an institution that may not fit every individual's present and future life goals. Getting into a marriage because of the benefits without considering the cost will be like hitching a brand-new carriage to a old horse, just because you have a horse and a carriage. Bad idea.

Having experienced marriage and divorce more than once, I hold the opinion that the emotional and financial toll a failed marriage can take on an individual is good enough reason to not hurriedly transform a committed relationship into a marriage.

Unless the two people involved have a clear and compelling reason to do so, marriage may not be such a great idea for the them. Of the compelling reasons (long-term companionship, having and/or raising children, and synergy), having one is fine; having two is good; having three is great. This recommendation of not hurriedly transforming a committed relationship into a marriage is intended specifically for divorced people who are considering remarrying. It could apply to people who've never been married.

For religious, cultural or personal reasons, the idea of two adults remaining perpetually in a committed relationship without getting married is uncomfortable for some people. However, depending on the stages of life or the circumstances of the couple in question, marriage may be more stressful than it is worth. Whether or not the two people choose to marry, their decision ultimately rests with them as two consenting adults in the relationship.

Let me also add that even though the decision to get married is ultimately between the two people involved, other people are impacted by that decision. That is another reason the decision to get married ought to be approached carefully. If there are children from previous relationships, their lives are significantly impacted.

To a lesser but also important extent, the lives of close friends and family members are impacted when two people decide to get married. Especially with people who fall in love later in life (and some of them with fully established individual lives), the traditional expectations of love and marriage going together have increasingly deserved a thoughtful evaluation.

I value commitment in relationships and admire the stability that seemingly happily married people have in their lives. However, my cautiousness about marriage is an acknowledgement of the fact that falling in love is a risk, and getting married is an even bigger risk. It is a risk individuals take in good faith. And like all risks, it is only prudent to thoughtfully assess the decision. With the right person and under the right circumstances, love and marriage going together makes perfect sense.

Love and Marriage

My mother once told me that if you're going to be a radio, you are better off being in stereo. Translation: two are better than one when it comes to living life as an adult. My mother is right that radio sounds better in stereo.

My parents seemed cordial towards each other for most of their marriage, but their marriage is not one that I would refer to as a model of love in a marriage. In fairness to them, love was not the reason many people in their generation got married.

My father was a kind and generous man who often opened our home to people who needed somewhere to live. My father, during the early years of my life, worked hard and took care of his family. My father's Achilles' heel, however, was how he viewed women – not with too much regard for their intelligence. For most of my childhood, I had no reason to believe my parents might not have loved each other. As I became a young adult, I experienced enough of their relationship to draw my conclusion. Eventually, their marriage ended.

For more than twenty years, my mother never remarried. She had a successful career, raised her children, and remained active in her community. My mother is a delightful and industrious woman who I think could have remarried if she had chosen to.

I asked my mother about being in stereo as far as her love relationship situation was concerned. She told me that depending on a person's age and station in life, marriage could be just a headache, so the person is better off remaining unmarried. She added that for her, focusing on raising her children meant more to her than a marriage that was likely going to complicate her life and her relationship with her children. I love and respect my mother in many ways, and respect her decision not to remarry. She tells me she is very content with her life, and I believe her.

Life In Progress: Winning Where It Matters

My mother is only one of many examples of people I know and respect who chose to roll solo. I would imagine that most of these successful and unmarried adults have at one point or another fallen in love, and might have even been presented with the opportunity to marry or remarry. I am sure that many of these individuals will tell you what my mother told me: that at a certain station in life, marriage could be just a headache and that person is better off remaining unmarried. I'm sure that if any of these people were children of my mother, she will be telling them two are better than one when it comes to living life as an adult.

Recognizing that marriage is essentially a merger of hearts, minds and resources, the decision to marry shifts from being a sentimental one to a practical one. At a certain age and stage in life, such a merger of two entities in the traditional sense could be complicated, and may end up exerting so much pressure on the otherwise loving relationship and lead to its demise.

On the other hand, if the two people are realistic about their circumstances, find a way to minimize the complications and see the benefits of marriage outweighing the benefits of remaining unmarried, it may be well worth it to invest the effort and resources required to transform the relationship into a marriage, and work on making it thrive.

Contrary to the dire statistics that indicate almost one out of every two marriages end up in divorce, good things can come about when love leads to marriage. However, that happens only when the two people share at least one compelling reason for getting married, and are motivated to put in the required work.

For the many years when I produced wedding videos, I often asked couples why they were getting married. Most couples almost always answered that they were getting married because they loved each other. On a few occasions, I would get an answer like the person was getting older and needed to settle down, or that his or her partner was the most responsible person and thought it'd be a good idea to "put a ring on it," so they could spend their lives together.

Sometimes, I would ask if there were reasons other than love for which they were getting married. Most of the responses boiled down to having found a reliable long-term partner with whom to experience life, having found the ideal person with whom to have and raise children, or merging resources to have the means to accomplish more than each person could by himself or herself. I have also received responses as candid as, "You know, I've never really thought of any other reason other than love."

Love is a beautiful, dominant part of the human experience. Love brings and keeps people together in loving relationships. Love often inspires people to get married. Love helps to keep married couples excited about each other. Most of the time, love helps the couple weather the storms that come about in the course of their marriage relationships.

Sometimes, love is not enough to keep marriages together. Sometimes, marriages come to an end.

One major disappointment of my early adulthood occurred when I found out that Babyface and his wife Tracey were getting a divorce. That shook me to the core because if you know the ten-time Grammy-winning singer-songwriter like I do (through his music), you would have been disappointed, too.

In a 2013 interview with Oprah Winfrey, Babyface had this to say about his "picture perfect" marriage to Tracey:

Life In Progress: Winning Where It Matters

"We wanted it to look like that. We felt responsible ... The reality is that there was a connection that wasn't really there. We loved each other, but we weren't really in love with each other. It was more the idea of it falling apart and me holding onto the image of what I thought we were. I don't feel like we were supposed to be together forever... I'm okay with it because I think she's okay."

Babyface is a hugely successful singer-songwriter who was behind most of the chart-topping love songs of the 1990s through the 2000s, and has an extensive catalog of love songs. I admire him for his talent, and I found a new level admiration for him for his honesty.

He loved his wife, but they were not really in love. They worked at the marriage for 14 years, and when it was time to call it quits, they handled it like grown-ups. And the classiness didn't end there. They remained cordial in a manner that is admirable. I saw an episode of Deion Sanders' reality television show that featured Babyface meeting his ex-wife's new boyfriend (Sanders) over breakfast; he spoke highly of Tracey and wished the new couple well in their relationship. Now, if that is not classy, tell me what is! Both men, but especially Babyface, earned more of my respect with that gesture.

In another example of love and marriage, there was a major scandal in Ghana when megachurch leader Archbishop Nicholas Duncan-Williams and his wife divorced in 2001, remarried and then divorced again in 2006. The scandal disturbed the faith of many of his followers who expected the fiery and charismatic leader to lead by example and stick with his marriage vows of "till death do us part." Of course, a great many of his followers defended his actions with some alleging that there was infidelity on the part of the wife, and that the preacher did everything humanly possible to stay married.

It is unfortunate that such a high-profile marriage that many people looked to as a model fell apart. I, however, do not get entirely surprised when any relationship comes to an end. For various reasons and despite a couple's best intentions and efforts, the demise of some marriages are sometimes inevitable. For certain individuals, under certain circumstances, divorce may be the only way forward. For the Archbishop, he's since remarried, seems happy, and continues to have a thriving ministry. I'm not sure what his current stance is on divorce and remarriage but it's my guess that his experience would make him more empathetic than before towards people who find themselves in situations where they believe divorce is the only option.

For people whose lives have been predominantly better because they married, it is reasonable for them to sing the praise of love and marriage, and recommend it to everyone. For people who believe their lives took a wrong turn because of marriage, it is understandable that some are cynical, blame love and even go as far as to say, "Never again." I have taken a measured approach in walking in the middle of that aisle, no pun intended.

I have examined my ideas about love and marriage. I have wondered if the benefits of marriage are worth the obligations and the work required. I have also wondered if my excessive optimism tends to make me overlook signals that compel me to exercise caution. It has crossed my mind that perhaps my view and expectations of marriage are so high that I inadvertently set myself up for disappointment.

My experiences have not changed my view of love as a beautiful thing, and that marriage is an integral part of the social structure. My experiences have provided me with a nuanced view of relationships. I have gained more clarity around some of the ideas that were previously fuzzy notions.

Being in a committed relationship with a reliable person with whom I share my heart, hopes and resources is vital for me. I'm made for community, and the most intimate community will be the one I have in a loving, committed relationship.

Whenever there is a love connection, it is possible that connection could turn into a marriage. It is also possible it won't. For this reason, it is incumbent on the couple in love to have the honest, open conversation about love and marriage rather than simply assume what the other person wants. Such conversations may not always be easy, especially when the two people do not share the same philosophies about marriage. Such conversations may be helpful in separating wants from needs, and will likely bring clarity to the future of the relationship.

Marriage has desirable benefits for those who commit to merging two hearts and minds into one, and also to nurturing the love that brought them together in the first place. Marriage is, however, not a way to prove or measure love.

Love and marriage, like horse and carriage, can go together – or not. There is utility in horses and carriages going together but not every horse is meant to be attached to a carriage.

In case you've been wondering how many times Sinatra made love and marriage go together in his own life, I found the answer for you - four times. He married Nancy Barbato (from 1939 to 1951), Ava Gardner (from 1951 to 1957), Mia Farrow (from 1966 to 1968), and Barbara Sinatra (from 1976 to 1998). His last marriage ended with his death in 1998. I suppose he loved each of the women he married, and they probably loved him, too.

The decision to get married has real emotional, financial, spiritual and physical consequences, sometimes favorable, sometimes unfavorable. Marriage may be a worthwhile endeavor for two people in love, but it's not necessarily the only expedient choice for every two people in love.

To those who have made the decision and are committed to putting in the work required for a fruitful, successful marriage relationship, I tip my hat. Likewise, I celebrate those who have thoughtfully abstained from marriage but have not given up on sharing their lives in committed relationships.

I hope that we each find what we're looking for in love. I hope that whichever way each person's love story goes, it is truly the greatest love story he or she will ever tell.

· EIGHTEEN ·

MY BROTHER'S KEEPER

> "Our chief want is someone who will inspire us
> to be what we know we could be."
> - Ralph Waldo Emerson, author and philosopher

There's something about men empowering one another – older men looking out for younger men, and younger men looking up to the older men – that strengthens communities. While a lot of credit for my upbringing is due the women in my life, and whom I have consistently acknowledged and honored, the men in my life have shaped my identity as a man. These men helped to shape me into the man I have become, so I am indebted to them for the roles they've modeled. Because it is not possible to pay them back, I pay it forward.

Before President Barack Obama launched his My Brother's Keeper initiative, which sought to build ladders of opportunity for young men of color by helping them stay on track and providing the support they needed to think more broadly about their future, I was the beneficiary of one such initiative, albeit an informal one. That informal mentoring for me started in my home in Accra, spread to my neighborhood, and followed me to school and beyond. These people lent me a hand and influenced my worldview as I developed from a boy to a man.

Kofi Agyare is one of my father's younger brothers. I also called him Ojuku or Novi. I don't know where he got the name Ojuku, a Nigerian name. Novi, however, is a word in the Ewe language from Ghana that means "brother." That became a name my siblings and I called him because we heard an Ewe family in the neighborhood call him that. Novi has his quirky ways and I, along with my siblings and neighbors, had our share of enjoyment from sharing and laughing out loud at his misadventures.

I had a special relationship with him, a relationship of trust. When he left for work, he would leave me the keys to his room because I had agreed to clean his room in exchange for the opportunity to listen to music on his sound system. He had a small cassette player as well as cassettes of A.B. Crentsil, Nana Agyeman Prempeh, and several other traditional and contemporary highlife musicians. The hours I spent camping out in his room listening to music were some of the most treasured memories of my younger years.

Because I did a fine job cleaning his room, he would sometimes bring me special snacks when he returned home, or he would give me the coins in his pocket.

Occasionally, he would ask me to dress up so we could just go hang out. We sometimes ended up at the then-Dimples Restaurant at Dzorwulu to have ice cream or at Ebony Restaurant at Kwame Nkrumah Circle to get meat pies and soft drinks. He would also share stories about Ghana's political history, and I would soak it all up. For the 10-year-old me, it was a really big deal to hang out with a grown-up who exposed me to some of the experiences that seemed like the preserve of rich kids.

Novi had a curiosity about religion that made him a fascinating man. One of the legendary Novi stories was about his praying at the door, asking the Lord Jesus to open the door for him. He was exercising his faith and taking a Bible verse literally - the one that says, "...knock and the door shall be open to you." He was also fond of welcoming our Jehovah's Witness neighbors into our home and showing a genuine interest in their teachings. While most people around the house dismissed his religious curiosity as "Novi just being Novi," the young me thought it was pretty cool that he would sit freely for hours and listen to religious views that seemed to conflict with the mainstream beliefs of most of the people in our home.

One Sunday morning, Novi and I wandered into a church at Tesano. Tesano is a quiet residential neighborhood about a 30-minute walk from my Alajo home. He didn't tell me where we were going, but I was happy to be with him. I don't remember the church's name, but I remember it was a gathering in a cafeteria that had wide, open windows. It may have been the cafeteria of the P&T Training School (now Ghana Technology University College). The person leading the session spoke calmly to a seated audience of about 100 people. About 45 minutes later, the service closed without much fanfare. I don't remember the words that were said during that service, but I remember the calm, refreshing nature of the meeting. There was no singing, drumming or dancing; no loud prayer or preaching - I don't even think they had microphones or speakers. The people were semi-casually dressed, most of them around Novi's age, and they all seemed very collegial towards one another. It almost seemed like a secret church - a church that operated below the radar as if to avoid drawing much attention to itself. What I experienced that morning was very different from the church services I was used to. Despite how brief that was, the calming nature of that experience has never left me.

Novi remained the easy-going, approachable and sometimes quirky man whom I could always count on. I'm not exactly sure how and why I transitioned away from cleaning Novi's room to spending less time with him. Even though the nature of our relationship changed, the experience contributed to setting me up for success in my future endeavors.

Although I may have been a nice and helpful kid, he didn't have to leave his keys with me. The position of trust he placed me in, small as that may seem, was a significant boost to my confidence. That someone other than my parents would entrust me as much with their personal belongings was an early lesson to me that helpfulness and honesty often lead to good things.

Later in secondary school, serendipity led to another mentoring relationship. I met Sammy Fiscian at WASS (West Africa Secondary School). While I was in Form 1, he was in Lower Six and five years my senior. This was in late 1987 after the school's relocation from Accra New Town to the new campus at Adenta. He was the sports prefect - which I didn't know at the time; and I was an opinionated kid who didn't think it was fair that a few of us were assigned to pick up stones and twigs from the soccer field. This assignment came about because Senior Fiscian stopped a handful of us on our way to class because we were late returning from lunch. I mumbled something as I walked away from him. He asked me to come see him in his classroom after we were done picking up the stones and twigs, for what I imagined was going to be an additional task as punishment for my subtle protest.

I spent most of the remainder of that day carrying his bag and following him around the campus. I was anxious because I didn't know what punishment he had planned for me, and I was counting down to the end of the school day when he would have no legitimate reason to detain me any longer.

The end of the school day came, and members of the soccer team entered the large room where I was sitting and waiting for Fiscian. The athletes changed from their school uniforms and into their soccer gear. It was then that I realized that he might have something to do with the sports team, and that may have been the reason he asked me and the other students to clear the field of stones and twigs. From what I observed of his interactions with the athletes, he seemed to command a lot of respect from these guys who were some of the toughest and most popular boys in the school. It dawned on me that the "detention" may work for my own good.

He was, in fact, the sports prefect, and he wielded a lot of influence. From my seat in the corner of the room, I noticed him pointing at me and telling one of the players to come give a bag to his "small boy."

An older student referring to a younger student as his "small boy" essentially meant that I was his mentee or protégée, so it felt really good to be referred to as that. I didn't think Fiscian even knew my name then. But he referred to me as his "small boy," which was enough to make me feel like he would be looking out for my best interest from then on. That was the beginning of a friendship that guaranteed me most of the perks of being an athlete, without being an athlete.

During the soccer and track and field seasons, which followed each other during the school year, I traveled on the same bus as the athletes, ate the same special meals as the athletes, and had access to areas of the stadiums and soccer fields restricted to only athletes. For two years, I enjoyed the perks of carrying the bag of a respected sports prefect, and had his "protection" due to the fact that he was one of the most influential people in the school.

I escaped a lot of the bullying that many of my peers experienced during the first couple years of secondary school. Most of these bullies often gave me a pass for being Fiscian's "small boy." It was very common for older students to bother younger students and put them through all sorts of juvenile torture. Some bullies confiscated the younger students' lunch money or sold the younger students' own property back to them as a form of extortion. Such bullying tactics were eventually eradicated from many secondary schools, but before they were, 12-year-olds like me cherished mentoring relationships that gave us a refuge.

There are things that I do well but being an athlete has never been one of them. However, when Fiscian graduated and left the school, I found other ways to "join" the sports teams, and continue to enjoy the perks of being an athlete (without really being one).

I was in Form 3 at this point, so I was technically now overqualified to be anybody's "small boy." Sonny Peasah was a muscular, athletic guy who transferred to my school at that time. He was in Form 4. Coincidentally, he lived in my Alajo neighborhood, so we rode to school on the same bus. Sonny was an aspiring rapper, and I was a poet transitioning into an aspiring rapper. Because he was skilled in regurgitating rap lyrics from

LL Cool J, Kool Moe Dee and other popular rappers of the day, I was trying to have him help me write my own rap lyrics. That is how our friendship started.

Sonny also ran track. With his unique physique and rumors that he was specifically recruited to our school because of his athletic skills, he quickly became the star of the track team. So, from what I knew about the perks of being part of an athlete's entourage, I gladly carried his bag.

My friendship with Sonny ended on a sour note because he cunningly fleeced me out of money he had borrowed from me. Despite that, our friendship was yet another example of informal peer mentoring relationships that helped to positively shape my secondary school experience. It was one of such relationships that happened merely by chance.

Also at WASS, I met Sam Laryea, a math teacher who exposed me to several meaningful experiences and helped to shape my professional ambitions. He started the Math Club to promote students' appreciation of math, and to show how the concepts can be applied to situations in real life. I signed up for Math Club thinking it was a group for math tutoring. I needed help with math and thought that would be an excellent way to get additional help. In the first meeting, there were three other students, and the activity of the day was nothing close to what I expected.

Mr. Laryea gave each of us a pencil, a ruler and a blank sheet of paper, and we drew graphs with x- and y-axes. We then drew lines to connect opposite points on each of the axes, from the first point on the x-axis to the last point on the y-axis, and then repeated the sequence. Slowly, the intersecting lines generated what looked like a curve; it was a parabola. I thought I was just drawing lines but ended up creating a curve. I came to the meeting expecting traditional math lessons, but I would be learning about how math is applied in real life. For the remainder of the meeting, we created several different geometric figures using the concept of parabolas.

It turned out that I was the only student in the room who thought spending two hours after school drawing parabolas was fun. At the next meeting, a week later, only Mr. Laryea and I were there. While we waited for the other students to show up, we talked about what I wanted to be in the future. I told him I wanted to be a pilot. He spoke at length about how math is applied in building airplanes as well as in flying them. I was fascinated by the information and soaked it all in. Math Club was more fun than any math class I had had up until that point in secondary school, and the calm enthusiasm with which Mr. Laryea described things held my attention. I secretly hoped the other students would not show up so that we could just keep talking. I secretly hoped Mr. Laryea would become my regular math teacher because he made math seem so cool and practical.

After the third Math Club meeting where, once again, it was just the two of us, Mr. Laryea disbanded the Math Club and focused his attention on the Pan-African Club where the student interest was greater. I was disappointed that Math Club was gone, but Pan-African Club seemed like a fun alternative. Sam Laryea started the WASS Pan-African Club with the purpose of exposing students to the idea that people of African descent have common interests and should be better connected. We went on field trips to the DuBois Center in Accra and listened to lectures about Pan-Africanism. Sometimes, we had poetry recitals where I performed poems I had written with inspiration from Kwame Nkrumah's speeches about Ghana and African unity. Nkrumah was Ghana's first president and an icon of the Pan-African movement. Nkrumah was famous for saying, "The black man is capable of managing his own affairs," as he championed political independence for Ghana and other African countries. His statement inspired a poem I wrote and titled "Managing our Own Affairs." I recited it at the DuBois Center as an ode to Africa's political leaders and the continent's bright future.

At one major Pan-African Club event, which took many months of preparation, we conducted an interschool mock Organization of African Unity (OAU) summit to commemorate the formation of the OAU (later it became known as the AU). The OAU was a group formed in the 1960s by African presidents and heads of state to promote economic and political cooperation among African nations, and to speed up the total independence of the continent from colonial rule. For the mock summit, my school was to represent Algeria. I wished my school had been selected to represent Ghana since that would have given me a shot at playing the role of Kwame Nkrumah. Instead, I was to be an Algerian president from the 1960s. A group of us spent some time in the school library researching Algeria and preparing for the big event. I spent additional time in the art resource room making a miniature flag out of paper and watercolor.

When the big day came, we were dressed in suits and other traditional African gear, and we put on a spectacular recreation of the 1963 OAU summit. Although I was disappointed that I did not get to recite my lines as the leader of the delegation from Algeria, it was still an awesome experience.

Moments like that, and others I experienced as part of the Pan-African Club, were some of the best parts of my secondary school days. I loved the deeper dive into Africa's political history and the opportunity to meet new people, both peers and famous adults. More than the activities, it was the manner in which Mr. Laryea guided and empowered the students that made the experience worthwhile. I was the club's secretary and a part of the leadership team. His approach in facilitating discussions, as opposed to dictating instructions, was refreshing.

Sam Laryea was one of the coolest teachers on the campus. I was impressed by his expansive knowledge. He seemed to know something about everything, and he appeared genuinely interested in sharing what he knew. In doing so, he nurtured my curiosity and showed me that my education didn't only happen inside my traditional classroom.

He took me to events at the DuBois Center. The DuBois Center in Accra is the home, library and final resting place of W. E. B. DuBois, an African-American civil rights leader and one of the NAACP's founders. The DuBois Center was an exciting destination for many secondary school students, and I was fortunate to go there many times. He also encouraged me to enter various essay competitions organized within and outside my school.

I relished the attention I got from the exceptional teacher and mentor that Mr. Laryea was. We remained in contact even after he took a new job at Ghana Airways. When I once visited him at his office, he gave me a tour and introduced me to his colleagues. I don't remember exactly what he did there, but it had something to do with computers. It seemed like a busy office, and people related to him in a way that made me believe he was an important man there. He could have told me he was busy and then turn me away, especially since my visit was unannounced. I just showed up. Rather, he made time to sit and chat with me, finding out how I was doing in school and what my plans were for the future. That gesture meant the world to me.

As if my mentors were exchanging batons in a relay race, my close friendship with Kwabena Bediako was gathering steam around the time Sam Laryea left WASS for his new job. My friendship with Kwabena would become a mentoring relationship that would significantly impact my teen and young adult years.

When I joined the Young People's Guild (YPG) at my local Presbyterian church, Kwabena was the group's president. I knew who he was because I had been friends with his younger brothers. But because he was not my peer and attended a boarding school, our paths barely crossed. At the time I joined the YPG, he had just completed Sixth Form and had been newly elected as the group's leader. Most of the members were, on average, about ten years older than I was. As a result, I felt out of place and did not have much interest in the group's activities. My mother insisted that I befriend Kwabena, explaining that he would be an excellent role model, both with my involvement in the church and with my education.

For the first few months of my following him around, we didn't have much to talk about. When we left YPG meetings to go home, I would often walk in his company, stop over at his parents' house for a few minutes, and then he would walk me to my house. Our limited conversations would usually revolve around how I was doing in my classes and what I wanted to do for work in the future. As time went by, the awkwardness melted away, and our conversations became more engaging. He talked about some of his experiences in secondary school, subjects he struggled with, and how he worked through those. He even gave me one of his old biology notebooks and spoke very highly of careers in science. He was planning on becoming a pharmacist and highly recommended that profession.

As our mentoring relationship grew, so did my admiration of him; I was very comfortable following in his footsteps. Although I did not wholly abandon my interest in flying planes or in journalism, I gladly embraced pharmacy as a career option. There was a point in time when I considered ways I could simultaneously practice all these professions.

Kwabena's father had a thriving pharmaceutical retail and distribution business where almost every member of their family partook either as an independent distributor or as salesperson in one of their retail stores. Kwabena had his semi-independent distribution business and was planning on studying pharmacy at the university. It made sense to me to want to become a pharmacist as well, following in his footsteps.

Chemistry plays a prominent role in studying to become a pharmacist, but I wasn't very fond of one of my chemistry teachers. He was very intimidating and I didn't enjoy what he taught. That chemistry class experience slowly alerted me that chemistry was going to get in the way of my pharmacy career, so I thought of alternatives. My interest in becoming a pharmacist waned, but my interest in the business of pharmacy grew.

On most mornings, I arrived at Kwabena's house to iron his clothes and polish his shoes as he got ready to head out into town. I would clean his room after he left, I would be back most evenings to hang out in their house. I would often share his meals with him or partake in a special snack or meal he brought with him from a fancy restaurant. There was a period of time when I spent more of my day at Kwabena's house than I did at any single location. With time, I went from being his inventory specialist to his delivery specialist (a.k.a. errand boy) and eventually to his business representative, transacting business on his behalf.

Through the years, I learned critical aspects of his business and proved myself to be dependable, so when Kwabena and Amakye, his brother and business partner, both left Accra for Kumasi to attend university, they put me in charge of much of their business activities in Accra. I was responsible for collecting substantial amounts of money from various retailers, depositing the amounts into a bank account, and keeping records of these transactions. I was transacting business with established businessmen and women, handling huge sums of money and making real-time supply-and-demand decisions. I often carried an old briefcase handed down to me by Kwabena, and I would travel around town like a real businessman. I looked legit. My 19-year-old self loved every minute of this experience and the related interactions I had with Kwabena and Amakye when I provided them with periodic updates.

The entrepreneurial skills and business savvy I acquired during this period laid a firm foundation for my future entrepreneurial ventures. Far more important than the business skills I learned was the opportunity I had to prove myself to be dependable and trustworthy.

Kwabena had a plaque on the wall of his room that read, "To whom much is given, much shall be expected." He told me the plaque reminded him that he needed to be accountable for the opportunities and resources he had been fortunate enough to receive. I, too, had been fortunate to have opportunities and resources, some of which came by way of my relationship with Kwabena. So, that plaque reminded me to act responsibly and not disappoint Kwabena, my parents, my other benefactors, or me.

The perks of the friendship included hand-me-down clothes with which I rolled around town in style. The regular cash stipend helped to keep my cash flow situation on the "up and up." Also, many people knew me as Kwabena's younger brother and therefore afforded me some of the exclusive courtesies that may not have ordinarily been extended to me, a middle-class teenager from Alajo.

Relocating from Ghana to the US was a bittersweet moment. Although leaving behind friendships like the one I had with Kwabena was tough, I was excited about the opportunities ahead of me in the US. Like the proverbial bird that had to leave its nest to fend for itself, it was going to be good for me to step outside of Kwabena's shadows and chart my life's course in a manner that was suited for my hopes and dreams.

As if by design, my friendship with Eric Amankwah picked up in New Jersey from right where my mentoring relationship with Kwabena Bediako left off. Eric and I bumped into each other in a store on Broad Street in Newark, New Jersey, where we both worked until the store closed down. I talked bout that in an earlier chapter, *The Pursuit of Happiness*.

A good friend over the years, Eric's guidance, encouragement and financial support played a major role in my pursuit of my undergraduate degree. We shared many ideas and experiences that helped me peel off some of my naivete about life. Even though he's several years my senior, he's always related very respectfully towards me and I've always reciprocated that gesture.

I've been fortunate to have someone like Eric in my corner to support my growth and development, hold me accountable, and help me get back on course when I missed my way. In the best way I know how, I have and continue to extend a similar kind of support to others - because people like him modeled that behavior.

The most unique and enduring mentoring relationship is the one I share with my brother Obeng Amoako. It started out by default, as in an older brother looking out for his younger brother; it eventually grew into a mutually beneficial relationship where I learned as much from him as he did from me.

Growing up in the same household with Obeng and my older brothers Oliver and Arthur, we created many great memories. We created photo albums of soccer stars from newspaper clippings, formed and managed a youth soccer team, went out at dawn to pick up counters (bottle tops) for counters ball, staged singing and dancing competitions, and found a host of other unique ways to entertain ourselves.

For many years during our childhood, I was the "people's favorite" until Obeng emerged as the star of the family due to his unusual brilliance. He was less than six years old when he entered Class 1. His grades, the quality of his writing and his exceptional level of understanding of concepts were miles ahead of his peers. With my parents' consent, he skipped Class 2 just after two months there. He maintained stellar grades through the rest of his elementary school years, and as was expected, he easily gained admission to PRESEC following his Common Entrance Examination.

Attending PRESEC was a big deal in my neighborhood. I had been unsuccessful earlier with my attempts at getting into the prestigious school, but I was elated when Obeng got in. I remember thinking to myself, "If there is only one spot at PRESEC for someone in my family, I'd prefer Obeng take that spot since he would make us very proud."

We would eventually both be students at PRESEC. However, before I did, Obeng had to endure several bullies on campus. I quietly wished I could have been there to look out for him. Of course, I was not going to be big enough to confront the bullies, but I felt that having an older brother around may have offered him some comfort. I was upset by reports of older students bullying him but as it turned out, he figured his way around those experiences and even helped me navigate my way around the campus when I got there some four years later.

Obeng and I shared many experiences, from entrepreneurial gigs around Accra to later jumping through hoops in pursuing our dreams as young men. As older men, we share a camaraderie that has its roots in the mutual trust and friendship developed over the years of looking out for each other.

Looking out for people is an idea that has always made sense to me. The idea reinforces the concept of community, and communities can only truly thrive when people are looking out for one another.

Kofi Agyare, Sammy Fiscian, Sonny Peasah, Sam Laryea, Kwabena Bediako, Eric Amankwah, and Obeng Amoako represent the many people who have directly and indirectly looked out for me. All these people, whether they were my family members, neighbors or strangers, instilled in me a sense of responsibility to look out for others as well.

Their actions reinforced the essence of the Ghanaian saying "*Obi biribi ni ne'a w'ayɛ no yie,*" which literally translates into "Somebody's someone is the person he or she has treated well." Said differently, the people you can count on are the people you treated well or looked out for, regardless of whether you're biologically related to them or not.

Sharing what we know to help uplift others, or granting audience to a younger person who may just need someone to listen and offer feedback, or saying a kind word to another person who seem to be in distress may be a single, simple action. But it could also be the one action that makes a life-changing difference in another person's life. Through my friendships and mentoring relationships with others, I have shared what I know and found ways to be of help to others as they sought to achieve their potential. I'm doing my part to make the world an awesome place.

Of course, there are people who may abuse the privilege of having others looking out for them. Others, with their sense of entitlement, may also behave in such a way that makes efforts at looking out for them become frustrating. It goes without saying that you cannot help everyone but you can help someone.

Maybe, all you have time for is one phone conversation with a young person who wants guidance on choosing a career. That phone conversation could mean guiding the next phenomenal teacher or the next Oprah Winfrey into their destiny. If you do that, and that next phenomenal teacher becomes next phenomenal teacher or that next Oprah becomes the next Oprah, you would have made the world a more awesome place - just by looking out for another person.

Others paid it forward by looking out for me, and I pay it forward by looking out for others. That is how I am my brother's, and sister's, keeper. And each of us can be, too.

· NINETEEN ·

MY DAUGHTER IN WHOM I'M WELL PLEASED

"I believe the children are our future, teach them well
and let them lead the way"

- From "Greatest Love of All," performed by Whitney Houston

In my early adult years, I had a mental picture of three as the perfect number of children to have in a family unit. I fantasized about the names of my children and what they would look like. I didn't care whether I had all sons or all daughters or whatever combination. All I wished and prayed for were healthy, adorable children who would be well behaved.

Afriyie Amoako was born in July of 2004. Her mother and I had been excitedly looking forward to her arrival. Her first name Afriyie means "you've come at a good time," so it is the perfect reflection of the excitement that her mother and I shared

My Daughter In Whom I'm Well Pleased

towards her birth. Her mother made a journal of the experience, and I took pictures and recorded videos.

Afriyie's first day on Earth was a Friday, hence her middle name, Afia, which in Ghanaian culture refers to a girl born on a Friday. It was around 6 p.m. As I watched her enter the world, I was consumed by the mystery of life and the fact that her mother and I are responsible for this new life we had created. Well, God created her but you know what I mean. These were literally the first moments of her life on Earth. Many exciting and hopeful thoughts quickly ran through my head, and I whispered to her mother with a gleeful smile saying, "She's really here!"

Her mother wanted to eat chicken masala from Olive Garden Restaurant, which was about 15 minutes away from the hospital. My excitement must have been obvious as I seemed giddy and eager to share the big news with anyone who would be willing to listen. A waiter at the restaurant asked if my day had been a good one; I nodded excitedly and shared the news.

In response, the restaurant's manager offered me the meal on the house. Although Olive Garden has good food and I would go there anyway, that gesture from the manager earned the restaurant a soft spot in my heart. In the years that followed, I have celebrated many important moments there, and have randomly stopped in there for lunch. I am a customer for life, all because someone who worked there spontaneously and graciously recognized an important moment in my life. The only reason for which I can think of ending my relationship with Olive Garden is if they stopped offering unlimited salad and breadsticks.

Many more special moments would follow Afriyie's birth. Friends and family members gathered for her dedication at church and a celebration of her birth. Since taking and sharing photos then was not as conveniently done as they are now in the age of smartphones and social media, I shared pictures via email and videos via DVD. From her learning to walk and talk, to her becoming a teen, the years seem to have flown by quickly. When I stumble on pictures or videos from when Afriyie was younger, I reminisce about those moments and remain grateful that I got to share in those experiences.

My parenting journey has been an adventure, i.e., more like a roller coaster ride. It's been a thrill ride with highs and lows, but a super fun ride. From the glorious highs of sharing unique experiences and laughing out loud, to the difficult lows of our family unit coming apart, and the related drama, being a father to my daughter has been one of the best things to have ever happened to me.

During her middle school years, she was catching a plane by herself to spend the summer with her mother out of state. When I left her at the John Glenn Airport boarding gate, I observed the maturity with which she handled the travel check-in procedure. It reassured me that she would be fine waiting at the boarding gate by herself. All that made it sink in that she was transitioning into adulthood. It also hit me that my baby girl is no longer a baby. I smiled and thought to myself, "We did well!" Afriyie noticed my smile and asked me why I was smiling. Without saying a word, I waved at her, kept smiling and headed towards the exit with an even bigger smile.

She's been a good child and is daily growing into a fine young woman. The parenting journey - from her first days as a bright-eyed newborn to her young adult years - has been filled with laughter, tears, optimism, frustration, celebration, disappointment, anger, and lots of love. It's taken a lot of work, patience and the support of others to get to the point where I can say, "We did very well!" But I suspect we are not done, yet.

Months after Afriyie was born, my previous idea of having multiple children began to slowly evaporate from my thinking because babies are not cheap; hospital bills and the steep cost of baby food gave me a reality check. Also, I poured a lot of my parenting energy into raising Afriyie that I was not so enthusiastic about going through the process again. I had a healthy, happy child who seemed to be hitting all the necessary growth milestones, so I was good with that. Helping her grow up and giving her every opportunity in life was, and continues to be, a responsibility that I embrace with all of my heart. I was satisfied and didn't feel the need to make another baby. Around that same time, her mother and I had hit a rough patch in our relationship. With the future of the relationship being as uncertain as it was then, having and raising another child didn't sit well with me.

I was well aware of the only-child stigma that is often directed at children in my community who have no siblings. Many times, well-intentioned friends, family members and strangers reminded me of what they perceived as a socially and psychologically disadvantaged position my daughter was in as an only-child. Some said it subtly; others were unapologetically direct.

There is a widely held but mostly subjective claim among mainly my Ghanaian family members and friends that, without a sibling, a child would not have someone to play with or someone close to count on in adulthood. As pragmatic as such an idea may sound, it contradicts the fundamental notion of community that suggests we all belong together. I believe that raising Afriyie with the skills necessary to develop meaningful friendships and strong social bonds will suffice.

Life In Progress: Winning Where It Matters

My goal as a parent has been to help Afriyie learn personal responsibility and develop a strong sense of community. If these two ideas sink in deeply, all the other important things will take care of themselves. So far, so good; but we still have ground to cover. So I, and the team of people helping to raise her, will keep working with her as she develops and masters the skills, and the mindset, necessary for her to thrive.

Her super-social personality reminds me of me. At school, she's almost always had more friends than she needs. Outside of school, she's always been surrounded by her many "cousins" and the children I tutor or mentor. Making new friends wherever she goes seems to be a breeze for her. It is also the one personality trait that got her into trouble the most in middle school. Having too many friends in middle school, we found out, can be quite distracting. She's, however, made progress managing her friendships.

While waiting to have breakfast at Bob Evans Restaurant two Decembers ago, we played a game where she had to pick two cards from a stack, and then talk about why they were important to her. One of the cards had to represent a wish, and another card had to represent a strength. Her first card had a picture of chocolate and her second card had a picture of hands piled one on top of the other. She explained that she picked the chocolate card because she wished to have chocolate in her pancakes. Her second card, she said, represented her ability to make friends easily, and quickly added, "Although I sometimes get myself into trouble over friends, I like having my friends."

Friendships are important and are to be treasured, I agree. But when friendships become a distraction, that's a problem.

My Daughter In Whom I'm Well Pleased

Mr. Green, her middle school guidance counselor, earlier that week, publicly recognized Afriyie for going out of her way to help a new student feel welcome. As part of our conversation at the restaurant, I reminded her that the recognition from Mr. Green was a testament to the fact that her ability to connect with people is a wonderful gift. I encouraged her to continue to use that gift of friendship to make others feel welcome and to create a positive experience for others; because the way to make the world a better place is through one human interaction at a time.

Since Afriyie places such a high premium on friendships and the giving of gifts for her friends' birthdays and at Christmas, there's usually the potential for such expenses to spiral out of control very quickly. As extremely important to her as friendships are, she's had to learn the economics of friendships, especially since she has limited resources.

Later that month, we discussed the number of friends for whom she was going to give gifts. She asked for $40, and I asked for a list of names. She came up with about 25 names and reminded me that was the shorter list. The longer list included about 40 of her classmates. She reluctantly cut it down to 13, and I gave her $20 since the gifts she was planning on getting were mainly candy. She went to the dollar store, bought $1 candies and boxes of candy canes, and she gave something to each of her more than twenty-five friends. I appreciated her resourcefulness. I also used that moment to remind her of the benefits of planning before spending - a.k.a budgeting.

Speaking of resourcefulness, we sometimes shopped for gifts on the day after Christmas. On one such day at the mall, she was reminding me that she would like to get two gifts for Lyberti since "we" did not give Lyberti a present on her past birthday, and had to give her something for Christmas. She wanted to get something for three more friends. Before she could say another word, my psychic ability - the parental kind - kicked in. I tactfully reminded her of the conversation about managing resources wisely.

With a Victoria's Secret gift card she had received earlier from one of my friends, she bought gifts for Lyberti. For the rest of her friends, we bought individually-wrapped Cheryl's cookies. And we were done.

Cheryl's cookies and candy worked as gifts then, but not so much during the teenage years. We graduated to gifts such as *Bath & Body* sprays, clothes, earrings, phone cases, and other accessories. Such things cost more money, so I've had to invoke the principle of managing limited resources wisely again, and again. So far, that principle seems to have taken hold, and I hope it sticks well into the future.

For the most part, Afriyie has been a relatively easy child to raise. As a healthy, likable child who welcomes new experiences, we've had the chance to participate in many activities. Her elementary school years were fantastic: summer camps, art classes, Girl Scouts, soccer, camping on the balcony, random craft projects, Saturday morning sing-along-and-dance moments, and more. Parts of Afriyie's middle school years were tough as she became more prone to testing boundaries and more easily distracted. Seventh grade was the toughest school year. Eighth grade has been much better. And with high school upon us, I am keeping my fingers crossed and being the best coach I can be for her. I hope the conversations about being personally responsible and putting her best foot forward will continue to take hold.

I know of several fathers and mothers who wish to be involved in the lives of their young children but cannot, either because the parents are feuding over custody and child support, or that the one parent and the children are separated by geographical distance. I, therefore, do not take for granted the fact that I can be involved in Afriyie's life as much as I am. I have had the pleasure of having front row seats, backstage passes and on-the-field roles in most of Afriyie's activities. This involvement has given me many opportunities to support her growth and development.

It is unfortunate when there is so much of difference in opinions between parents that civility gets thrown out the window. I have had my share of drama related to shared parenting when Afriyie's mother and I didn't agree on many things. I am thankful that I maintained my resolve to do everything within my means to be actively involved in Afriyie's life.

Even though the differences haven't gone away, our shared responsibility and privilege of raising Afriyie often triumph over our respective egos. When Afriyie's best interest prevailed, we all tend to better off.

To get to a state of relative cooperation between her mother and me, it took the wrestling of ideas to iron out our differences. It also took the passage of time for meaningful agreements to be reached. Sometimes, the disagreements became extremely contentious and at other times very expensive. But whatever it takes for both parents to have a role in their child's life is a worthwhile effort. That is because there is a limit to the things one parent, father or mother, can teach a daughter about becoming a woman or a son about becoming a man.

Life In Progress: Winning Where It Matters

I believe Afriyie won the parent lottery by inheriting the best traits of both of her parents. She's also been endowed with natural talents that are uniquely her own. I am proud of her academic and social accomplishments. I'm impressed with her reasoning, the quality of her writing, her appreciation of art and music, and her thoughtfulness towards others. She's also developing some fine culinary skills by which I have tasted many experimental meals and I've also been pleasantly surprised by some delicious meals she's cooked. I'm sure that in the future, she'll also master the art of cleaning her room without being asked to do so.

As much as is within my power, I'm giving her every opportunity to be successful. She knows that. She also knows that much is expected from her because she has been given much. My expectations are clear and reasonable: for her to put her best effort into things that matter.

I look forward to good things in the years ahead. Just as the years between the day she was born up until now have been filled with many fine moments, I'm quite certain that the years ahead will be filled with good things. Some of those moments will be celebratory, and some may leave her scratching her head wondering, "How did that happen!?!"

Through it all, I hope she remember the words of the LeeAnn Womack song her mother used to play for her as an infant:

"I hope you never lose your sense of wonder
You get your fill to eat but always keep that hunger
May you never take one single breath for granted
God forbid love ever leave you empty-handed
I hope you still feel small when you stand beside the ocean
Whenever one door closes I hope one more opens

Promise me that you'll give faith a fighting chance
And when you get the choice to sit it out or dance,
I hope you dance. I hope you dance.
I hope you never fear those mountains in the distance
Never settle for the path of least resistance
Living might mean taking chances, but they're worth taking
Loving might be a mistake, but it's worth making
Don't let some hell-bent heart leave you bitter
When you come close to selling out, reconsider
Give the heavens above more than just a passing glance
And when you get the choice to sit it out or dance,
I hope you dance. I hope you dance."

I hope, too, that you dance, Afriyie.

In the words of Kid President, "We were all made to be awesome ... and it is everyone's duty to give the world a reason to dance! ... Create something that will make the world awesome and let's dance!"

Let's dance, young lady! Let's dance!!

· TWENTY ·

GHANA. CULTURE. ME.

"Maybe in our haste to belong to an oncoming future,
we inadvertently leave the greatest parts of ourselves behind,
and soon ignore any value therein."
- Agya Koo Nimo, musician and educator

Every person who arrives at a Ghanaian social function or a Ghanaian home is expected to make a reasonable effort to locate the elders or the older people and greet them. At traditional formal functions, greeting the elders with a handshake is expected, especially when they are seated at the head of a table and receiving guests. Neglecting to do this may not only be considered rude but would also reflect poorly on the individual's cultural intelligence. It may also reflect poorly on the individual's parents or extended family.

Greeting elders is just one of the hundreds of cultural practices I had to get used to from a very early age. Such traditional greetings at social functions often involved walking up to an older person or a group of older people, some of whom I knew and some of whom were complete strangers. It was uncomfortable for me at first. My parents, however, maintained that proper etiquette required a child to greet his elders at social functions. I would often wonder why it was necessary to do that. It seemed important to my parents that I conducted myself in a manner consistent with our cultural norms, even when those norms seemed unnecessary to me; so I would grudgingly comply. My mother would often say that when a person ignores a basic cultural protocol such as properly greeting the elders at a traditional function, it is akin to the person's telling the world that he or she is being reared like a farm animal rather than being nurtured like a human being.

Ghanaian culture is a mixture of several distinct, but similar, traditions of the various tribal and ethnic groups located in this country of more than 30 million people. Ghanaian culture is often exhibited through our colorful traditional outfits, our expressive response to music, our fond appreciation of spicy, delicious Ghanaian cuisines, and how we gladly welcome others into our homes and communities. There are other significant aspects of Ghanaian culture that have to do with chieftaincy and traditional rulers, marriage and family, names and their significance, rites of passage, religion, festivals, burying the dead, and many more. I speak of Ghanaian culture in general terms knowing fully well that there are differences and nuances in the various tribal, ethnic and regional cultures. Ghanaian culture, like most cultures, is too vast for me to address fully in one chapter of a book about many things. So, I'll share just a few key thoughts on the subject.

Anthropologists Daniel Bates and Fred Plog describe culture as the system of shared beliefs and customs that members of society use to cope with their world and with one another, which is passed on from generation to generation. The main ideas I take away from this definition are the facts that culture is shared and is used to cope with our world and with one another, and is passed on through education.

My curiosity about the rationale behind cultural protocols prompts me to ask a lot of questions, and I get answers sometimes. Why is greeting elders at a social function or when you arrive at someone's home such a big deal? Elders are revered in Ghanaian societies for their longevity and wisdom; it is therefore expected of the community members to acknowledge that. As a Ghanaian saying goes, "*Opanin nni whee mpo no, ɔwɔ abakyɛ*," which translates into "An elder has longevity [and experience] even if he or she has nothing else." My parents explained that walking up to elders (instead of expecting them to walk up to you or you just waving at them from across the room) is the proper way to acknowledge and show respect towards such important people. That explanation made sense to me. My discomfort with walking up to elders at social functions and greeting them, and sometimes engaging in "small talk," went away eventually.

Contributing to the greater good of the community, maintaining a strong connection with our history and our ancestors, respecting one another and authority, and acknowledging the providence and protection of supernatural powers are all ideas that are fundamental to Ghanaian culture. These ideas are often embraced and practiced by most people of Ghanaian heritage. Many Ghanaians, however, perceive certain aspects of the culture as an unnecessary drain on limited resources.

The devotion to extravagant funeral ceremonies is one example that readily comes to mind. In my interactions with Ghanaian culture, I have upheld, complained or confronted the ideas that underlie many of the customs. Sometimes, I've been mildly successful at getting others to pay attention when I complained about or confronted the customs I deemed unnecessary. Other times, my complaints fell on deaf ears.

I have observed that if we, Ghanaians and Africans, applied as much commitment to mourning and burying the dead as we did to research and development, it is very possible that Ghana and most African societies would experience a significant innovation boom like we've never seen. The situation, however, is not totally hopeless. It's just that some things take time to change, and tradition is one of those things.

Ghanaian culture primarily emphasizes two big ideas: social hierarchy and community. My parents did their part in emphasizing important aspects of Ghanaian culture, specifically those of the Twi-speaking Akans. They sowed in me the seeds of cultural awareness and sensitivity, and provided me guidance on what's culturally appropriate and what's not. In absorbing these cultural lessons, I usually asked why one thing was appropriate and why another was not. My parents have usually been gracious in sharing the reasons behind our customs and have admitted it when they didn't know the reasons.

As a child growing up in Ghana, you learn about social hierarchy very early, especially when you have siblings, or when you grow up around neighbors who are just a few years older than you. When parents had to share something among their children or assign responsibility, age is often the default-determining factor. Sometimes, the oldest child is sidelined when there's not enough of whatever is being shared to go around. Other times, the youngest child gets left out when there's not enough to go around. Many times, the oldest child bore all the responsibility just because he or she was the oldest on the scene when something inappropriate happened. Age is often a determining factor of whether or not a person is invited to join a conversation or when the person is expected to speak during a conversation with his or her elders. These ideas about social hierarchy and community stayed with me through my young adult years and into adulthood. Putting these ideas into context has been very helpful in honoring the essence of the cultural practices and not simply going through the motions just for the sake of tradition.

When it comes to cultural protocols, I tend to focus on the purpose and not just the practice. For example, the purpose of younger people being expected to know when to speak and when not to speak at a gathering with adults is often to extend the courtesy to older people, and hopefully, allow more experienced voices to speak first. A popular Ghanaian saying suggests that if a child learns to wash his or hands properly, he or she can dine with the elders. Another one states that to have been present at a gathering and to have said nothing is almost as good as not having been present at all. These sayings together affirm the idea that there are respectful ways to speak up when in a meeting with elders, and even disagree with them when necessary, and get opposing ideas across.

Operating within the Ghanaian cultural context, one is bound to encounter protocols that dwell heavily on hierarchy. In my humble opinion, some of these protocols are time-wasting steps that do not add much value to what needs to be done. Nevertheless, navigating such hierarchies and protocols require wisdom – wisdom that is rarely found in books. I have found that this wisdom is often acquired by engaging with elders in the community. As frustrating as these hierarchy-laden interactions can be, engaging with the most ardent practitioners of the culture is usually necessary for understanding the purpose behind the practices. And if one is going to influence the culture, that cannot be done remotely or from the sidelines.

It is important that a society has structures that acknowledge and celebrate its elders, and honor social hierarchy. It also matters that cultural protocols are observed in ways that do not impede progressive thinking. It is possible to appreciate culture and practice it in a way that makes the community progressive. As often as I have the opportunity, I do my part to help put the focus on the essence, and not merely on the practices.

The other area of emphasis in Ghanaian culture is community. It is premised on the idea that even though each person comes into the world alone, no person is entire by himself or herself. Our strong tendency for being connected to one another often manifests itself in our predisposition to belong to groups. In addition to the natural groups of nuclear families and extended families, the typical Ghanaian is very likely to be a part of a church, a group of friends, a civic or ethnic association, or an informal association based on work relationships. It is very common to find people who actively belong to all of the above groups. The typical Ghanaian embraces the idea that "it takes a village" to do almost anything worth doing. It takes a village – the entire community – to do many of the things Ghanaians deem important. It takes a village to raise a child; it takes a village to have a thriving economy; it takes a village to protect the public's best interest; it takes a village to hold social ceremonies; it takes a village to have a good soccer team; and it takes a village for individuals to find advancement opportunities, especially when those individuals were not born with silver spoons in their mouths.

Sometimes, that village may be two people or a thousand people, but the underlying idea is that you'll get further and get more out of your endeavors when you don't roll solo. As a result, the level of an individual's involvement or contribution to the proverbial village often determines the level of enthusiasm the village shows towards that individual. The idea of looking out for one another and contributing to the well-being of others within the community is so fundamental among Ghanaians that many people expect that by default. But to avoid an abuse of the communal goodwill, a person's commitment or contribution to the community is often a primary determining factor of how members of that community look out for that individual. A popular Ghanaian saying in that regard implies that others do for you just as you do for others. And by extension, a successful individual whose success is not deemed to be of benefit to others in the community is often an individual who is not held in high regard. On the other hand, generous and benevolent people are often celebrated even when their benevolence go only as far as helping their own extended families.

Passing on the essence of a practice makes that cultural practice less of a burden and more of a practical matter. For instance, the recommended sequence of handshakes with groups of two or more people is from my right to my left because that order fits the natural flow of how the palms of our hands fit together in successive handshakes. On the other hand, the insistence on honoring the dead with elaborate funeral rites at whatever cost or inconvenience is a practice that baffles me and frustrates others.

Customs are not always convenient, but when necessary, all reasonable accommodation must be made to honor the tradition. However, customs and traditions are man-made, and should be appropriately modified as necessary. Even with the customs that we believe are ordered by our ancestors, there are ways to make modifications to honor their essence without harming the social relationships that these customs ultimately serve.

The emphasis on community also manifests itself in the naming system employed by most Ghanaian tribes. Children are named after elders or prominent people in the community. For example, I'm named after one of my father's uncles; Afriyie is named after my grandfather; and one of my older brothers is named after one of my father's benefactors. Naming a child after an elder in the Ghanaian community is an honor extended to a respected individual, and it also conveys to the world who our heroes are. A person's name is often the most obvious part of his or her identity, so it is one of the ways many Ghanaian parents choose to always remind their children of their heritage. That is one way parents ensure a strong connection with one's ancestry.

Of course, there are several different considerations that go into parents' decisions about the names they give their children. Some keep it simple by using the default day name (name given based on the day of the week on which a person is born), plus the given name (usually the name of a respected person), and then the last name (or surname or family name). Some load up their children's names with two Western or Christian names, the default day name, the given name, the last name, and sometimes with a title (such as Nana, Sir or Maame) or a suffix name (such as Junior or II). Generally, most Ghanaian parents take the naming of their children very seriously, whether they keep the name structure simple or complicated. While most naming systems establish an individual's identity, naming systems in Ghanaian culture go beyond that. A Ghanaian's name is often intended to reflect the community to which he or she belongs.

During my early years in America, when I had to explain to people at every turn how to say my name correctly, I contemplated changing the spelling of my name from its correct spelling to its phonetic spelling. There's almost no way you will see "Kyei" for the first time and think it sounds like "Chay" if you're not familiar with the Twi language. I have almost always graciously offered the phonetic lesson about there being no "C" in Twi, and that the "K-Y" combination is how you make the "Ch" sound. I thought changing the spelling of my name would save me the trouble of having to repeat that explanation again and again. Changing the spelling of my name meant I was going to have to update all my official documents and pretty much abandon everything I owned that had the correct spelling of my name on it. That seemed too tedious. The way people said my name, especially in transient situations, didn't bother me enough to have to go through all that trouble of changing the spelling of my name.

As it turned out, sticking to the original spelling of my name has been a very good thing. Many Ghanaians familiar with the origin of my first name, Kyei, often respectfully pay homage to it by acknowledging the name's royal significance. Especially among people from my paternal hometown of Agogo in the Ashanti Region, my name holds that significance because several chiefs and prominent people have had that name in the past.

Sometimes, for simplicity sake and on temporary name tags, I write only the phonetic spelling of my name, if I deem that expedient for the situation. That is a case of purpose over practice.

And it is worth adding that explaining how to say my name to people I meet for the first time is often an effective icebreaker and a conversation starter, and I am happy to engage that way.

The motivation to adapt the spelling or pronunciation of one's Ghanaian name when you live in a Western culture can be very high. The convenience of everybody saying your name without a phonetic lesson and the pressure to fit in can lead to the mispronunciation and misspelling of many Ghanaian names. The best thing about not changing the official spelling of my name is how the original spelling affirms my connection with my ancestry and keeps me connected to my roots.

I can empathize with young people who choose to Americanize their names. The pressure to fit in, by making your name easy to pronounce, is real. Also, because most of us live in multicultural societies, we are bound to mispronounce names that we're not familiar with. However, when a person with a Ghanaian name introduces himself or herself and says his or her own name incorrectly, that gives me a little heartburn. It is my opinion that if you bear a Ghanaian name, you have a duty to your heritage to at least pronounce your name correctly. It's been my experience that most people appreciate the opportunity to say a person's name correctly, and expect that person to politely correct them when they are way off with the pronunciation.

Nana Asante-Frempong is an elder who took great interest in insisting that Ghanaians introduce themselves and other Ghanaians properly. With his deeply informed perspective on the Asante culture, he took great pride in thoughtfully explaining the essence of the customs we practice.

I first met Nana Asante-Frempong more than a decade ago when his daughter Akosua hired me to produce a wedding video for her. From our conversation, I picked up on how well-read, well-traveled, and how culturally astute this man was. As a two-term parliamentarian in Ghana and an international businessman, he had a refreshing perspective on the good, the bad, and the ugly of cultures around the world. Our subsequent conversations revolved around elements of Ghanaian culture, politics, and our mutual disgust for the phrase "African time" and the tardiness that it represents. He made clear his frustration with many Ghanaians who seemed to have no value for their culture and who copy other people blindly.

About a year from our first meeting, we met again at the wedding of his other daughter, Ama. The MC at the reception event, doing his part to be courteous and respectful, referred to him as Mr. Nana Asante-Frempong, and he was not happy about that. In a side conversation, he pointed out the fact that it was tautological to tag on "Mr." when addressing someone whose name starts with the royal title of "Nana." In many cases, "Nana" is used in a non-royal context as part of the name of a grandparent or a child who was named after a grandparent. More often than not, "Nana" at the beginning of an older Ghanaian male's name signifies status. It is, therefore, a safe bet to not tag on a "Mr." And as it was the case in this instance, Nana Asante-Frempong was a real chief in his village of Wonoo, so the royal title was very significant to him. He deemed it forgivable when a non-Ghanaian addressed him as "Mr. Nana Asante-Frempong" but considered it extremely careless if a Ghanaian did that, especially over the microphone.

We talked about Ghanaian languages and the importance of passing it on to the next generation. As far as he was concerned, it is a problem when children born to Ghanaian parents don't speak any Ghanaian language. He pointed out that there are people in Ghana today who do not think that being fluent in a Ghanaian language is important. He added that if such a person should find himself or herself outside of the country, and gives birth to a child, he or she is highly unlikely to teach his or her child any Ghanaian language. He called it a big shame for a Ghanaian couple who both speak a Ghanaian language fluently to have children that do not speak or even understand their parents' native language.

He passionately added that, "It is a tragedy because language is a key element of culture. If children are not able to speak, or at a minimum, understand the language of their parents, it is the fault of their parents. To me, such parents have disinherited their children."

Our conversations, some of which he agreed to record on video, covered various aspects of culture and society. In closing, I asked for three recommendations he had for every Ghanaian parent, whether living in or outside Ghana. Here's what he said:

"First of all, you the parent have to honor the customs and culture that you want to pass on. You should decide that it is important to you. After you make that decision, you can then continue to educate yourself by seeking out elders here and at home and learning from them. You cannot teach what you don't know. And if you don't know, you ask. If you don't know your culture, you ask your mother or your father or your elderly neighbor. Most elders are more than happy to share this knowledge."

He continued passionately.

"Secondly, belong to your community – community in terms of your nuclear family and community in terms of the social community around you. The nuclear family is the foundation of culture, so maintaining ties with your siblings, your parents, your biological uncles and biological aunts is critical. Show an interest in the well-being of these people and make an effort to meet or talk over the phone every now and then. You may not realize it, but your children will be taking note, and that's one of the ways they will notice if your cultural values are important to you. Expose your children to members of your community. When you're at a funeral or outdooring or any other event, explain to your children what the customs mean. Don't leave it up to the community to pass on your culture to your children. The community can help, but it is part of your job as a parent to educate your children about the things you consider important. If the parent is not taking the lead, then I'm afraid we're fighting a losing battle."

He ended with what he considered the most vital behavior.

"Thirdly, speak the language, and speak to your children in your language. If your child is not confident about speaking the language, encourage him or her. Break the sentences down into simpler parts and help them put it together. Your children can speak your mother tongue fluently and at the same time be able to speak English fluently. But that is not going to happen by accident. You have to be mindful when you're speaking to your children and choose your language purposefully."

As the parent of a child growing up away from the direct influence of her extended family, I recognize my responsibility to draw her attention to aspects of our culture which explain her heritage and enhance her relationships with her extended family and other Ghanaians.

Traditionalists often have a hard-core adherence to aspects of the culture that liberal progressives might dismiss as primitive and irrelevant. But because culture is dynamic, many aspects of Ghanaian culture will continue to evolve. This evolution will continue especially as world cultures continue to interact with one another, and borrow from one another. However, the degree to which an individual preserves the essence of his or her culture will depend on the appreciation that person has for the rationale behind the practices.

A Ghanaian saying states that when water stays in a bottle for too long, it goes stale; another states that nobody throws away the bath water with the baby. Taken together, these two ideas suggest that aspects of culture that hold us back ought to be reformed and the aspects that embody our essence are worth the conscious effort it takes to preserve and pass on to the generations that come after us.

Essentially, culture is a set of courtesies we afford one another so we can celebrate shared values and live peaceably with one another. At the end of the day, when any of us chooses to uphold, complain about, or change aspects of Ghanaian culture, I hope that we do so thoughtfully rather than out of ignorance. In this way, we would neither be holding stale water in a bottle nor throwing away the proverbial bath water along with the proverbial baby.

PART IV: I BELIEVE THAT WE WILL WIN

· TWENTY-ONE ·

ALL I DO IS WIN

"I believe that we will win... I believe that we will win..."
- Team USA chant at soccer games

The question of what it means to win in life is a big one, and the answers may vary from person to person. To some, winning means accomplishing goals. To some, winning means overcoming hurdles. To some, winning means being recognized by others for doing something well. To me, winning means all of the above: accomplishing goals, overcoming hurdles, and being recognized by others for the things I do well.

Sports, as a metaphor for life, offers examples that can shed light on what winning can mean to each of us. In a successful athlete's career, he or she is often accomplishing goals (staying in optimal physical and mental shape, improving essential skills, winning games, etc.), overcoming hurdles (recovering from injury, confronting self-doubt, beating opponents, etc.), and being recognized (being paid well, winning awards, being celebrated by the public, etc.). The athletes who do these things well, are often the athletes we know to be winners. The goals they accomplished and the hurdles they overcame may have been private and unknown to us. But when you hear them tell their stories, there is rarely a winner who didn't accomplish goals or overcome hurdles.

When we take stock of our respective lives to determine whether or not we are winning at life, most of us are very likely to point to goals we've accomplished, hurdles we've overcome, and recognitions we've received. On the other hand, not accomplishing our goals, hurdles standing in our way, or not getting enough recognition for the things we do well can be very frustrating.

From watching the very best professional athletes and teams, I realized that they do not limit their definition of winning to the outcome of a single event. Winning involves progress towards a major goal. They obviously like to win as often as possible. But even when they lose, they dust themselves off and then begin getting ready for the next game, looking for ways they can improve. They tend to have the habits and routines that reinforce their always-getting-better mindset. It was a moment of clarity for me when I learned that winning, to the very best athletes, is a habit and not just an event.

A game is a single event in an athlete's career. As important as every event is, success in sports is often determined by the net effect of relevant events. So a win or a loss per se is not conclusive but the net effect of relevant wins or relevant losses could be. And what an athlete or a team learns from their wins and losses matter just as much as the wins or the losses.

Likewise, success in life depends on how many relevant wins or losses a person experiences, and the lessons he or she take along with him or her. Therefore, any event in a person's life, whether with a favorable or an unfavorable outcome, can matter if the person can at the least learn something from that event. A single event may or may not matter in the grand scheme of things. However, if that event impacts a goal or hurdle or a recognition, then that event is relevant enough and counts towards whether the person is winning or not in the metaphorical game of life.

As most serious athletes often do, ask yourself reflective questions that encourage introspection and learning. You may start with: Is the experience moving me closer or away from my goal? Is it creating or removing a hurdle? Is it bringing or getting in the way of a recognition?

If that experience is doing for you what you need, then great. If not, then you have a situation that needs more attention.

Also, the very best athletes trust their instincts most of the time. Instincts are the inherent natural impulses that guide our actions. In sports, there is what is referred to as "killer instinct" which is a ruthless determination to win, even if it means "killing" everything standing in the way. I'm not a big fan of that phrase. I prefer "winner instincts" which is the thoughtful determination to win by finding creative means to surpass everything standing in the way. The phrase "killer instincts" might work for most people in the arena of sports, but "winner instincts" works better for me in the arena of life. "Winner instincts" drive winning behaviors.

The outcomes of several personal development pursuits in the last several years have taught me to trust my instincts more. I have learned to recognize when I am making the right decisions even when I cannot eloquently explain the decision. I am also learning to cautiously retreat when I have a premonition of an oncoming disaster. In trusting my instincts, I have made decisions that have turned out very well, and I have also made decisions that have not turned out so well. In either situation, trusting my instincts enabled me to act confidently and not to second-guess myself as much as I have done in the past. Whether the outcomes were favorable or not, I made progress in learning to trust my instincts more.

Winning is not easy but winning is possible. Winning does not happen by default but rather as a result of deliberate actions. Winning requires showing up and putting up some effort. And with some personal effort, the support of others, and some luck, almost everyone can make progress towards a goal; and that's a good enough place to start.

As long as I am making progress, I am winning.

I am winning in my life not because I have accomplished every goal, overcome every hurdle, or have been unanimously recognized for all the things I do well. Instead, it is because I am making progress with my short-term and long-term goals, and overcoming small and the big hurdles daily.

Along my journey, three actions have guided my mindset about winning:

1. Own your story
2. Practice the process
3. Have a plan

1. OWN YOUR STORY

As a younger man, my definition of what it meant to win in life was heavily influenced by the expectations of my parents, family members and friends. I lived my life according to a storyline that was heavily influenced by what others thought, what others expected of me, and my perception of what others thought and expected of me. The process of me owning my story started with me thinking through some big questions, many of which I have written about in this book, and how those questions relate to my beliefs about me and about the world around me. Even though I am still working through the answers to some of these questions, I am much better off because I sought answers to those questions. The more answers I received to these important questions that underpin my beliefs, the more empowered I became to update the narrative by which I'm living my life. Those answers inspired me to take more ownership of my story.

The things we believe inform the decisions we make in life. When others write the storyline by which we live our lives, the beliefs that inform our thoughts and actions may not necessarily be our own beliefs, but rather handed-down and unexamined beliefs that may not be serving us well. In my case, my parents, family members, and some other well-meaning people wrote the original storyline. As grateful as I am for the influence of many of these people, it was vital for my growth and development that I took a closer look at that storyline and make the necessary adjustments.

Writing this book gave me an opportunity to reexamine many ideas and refine them in my life as necessary. While I recognize that the task of writing a book is a huge undertaking that many people may not have the time for, examining the ideas that form the framework of our decision-making is the least each of us can do. So write a book if you choose to; write a personal essay if that works for you; have a conversation with a counselor or a with trusted advisor if that's what you're comfortable with; do what is necessary to examine, affirm or refine the ideas that inform the decisions you make. And plan to engage in that exercise from time to time, taking stock of the ideas and behaviors that hold you back or confine you to living life on other people's terms.

Until I defined for myself what it means to win, I was focused on doing things that made other people happy but not necessarily what I wanted to do, needed to do, was good at doing, or that which made me happy.

By defining for myself what it means for me to win, I cultivated a clearer sense of my strengths and weaknesses, celebrated the things that I do well and invested my time and energy in ongoing personal development. That definition of what it means for me to win also made me aware of some critical areas of my life where I was already winning.

In writing my own story, I identified areas in which I needed to develop. As an adult, I am responsible for my development. My growth will happen automatically with the passage of time, but my development requires a thoughtful effort towards improving myself. My personal development program involves various actions that improve my self-awareness and help me develop my talents.

Personal development could come about through obtaining more information or education. However, getting more information or education in itself is not personal development. It is the application of that information or education to create value - that is what counts as personal development. So I expose myself to experiences that expand my thinking and worldview. That expanded thinking and worldview, in turn, informs the narrative by which I live my life, and that gives me the tools necessary for creating value for me and for the people around me.

As each of us writes the storyline necessary for us to win in the areas of life that matter, each of us is responsible for our personal development. A big part of the process, however, involves associating with people who add value to our lives by way of their ideas, insights, and feedback. Life as an adult is an individual sport, but each of us still needs a team; just like a professional tennis player, a boxer, or a NASCAR driver does. My success depends on my individual effort, and I have people I rely on to play key roles.

The story you tell yourself about you is the most important story you will ever tell. When I own my story, I pay attention to the storyline and modify it accordingly in order for me to win when and where it matters.

2. PRACTICE THE PROCESS

Most of us have bucket lists, that is, the list of things we'll like to do before we kick the bucket and die. Others have a dream list or a dream board which is a compilation of ideas by which they're going to impact their world or accomplish a personal goal. Having a bucket list or a dream list is a great exercise that gives an individual something worthwhile in the future to look forward to. Much more than making these lists, taking steps to accomplish each task is what matters most, and what will bring the individual the most fulfillment.

Dream lists or bucket lists are merely wishes until we pursue them. And because pursuing dreams require that we follow a process, whatever the process is for that particular dream, most of us who don't find the time and discipline to do so never make any progress on our dreams. I have heard stories of people who, on their deathbed, reportedly expressed regret for not pursuing their dreams. When asked why they did not pursue their dreams, some cited their lack of resources and others said they were waiting for the right time. I think that at the center of every dream that remains unpursued is a man or woman who has not committed to the required process. The process often involves specific behaviors but it almost always involves taking action.

I learned an important lesson about process and practice when I sought to learn to play the guitar. Playing the guitar in front of a live audience is one of the items on my bucket list. In years past, I've had unsuccessful attempts at learning to play the guitar mainly because I did not make enough time to practice. I saw my friend Eugene Osei-Boateng perform at an event, singing and playing the guitar simultaneously. He started learning a few years earlier so I asked him for the secret formula.

"Unfortunately, there's really no short-cut," he told me. "It is about learning the process and then practicing the process."

If I was ever going to learn to play the guitar, I had to commit to the process. With his guidance, I learned a few notes and chords and I am slowly-but-surely taking baby steps, and making time to practice. My finger tips hurt but I feel like I'm making progress.

Having a dream is the start. Pursuing the dream requires learning the relevant processes (or principles) that govern the dream. Knowing the process is necessary for knowing the steps you need to take. Knowledge is more useful when put into practice, so action is required. It is the practice of the process that will make you better.

People who win in life pursue their dreams. They figure out the process, and they practice the process.

3. HAVE A PLAN

I think of a plan as the "What," the "Why," the "How," the "Who," and the "When" for the dreams each of us would like to pursue. A plan can be as simple as a single-page document or as thorough as a billion-dollar business plan. My plans, whether short-term or long-term, tend to be simple and in response to the what-why-how-who-when questions. I try to write them down as often as possible.

Writing down my plan prompts me to be specific about my goals (what), my compelling reason (why), key actions I will need to take (how), my or others' role (who) and a timeframe (when). A good plan could help you see a path towards the goal. If you can't see the path towards your goal, then the "how" and the "when" of your plan, and maybe the entire plan, may need evaluation. Also, because dreams usually take time to come true, you are likely to be less frustrated when you have a plan.

In instances where I've tried to proceed without a plan, it was easier for me to give in to the temptation to quit when things got difficult. In instances where I operated without a plan, I became distracted much more easily and didn't accomplish as much as I could have.

Plans are like maps; they help you get to where you're going and help you find your way when you get off course. Sometimes, things will happen that you did not anticipate. If that happens, having a plan gives you a reference point for where you were trying to get to in the first place, and then course-correct.

Boxer Mike Tyson once said, "Everyone has a plan until they get punched in the mouth." I picked up on two ideas from that statement: 1. Tyson expects you to have a plan if you're going to fight him; 2. Sometimes, you'll get punched in the mouth, and you'll need to change plans. Nevertheless, you'll need to start out with a plan, if you're going to fight Mike Tyson.

I have no intention of ever fighting Mike Tyson, but I have intentions of doing things that are as intimidating as fighting an undisputed world heavyweight champion. I intend to win so I plan on having a plan in each of those endeavors. When I do, I'll do my best to avoid getting punched in the mouth, and I'll also stick with the plan, or adjust accordingly, even if I get punched in the mouth.

Planning takes time and effort, and sometimes require other people helping you figure things out. A plan will likely be the most rewarding thing you invest in. So, whether you do it all by yourself or enlist others to help, have a plan.

Have a plan if you're serious about winning. Have a plan because you'll need one.

I BELIEVE THAT WE WILL WIN!

I sincerely believe that most individuals are capable of living the life they imagine for themselves. I also believe that to receive anything of value, you will have to give something of value. The desire to win is important, but your commitment to winning is more important. That commitment will determine how much value you are willing to exchange for what you want.

That something of value which you give in exchange for the things you want could be money, time, effort, or a combination of those. In order for each of us to live the lives we imagine for ourselves, we will be required to give our effort, our time, our money, or a combination of those. Sometimes, that thing of value you give in exchange for the value you want is paying someone for their time or expertise.

Life In Progress: Winning Where It Matters

Sometimes, that value required from you is your mental fortitude, which involves making up your mind and sticking with the mindset of winning against all odds.

At the 2014 World Cup, the US Men's Soccer team was not one of the very best in the world. Matched in the "Group of Death" with Germany, Ghana, and Portugal, the US team was not expected by most people to make it out of the tournament's groups stages. Even the US coach, Jurgen Klinsmann, seemingly conceded that fact when he said his team "was not currently capable of winning the World Cup." Whether that statement was meant to prompt the US' opponents to underestimate them or not, the fact remained that it would take a plan and a tenacious commitment to winning for any of the four teams to make it out of that group and to the next stage of the tournament.

Buoyed by a winning mindset cleverly articulated by Klinsmann (that they were considered in group of death because each of the four teams had an equal chance of winning or losing), the US team finished second in the groups stage before eventually losing to Belgium in the Round of 16.

While I have no definitive proof that the chants of the US cheer squad was a factor in the team's success in each of their games in the groups stage, I believe the affirming nature of those words gave the US team a slight boost in confidence and enhanced their mental fortitude in the face of a seemingly insurmountable challenge.

You can test my theory for yourself by enthusiastically repeating, "I believe that we will win!" for about thirty seconds.

Affirmations play an important role in enhancing mental fortitude. I am convinced that hearing "I believe that we will win!" over and over again helped them trade in the thoughts of inadequacy in exchange for thoughts of competence. With that mindset, they stuch with their plan and practiced their process.

Mindset shifts and mental fortitude do not occur automatically or simply because we wish for them or because someone prayed for us. Shifting your mindset is a process that must be practiced. Mental fortitude - the ability to maintain your focus and remain calm in difficult situations - is a process that must be practiced. With practice, each of us can get better at shifting our minds when needed and remaining resilient to persevere in difficult circumstances.

I believe each of us can win where it matters - by focusing on our decision, both big and small. That is why I have committed myself to sharing the principles and ideas that have helped me along my journey. Just as others shared and helped me get on a winning path, I hope that what I'm sharing will inspire you to take at least one action or affirm a decision that moves you towards winning.

Each person makes hundreds of decisions each day. Some of the decisions are easier to make, so we make them without even blinking. Other decisions have major and long-term consequences and might require more thoughtful consideration. If you take nothing with you from reading this book, I hope you remember that your decisions will continue to play an important role in the outcomes that you will experience in your life. Even when you don't control all the circumstances you have to confront, you can make more out of the situation by controlling what's within your control - your decisions.

You may think of yourself as a boxer in a ring or as a professional tennis player on a court or as a NASCAR driver on a racetrack. You'll receive input from your team, but ultimately you will have to make the big and small decisions based on what you've planned and practiced. Sometimes you'd have to draw on your instincts but each time you'll need to make a decision.

Becoming who you want to become is the result of a series of decisions. I used to – and sometimes still do – hesitate in making decisions for fear of making the wrong decision. With more practice at making consequential decisions, I have developed a mechanism for making decisions. I assess, think, plan, do and learn.

My mechanism involves getting enough information about the decision to be made, considering the worst thing that could happen from my decision, and seeking the opinion of a trusted advisor if necessary. I have also learned to trust my instincts.

I am yet to meet a person who does not want to win where it matters. However, I have met many nice and well-meaning people who are not making decisions necessary for winning where it matters. For many years, I was one of the people who made decisions based on ideas that did not serve me well.

I am in recovery from years of making weak decisions. I am also in recovery from years of avoiding consequential decisions. My recovery has thus far been going well, and I do not take my progress for granted. As it is the case with any addict committed to a successful recovery, I have made my recovery a priority, taking it one day at a time. I strive to make better decisions each day and I don't beat myself too hard when I make a not-so-good decision. I learn from it and do better the next time drawing from the Maya Angelou quote that says: "Do the best you can until you know better; then when you know better, do better."

So, whether I am chanting the Team USA slogan or singing along with DJ Khaled proclaiming, "All I do is win," it is because I realize that winning where it matters is the only option for me.

I hope it is the only option for you, too.

I have decided to win where it matters and I have a plan. I am practicing the process and doing the best that I can. I own my story and I'll tell it to myself throughout my life's span. And like the man in the arena, I am my biggest fan.

So, until next time, keep winning where it matters!

• TWENTY-TWO •

MY APPRECIATION

"Someone is sitting in the shade today because someone planted a tree yesterday!"
- Les Brown, life coach and entrepreneur

The legendary Ghanaian musician Agya Koo Nimo once said we struggle to build a foundation so that the people who come after us don't have to go through the same struggles, but have a head start. I have been the beneficiary of the kindness of many people, some of whom I have spoken about earlier. There have been mentors and champions, the people who shared their insights to guide me along my way. There are people who spoke on my behalf. There are the giants on whose shoulders I stood, and who gave me my opportunities to succeed.

Expressing gratitude is an important aspect of living with others, so I do my very best to show genuine appreciation as often as possible. That is one of the reasons for which I prefer writing thank you notes in my own words rather than sending pre-printed words in a greeting card. The personal nature of ap-

My Appreciation

preciation is another reason this is one of the chapters I've added to the most, even at the eleventh hour.

I have a feeling that I am going to miss some names despite my best efforts. To the people whose names I missed, please know that your names are written in a more important place – in my heart!

This is the shout-out chapter and my appreciation for the roles many people have played in my life. So, here we go!

I had a team that helped to bring this book to life. Jen Doron, Silvia Opoku, Charles Teye, Obeng Amoako, Kofi Honu, Ryan Magada, Chris McAlister, Johnson Ayoka, Bernard Afriyie, Ron Mead, and Mrs. Akyeampong, thanks again for all the help.

My mother, Rose Ama Efi Afriyiye, is awesome. I know most people believe their mothers are awesome, but my mother is the best mother in the whole wide world. From the humble streets of Alajo through the years up until now, my mother has been my biggest cheerleader and my rock in the midst of life's storms. Many of the tactics I use in raising my daughter Afriyie come from my mother's playbook. In many ways, I have said thank you to my mother, so this is just one more way. Much love, Mama!

I consider two distinguished women, Elizabeth Amoafowaa Bediako (a.k.a. Sissi Bediako) and Diana Nana Aso Yamoah, as my "mothers" as well. These women looked out for me in significant ways and have taken care of me as they did for their own children. Sissi and Mama, thanks for everything.

My father was a fascinating man. He was a kind-hearted man whose good intentions did not always manifest in his actions. I have my father to thank for my diplomatic tendencies and my entrepreneurial aptitude. Although our relationship was strained at times, I'm still my father's son. His accomplishments served as my inspiration while his mistakes served as a cautionary tale for me. I have many fond childhood memories and experiences that set me up to be a successful adult, thanks to my father, Peter Buonti Amoako (a.k.a. Wofa Akwasi Buonti Sikrim). It was an honor to lay your body to its eternal rest, and may your soul rest in peace. "In a sky full of stars, I think I see you."

My uncle Yorke Afriyie is a calm-mannered and principled man, who models leadership and empathy. Frank Afriyie, my mother's younger brother, is often misunderstood for his sometimes hardline views. He is a good man who I'm honored to have in my circle of influence. Kwabena Sampong Bediako is a dear friend who I will always credit for guiding me into becoming an adult. Yaw Amakye Bediako is an honorable man who modeled humility and respect for others. Eric Amankwah is one of the most selfless people I've known, and he's always believed in me.

Dr. David Yamoah is thoughtful and generous with his time; he always made time for me whenever I was "just in the neighborhood." Mr. Akoto and his wife, Margaret, welcomed me into their home on many occasions. Mrs. Charlotte Akyeampong is my favorite teacher and a "gift of God without measure."

William Ampadu is the D-Wade to my LeBron James; my brother for life! Bernard Afriyie is insightful, and I can always count on his constructive feedback. Daniel Afriyie makes me laugh out loud with his candid commentary about human behavior. Peter Ntiamoah calls me Wofa Kyei; he is always kind towards me, and I never take that for granted.

Albert Edusei, Benjamin Boateng, Kwame Marfo, George Afful, Francis Andoh, Elvis Boamah, Ed Mettle, Rev. Preston Terrell and Miss Ethel Eaddy are some of the people who paid it forward to help me find my footing in my early days in America.

My Appreciation

Rev. Paddy Brew, Rev. Fitz Odonkor, Rev. Ogbarmey Tetteh, Rev. Emmanuel Titi-Lartey, Rev. Joe Ammah-Tagoe and Rev. Kwesi Dickson helped me build a spiritual foundation that will always be a part of me. Elder Sammy Nkansah, Elder Bethel Donkor, and Elder Kojo Folson generously invested in my development. Elder Frank Asante is an extraordinary man who makes time for me whenever I need his input on a matter.

James Appiah, Kofi Sarpong, and Akoto Bamfo inspired me to dream. Sam Laryea, Sammy Fiscian, Frederick Opare-Ansah, Tony Darby, Solomon Brobbey, Samuel Atta-Mensah, and Cyril Heyman nurtured my curiosity.

Barbara Amoako, Gloria Agyapongmaa Amoako, Joe Glover Amoako, Oliver Buonti Amoako, Kofi Tawiah, and Fred Arthur provided a covering that only older siblings could offer, and always made me feel a strong sense of belonging. Obeng Amoako, Francisca Amoako, Fredrica Okyere, Daniel Bonsu, Belinda Gyampah, and all my siblings gave me reasons to be thankful.

Paapa John Wilson Afriyiye, Maame Cecilia Asor Afriyiye, Proper Afriyiye, Julie Afriyiye, Doreen Afriyiye, Gene Afriyiye, Baffour Asare, Charles Afriyie, Daniel Afriyie, Bernard Afriyie, Helen Afriyie, Emily Baffour Asare, Kenneth Afriyie Asare, Nana Ama Afriyie, Nana Akua Afriyie, Frank Afriyie Jr., John Wilson Afriyie, Nana Kwasi Boatey, Jerry Afriyie, Elvis Martinson, Kwame Afriyie Okrah, Juliet Boye Edmonds, Lebene Afriyie, Linda Afriyie, Alice Vivie, Nana Yaw Sarpong, Alex Okyere, Lyric Maame Gyamfuah Gambrah, Michelle Okyere, Manuel Okyere, Charisa Okyere, Nana Kwaku Bonti-Amoako, Akrofi Obeng-Edmonds, Eva Afriyie, Anna Afriyie, Seli Aba Afriyie, and my Akyem Awisa ebusua have contributed in diverse ways to the experiences that shaped me.

Life In Progress: Winning Where It Matters

E.K. Addae, Paul Amoakohene, Joseph Pinaman, Mary Amoakohene, Kofi Agyare, Yaw Owusu, Bernard Amoakohene, Belinda Afram, Kwame Baah Williams, Mary Adomah, S.K. Amoah, Kakabo Kwaku Amponsah, and my Asante Akyem Agogo ebusua helped to raise me, and I will always remember that.

E.S. Bediako is a visionary leader whose selflessness made many lives better. Yaw Osae Kwapong, A.A. Abedi, Michael Owusu Ansah, Nana Ampomah Gyebi, and several fine people made it cool to be from Alajo.

Grace Osei Bonsu, Mercy Afriyie, Joana Asante, Comfort Asamoah, Mercy Laryea, Paulina Asiamah, Beatrice Bampoe, Victoria Asamoah, Emelia Acquah and Agnes Kissi Yeboah are extensions of the love and support my mother provides me.

Kwabena and Juliana Boamah-Acheampong, Kingsley and Joyce Ohene, and Oheneba Kofi and Faustina Amponsah have stood by me through good and bad times. Ben Opoku has taught me valuable lessons about humility. Kwasi Dadie Amoah offers no-pressure counsel that allows me to learn and grow at my own pace. Kwabena Ayisi has insights that help me focus on what matters most.

Roslyn Abbiw-Jackson cares about people and is available whenever I call. Veronica Hairston is full of wisdom and is always pleasant to talk to. Dave Hill gave me an opportunity and valued my work. Linda Brown leads by example and holds me accountable. Barbara Benham has an open door and always welcomes me with a smile. Glen Zehr is a Renaissance man and a source of inspiration. Scotty McKinnie is my brother from another mother. Chris McAlister knows a lot about identity, mission, and community, and he's helped me "figure that shift out."

My Appreciation

Mike and Wanda Phillips are special elders in my "village." Thank you, Manuela Brown. Thank you, Miss Moody, Miss Sherry, Miss Gina, and Miss Aisha. Todd Keenan is a good man.

Tom Dearing was a beautiful human being, and I will always remember him for his big heart. Thank you, Laralyn.

Egbert Ayim, Eric Ayim, James Opare Asamoah, and Francis Aikins are the best roommates, ever. Debbie and Benjamin Boampong are always happy to open their home (and kitchen) to me. Big bear hugs to you, Abena Nyanteng, Baaba Pettingle, Elizabeth Armstrong-Mensah, and Elsie Osei-Tutu.

My team is huge, and have over the years included Kofi Owusu Ansah, Victor Coker-Appiah, Eugene Osei-Boateng, George Aduhene, Kwabena Asante Agyei, Angelo Akyeampong, Adrian Akyeampong, Bernard "Degor" Laryea, Kofi Honu, Yaw Pare, Kwame Agyakwa, Kenneth Okyere, Michael Commey, Fred Kwawuvi, Seth Ofori Quaye, Aristotle Socrates Olympio, Kwamena Gilbert-Arthur, Alfred Opare Saforo, Oboshie Badger-Plange, Nadia Agudu-Sam, Angela Gyamera Gyasi (nee Anaafi), Maame Saah Oduro, Jemila Mahama, Gloria Nunoo, William Adjei, Nathaniel Aguda, Fuseini Issah, Gilbert Abadji, Richard Adu, Derek Wright-Hanson, Ernest Nimako, Samuel Asiedu Obeng, Andrews Obeng Darko, Mark Bekoe Yeboah, Yakubu Kassim, Gideon Addae, Fred Ebeneku, Emmanuel Osei, Muftaw Giwa, Godwin Dogbey, Rudolph Mensah, Edwin Opare, Kwame Buabeng Frimpong, Jibriel Ibrahim, Richard Kudiabor, Wisdom Gomashie, Johnson Ayoka, Godfred Osei-Boakye, George Dei Danquah, Thomas Sasraku, Asare Dakwa, Albert Odei Quansah, Opoku Kyei Nimako, Baffour Kyei Nimako, Kwabena Obeng, Augustine Tweneboah-Koduah, Henry Ayensu, Elsie Osae-Kwapong, Joycelyn Osae-Kwapong, Isaac Osae-Kwapong,

Life In Progress: Winning Where It Matters

Kwaku Osae-Kwapong, Jeffery Quayson, Reginald Atta-Kesson, Raymond Atta-Kesson, John Amoatta, Anderson Amoatta, Alex Tetteh, Michael Siaw, Kwabena Sasu Bediako, Kwame Sampong Bediako, Kwaku Sampong Bediako, Yaw Opare Asamoah, Joe Appeah, Nana Boamah, Abena Boamah, Shemaine Bakir, Ama Anim, Trish Dogbey, Josephine Effah, Elizabeth Effah, Theresa Obeng, Serena Moro Shores, Albert Ampah, Elisa Bannerman, Adjoa Fobi Duffour, Sheila Sowah, Ama Oduro Manu, Harriet Hawa Asamoah, Akosua and Fiifi Anthony, Thomas and Ama Brew, Yaw and Delali Agyekum, Theresa and Akwasi Agyapong, Peter and Anna Womber, Francis and Sylvia Cobbinah, Chief and Sarah Opoku Agyeman, Tricia and James Quartey, Bernice and Kennedy Asamoah-Adom, Angela Ohene, Nana Kwame Addo, Denise Early, Kari Palmer, Michelle Martin, Lachandra Baker, Dave Coleman, Tiffany Lyons, Paige Banks, Marcus and Stephanie Hazelwood, Keishay Moore, RJ McVane, Cheryl King, Brent Wilder, Shannon Cote, Adetutu Olatawura, Femi Obikunle, Dennis Massawe, Sissy Armah, Linda Amoah Owusu, Linda Osei Akoto, Abena Antwi, Akua Antwi Boakye, Sean Oriordan, Frank Appiah, Charles Teye, Sam Stephens, Adu Kakra Ayensu, Nana Ampem Darko, Eric Wireko, Kwasi Amoakohene, Isaac Osei Tutu, Tony Hammond, Nana Yaw Timpoh, Ampofo Asare, Nana Kwame Owusu and Selina Ampadu Badu, Samuel Obeng, Rev. Joshua Kest, Rev. Justice Ofosuhene, Rev. Rebecca Tollefson, Rev. Margaret Asabea Aboagye, Rev. Joseph Amponsah, Rev. Bismark Akomeah, Rev. Ofosu Atta, Rev. Alfred Nyamekye, Rev. Adarquah Yiadom, Rev. Alphonse Kattah, Rev. Joseph Antwi, Rev. Emmanuel Gyan, Rev. Prince Bonsu, Rev. Seth Asante, Rev. Ababio Gyebi, Adjoa Amoako Gyebi, Kwaku Dua Berchie, Terry Bright Ofosu, Eric Ansah Brew, Fred and Julie Gardiner, Sheila

My Appreciation

Bekoe, Afia Agyei and Maxwell Oppong, Yaa Sarpong, Cynthia Sakyi-Hyde, Yaw and Olive Antwi-Dadzie, Baffour Abankwah, Francis Quaye, Jocelyn Atiase-Wobil, Vivian Atiase-Anochie, Esther Asamoah, Yvonne Zuta, Stella and Michael Larbi, Anna Arhin, Linda and Jonathan Yawson, Maame Yaa Ampadu, Nana Agyeman Frimpong, Nana Konadu and Kwesi Wiredu Boateng, Nana Twumasi, Sandra Abanquah, Cynthia Essuman, Leslie and Faustina Opoku, Emmanuel Yamoah, Chanda Riddick-Yamoah, Kwabena Yamoah, Diana Yamoah Brown, Patrick and Nana Achiaa Acquah, Kofi and Serwaa Boateng, Ashiokai Akrong, Ernest Yankson, John Ammah-Tagoe, Andy Okaikoi, Adrian Awuah, Leonard Awuah, Ernest Opuni, Elikem Kattah, Kodjo Somana, Talle Bamazi, Sam Adjin-Tettey, Katrina Hairston, Martha and Kwabena Manu Baffour Awuah, Patrick Asamoah, Kaykay Amponsah, Kwabena Adusei Poku, Benjamin Okley-Anyanume, Tasha Lomo, Nora Lomo, Solomon Aborbie, Christian Aborbie, Solomon Aborbie Jr., Daniella Akomeah, Bismark Akomeah Jr., Yaw Owusu Appiah, Rita Kusi, Kwaku Boafo Agyeman, Gideon Segbefia, Malik Moore, James Nutor, Paapa Yeboah Agani, Mike Bampoe, Otu Amankwah, Annabell Adjei, Steve Antwi, Anna Maria, Ruth Ankrah, Sonia Ansong, Emmanuel Caster, Anita Caster, Prince Caster, Jacob Buaful, Caleb Buaful, Kofi Mensah Asamoah, Brian Asamoah, Emmanuela Asamoah, Jude Adjei, Justina Afful, Ronnie Oppong, Renee Oppong, Boniface Womber, Ama Dufie Karikari, Ezra Wireko, and Erwin Boateng. This is a long list, and it can go on and on.

There are also many young people who've enriched my life: Tryphena Awuah, Benjamin Ohene, Vanessa Ohene, Michele Ampadu, Natalie Ampadu, Valerie Ampadu, Jada Adjabeng, Lyberti Chandler, Amara Peters, Marlie James, Rayna Ansah,

Trenyce Twumasi, Trishelle Twumasi, Tyler Twumasi, Kwame Boateng, Kofi Boateng, Naana Boateng, Jayden Yawson, Janelle Yawson, Jonathan Yawson Jr., Myron Kobson, Adeline Kobson, Gabrielle Amankwah, Danielle Amankwah, Michelle Amankwah, Eric Amankwah Jr., Joshua Boampong, Brooke Boampong, Alfred Boakye Amankwah, Kwaku Ofosu Amankwah, Kwasi Bediako Sampong, Mimi Bediako Sampong, Efua Bediako Sampong, Ewurabena Bediako Sampong, Elsie Kusi, Erick Mensah, Lilian Mensah, Angela Ofosu, Anthony Ofosu, Andrew Ofosu, Michelle Saka, Jesse Opoku, Benjamin Opoku, Angel Ikem, Myra Oduro, Bridget Womber, Reggie Amanor, McKenzie Amanor, Stacy Sackey, Chelsea Sackey, Eliezer Nana Yeboah, Francisca Peprah, Francis Peprah, Stacey Baffour Awuah, Sam Baffour Awuah, Paulissen Owusu Ansah, Thaddeus Kyeremeh, Angela Adu, Kendra Adu, Nana Baffour Awuah, Abena Baffour Awuah, Glory Anokye, Daniel Fosu, Dave Mensah, Eve Konadu, Eliora Konadu, Euclid Konadu, Jocelyn Owusu, Janella Owusu, Janita Owusu, Daylin Apraku Djan, Charles Antwi, Elton Adu-Gyamfi, Jannelle Adu-Gyamfi, Perry Nimoh, Pearl Nimoh, Jayda Nimoh, Emmanuel Boakye, Emmanuela Antwi, Miriam Akomeah, Joella Akomeah, Miles Amoah, Michael Amoah, Theodore Amoah, Paula Quartey, Jaysen Quartey, Johnathan Quartey, Petra Quartey, Gideon Boahen, Reuben Boahen, Kofi Ofosuhene, Nathan Majeed, Ansoumane Kaba, Precious Antwi, Kevin Ansong, Enoch Okyere... and this is another list that can go on, and on, and on.

To all the people listed above and those I missed, thanks for being a part of my story.

Meda mo ase papa paa! Thank you all very much.

LET'S CONNECT!

Thanks for reading. I hope my story and the thoughts shared here have stirred up something within you. If there's any way I can be of help, kindly let me know. If you have any questions or suggestions, I'll be happy to hear them. If you want to link up to talk about what you're doing, feel free to do so.

I work with individuals and groups interested in:
- personal & professional development
- marketing & communications, and
- book publishing.

I will like to hear from you, so don't hessitate to reach out. By email, you can reach me at **KyeiAmoako1@gmail.com**. On social media, search for me under my full name. You can also find me on **KyeiAmoako.com**.

Talk with you soon.

INDEX

Symbols

4Him 206
360-degree feedback 143
401(k) 122, 157

A

Acting 22, 39, 61, 120
African 42, 74, 88, 262
African-American 41, 89, 264
African Students Association 78
Afriyie Amoako 224, 273
Agogo 291
Agric prefect 36
Agya Koo Nimo 283, 309
Alfred Nobel 195
Alfred Tennyson 231, 242
American Dream 73
Andre Crouch 206
Anointed 202
A.N.T. 1 12, 23
Apostle Bismark Akomeah 89
Archbishop Duncan-Williams 251
Arthur Ashe 57
Arthur Brooks 97
Ashesi University 137

B

Babyface 251
Barack Obama 71, 87
BBC Radio 10
Belief 162
Bible 164, 182
  Book of Proverbs 183
  Psalm 183
Billy Ocean 235
Birthday 1, 4
Blue County 206
Bob Marley 201
Bono 86
Bucket List 303
Buddhism 168

Bullying 15
Business 16, 51, 60

C

Career 115
Carlton Pearson 167
Casper 31
Cece Winans 209
Christian 113
Christmas 278
Church 105
  Catholic Church 185
  Jehovah's Witnesses 167
  Presbyterian Church 265
  Seventh Day Adventists 167
Coming to America 77
Commitment 244
Common Entrance Examination 27
Counters Ball 9
CPA 82, 116
Culture 274, 283
Cyril Heyman 59

D

Dadaba 20
Dance 282
Daughter 88, 121
Dave Ramsey 156
Death 2, 194
Declaration of Independence 91, 100
Degree 117
  Accounting 118
  Communications 80, 117
  Marketing and Communications 123
  MBA 120
Diane Ackerman 91
Divorce 246, 250, 252
DJ Khaled 308
Doubt 186

INDEX

Dr. David Yamoah 80
Dr. Dre 158
Dr. Gary Chapman 239
Dr. Helen Cooks 38
DuBois Center 262, 264

E

Eddie Murphy 71
Elsie Osei-Tutu 46
Eminem 2, 208
Eric Amankwah 74, 79, 268
Evangelical 167

F

Facebook 1
Faith 150, 153
Family 18, 150, 151
  Brothers 9
  Children 273, 276
  Daughter 8, 88, 161
  Father 54, 193, 248, 297
  Grandfather 16
  Mother 10, 53, 56, 248
  Siblings 53
  Sister 9
Fear 129
Filmmaking 121, 135
Finances 150
  Money 155
Folktale 99
Franklin-St. John United Methodist Church 79
Franklin University 120
Frank Sinatra 243, 253

G

G.C.E. 18, 27
  A-Level 27
  O-Level 18
George Carlin 178
George Darko 209

Ghana 8, 41, 84
  Accra 40
  Accra New Town 258
  Adenta 20
  Alajo 8, 40
  Kumasi 267
  Legon 25
  Tesano 257
Ghana Airways 40
Ghana Broadcasting Corporation 16
Ghanaian 74, 85
Ghanaian Culture 284, 286, 293, 295
Ghanaian Languages 293
  Ewe 256
  Ga 8
  Twi 8, 60, 85, 205
Ghanaian Saying 2, 270, 285, 287, 289, 296
Ghost 193
Girls 31
God 155, 162, 174
  God of the Bible 177, 178
Google Analytics 125
Goo Goo Dolls 203
Greeks 232

H

Happiness 91, 92
Heaven 165, 167, 171
Hell 161, 164, 171
Highlife 9

I

Identity 86, 88
Immigrant 71
Infatuation 235
Inroads 81
Insights 145
Instinct 7, 299

INDEX

J

Jay Z 2, 208
Jesus Christ 161, 167
John Mayer 134, 207
Jonathan Larson 207
Journalism 57, 58, 80
Journalist 16, 57, 104
Jurgen Klinsmann 306

K

Kanye West 137, 203
Kean University 78
Kofi Agyare 256
Kofi Kinaata 99
Kojo Antwi 193, 204
Kwabena Bediako 51, 265
Kwame Nkrumah 262
Kwame Nkrumah University of Science and Technology 59

L

Lao Tzu 141
Leadership 35, 37, 109
LeBron James 110
LeeAnn Womack 281
Les Brown 2, 103, 309
Lou Gehrig 94
Love 132, 179, 231, 237, 242, 250
Love and Marriage 247
Love Languages 239

M

Mae West 189
Mariah Carey 205
Marriage 243, 244, 249
Martin Luther 164
Martin Luther King Jr. 94, 177
Math Club 262
Matthew Spalding 90
Maya Angelou 161

McCrory's 74
Mensa Otabil 25
Mentor 265, 266
Mike Tyson 305
Mr. Hudson 2, 208
Mrs. Charlotte Akyeampong 23, 29
Muhammad Ali 141

N

Naming 290
Nana Asante-Frempong 292
NanaBcool 209
National Service 45
Nationwide Insurance 118, 131
Neale Donald Walsch 183
Nelson Mandela 7
Nietzsche 137

O

Obeng Amoako 269
Obituary 192, 195
Obrafour 205
Ohio University 118
Oprah Winfrey 271

P

Pan-African Club 263
Patrick Awuah 137
Pharmacist 58
Pharmacy 58
Pilot 57
Playlist 201
Pope Francis 185
Prefect 35
PRESEC 19, 25
  Drama Club 23
PricewaterhouseCoopers 81
Progress 146, 300, 308
Protestant 163
Purpose 104
Pursuit of Happiness 91

INDEX

R

Radio Station 59, 105
  Joy FM 60
  Sahara Radio 124
Ralph Waldo Emerson 255
Reggie Rockstone 63
Relationships 151, 233
Religion 178
Risk 136
Rob Bell 168
Robert N. Test 198
Robin Sharma 129
Romantic Love 232
Romantic Relationship 239, 242

S

Sam Laryea 261
Sammy Fiscian 258
School of Performing Arts 62
Self-awareness 142
Service 109
Shared parenting 280
Sixth Form 19
Snoop Dogg 158
Sonja Lyubomirsky 97
Sports 297
Steve Jobs 115, 127, 189
Subjects 17, 27

T

TEDx 136
The Search 37, 218
The Wizard of Oz 134, 139
Tinny 205
Tom Dearing 196
Tony Robbins 143, 149
Tour 33, 39, 264
Travis Greene 203
T-shirts 63
Tutor 18, 79, 86, 107

U

United States of America 40
  Cleveland 111
  Columbus, Ohio 83
  Newark, New Jersey 73
  New York 72, 73, 120, 121
  Ohio 38, 40
  Toledo 41
University of Ghana 38, 59
  School of Performing Arts 62
University of Toledo 38
  Toledo Excel 38

V

Valentine's Day 237
Victor Frankl 93
Video Producer 86
Visa 63
Vocation 150, 158

W

WASS 14
Wayne Dyer 96, 173
W. E. B. DuBois 264
Wedding Videos 249
Whitney Houston 205, 273
Winning 297, 300, 307
Work 115
Work of Art 241
World Cup 306

www.ingramcontent.com/pod-product-compliance
Lightning Source LLC
Chambersburg PA
CBHW030430010526
44118CB00011B/572